writing
in
context

writing in context

MARY ELLEN S. CAPEK

Princeton University,
Program in Continuing Education

Harcourt Brace Jovanovich, Inc.

New York   Chicago   San Francisco   Atlanta

ISBN: 0-15-597896-9

Library of Congress Catalog Card Number: 75–44874

Printed in the United States of America

COPYRIGHTS AND ACKNOWLEDGMENTS

For permission to use the selections reprinted in this book,
the author is grateful to the following publishers and copyright holders:

CHATTO AND WINDUS LTD. For "The Arts of Selling" from *Brave New World Revisited* by Aldous Huxley. Reprinted by permission of Mrs. Laura Huxley and Chatto and Windus.

CANDIDA DONADIO & ASSOCIATES, INC. For "New York" by Gay Talese. Copyright © 1960 by Gay Talese. First published in *Esquire* magazine. Reprinted by permission of Candida Donadio & Associates, Inc.

FARRAR, STRAUS & GIROUX, INC. For the excerpts from *The Pine Barrens* by John McPhee. Copyright © 1967, 1968 by John McPhee. This material originally appeared in *The New Yorker*. Reprinted with the permission of Farrar, Straus & Giroux, Inc.

HARCOURT BRACE JOVANOVICH, INC. For the excerpts from *The Five Clocks* by Martin Joos. Copyright © 1967 by Martin Joos. Reprinted by permission of Harcourt Brace Jovanovich, Inc.

HARPER & ROW, PUBLISHERS, INC. For "The Arts of Selling" in *Brave New World Revisited* by Aldous Huxley. Copyright © 1958 by Aldous Huxley; and for "Balloons" from *Ariel* by Sylvia Plath. Copyright ©1965 by Ted Hughes. Both reprinted by permission of Harper & Row, Publishers, Inc.

OLWYN HUGHES. For "Balloons" from *Ariel* by Sylvia Plath. Copyright Ted Hughes, 1965. Published by Faber & Faber, London. Reprinted by permission of Olwyn Hughes.

ALFRED A. KNOPF, INC. For "When Sue Wears Red" from *Selected Poems* by Langston Hughes. Copyright 1926 by Alfred A. Knopf, Inc. and renewed 1954 by Langston Hughes; and for the excerpts from *All God's Dangers: The Life of Nate Shaw* by Theodore Rosengarten. Copyright © 1974 by Theodore Rosengarten. Both are reprinted by permission of Alfred A. Knopf, Inc.

SCOTT MEREDITH LITERARY AGENCY, INC. For the excerpts from "Ego" by Norman Mailer from *Life*, March 19, 1971. Reprinted by permission of the author and the author's agents, Scott Meredith Literary Agency, Inc., 845 Third Avenue, New York, New York 10022.

THE M.I.T. PRESS. For the excerpt reprinted from *Language, Thought and Reality: Selected Writings of Benjamin Lee Whorf*, edited by John Carroll, by permission of The M.I.T. Press, Cambridge, Massachusetts. Copyright © 1956 by The Massachusetts Institute of Technology.

preface

Language is at once one of our greatest cultural resources and one of our most complex cultural barriers. The effective use of language is an essential tool in seeking to learn more about ourselves and our culture; yet no scholars have been able to explain conclusively how we assimilate language or how, in fact, we exploit what we already know. No sooner is a text in print than new research and new experiments in teaching methods seem to outdate it. Despite all the experimentation, language remains a stubborn mystery.

In light of this fact, producing a text that attempts to "teach" writing is a challenging experience. The success of that experience depends on how effectively an author communicates with many different students and instructors, whose experiences and expectations are unique. Perhaps the most realistic expectations for any writing text are that it generate and encourage attitudes of experimentation, questioning, humor, and patience.

The form that this text has finally taken is a product of many individuals and opportunities. I would like to thank, first, the students at Essex County College in Newark, New Jersey, who helped shape the foundations of this book. Their questions, their ambition, their patience and enthusiasm, their demand for better answers, and their criticisms provided the challenge to create more effective, realistic teaching materials. Numerous colleagues at Essex—especially Charlee Irene Trantino and Lyn McLean Quiroz—offered consistent support and shared many suggestions and materials in the preparation of the manuscript.

I would also like to express appreciation to Clifford A. Hill of Teachers' College, Columbia University; Mary Ann Cook of Forest Park Community College; and the late Albert H. Marckwardt, formerly of Princeton University, for their thorough readings of the manuscript and their valuable criticisms and suggestions. They not only helped "debug" the text but supplied the necessary diverse perspectives so essential in considering options of chapter arrangement and the tone of the text narrative. I am especially grateful to my husband, Michael J. Capek, for his critical reading of the manuscript at several stages of production and for his encouragement throughout the project.

A grant from the National Endowment for the Humanities generously provided a year's sabbatical and sufficient funds to update research on current linguistic scholarship. The Endowment's support enabled me to expand and considerably revise earlier drafts of the manuscript.

Finally, I would gratefully like to acknowledge the efforts and support of my editors at Harcourt Brace Jovanovich—specifically Gordon R. Fairburn and Eben W. Ludlow, with special thanks to my manuscript editor, Elaine Romano, whose expertise, interest, and unerring attention to detail taught me much about writing. I hope the text is as challenging and rewarding to use as it was to produce.

MARY ELLEN S. CAPEK

contents

PART TWO

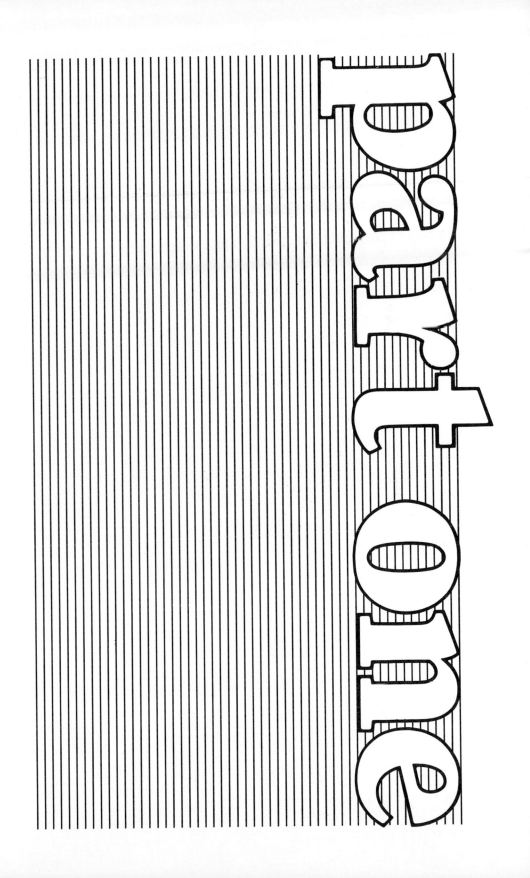

part one

introduction

As you begin to read this book, you should realize several important facts about our language. First, as someone who has been speaking English most of your life, you are already an experienced user of language. You have been talking since you were two or three years old. You understood language even before you could talk.

Because language is such a commonplace thing, however, you probably tend to overlook your own experience, just as you don't take too much credit for breathing or pumping blood while you sleep. But consider what you already know. You know, for example, that the following two messages mean the same thing:

> The dog bit the man.
> The man was bitten by the dog.

And you know these two are very different in meaning:

> The dog bit the man.
> The man bit the dog.

You also know that when someone shakes a fist at you or yells, he or she is probably angry. Or if someone raises an eyebrow, that person may be puzzled. If these seem rather obvious, it might be because you never tried to analyze them before. In fact, they are quite complex features of communication.

As a child, you learned to make sense of long stretches of sound which, to a non-English speaker, would be just so much confusing noise. You learned to interpret the slightest change in someone's expression or gestures. In fact, you have developed a skilled instinct for sorting out—and creating—all kinds of language. You have in your brain a set of blueprints, a sort of built-in "grammar." With it you not only reproduce copies of words and sentences heard or read before, but, much more remarkable, you also turn out endless variations and modifications, entirely *new* models you never actually used before. You've done this every day of your life since you started speaking, and you probably never even knew it.

3

As a child, you learned to speak the language around you, just as you learned to walk and eat and laugh. But you also learned more: the second important fact you should realize is that besides learning to *use* language, you have also learned to *control* and *manipulate* language. You discovered very early how to convince someone to give you what you wanted. That's manipulating language—exercising control over your choice of words, your tone of voice, the gestures you use to communicate your message.

If you need to be convinced that, as an adult, you are already a very subtle manipulator of language, just say the sentence "He's a very ambitious person" out loud in order to communicate that:

1. You are simply stating a fact
2. You are friends and really like his ambition
3. You can't stand the guy and his ambition really gets on your nerves
4. The extent of his ambition is amazing
5. Ambition is the *only* thing he's got going for himself
6. You're questioning someone else's judgment; you can hardly believe your ears

Manipulating language—communicating meaning—is probably the most important thing you do every day. Language is a very pervasive and influential part of life. Every waking minute, you define your world by language. Language is the way you share yourself with others and are known. Language also labels you. Your use of language can reveal the region you come from; it can identify your class or ethnic origins; it can reflect your education, your aspirations, or whatever you have defined yourself to be.

Such use and manipulation of language is one of the essential things that makes us human. Yet in spite of—or perhaps because of—the fact that language is so much a part of us, no one really knows how we learn language, or how language really works, or even when language first came into use in human history. It is one of the least understood and most complicated human characteristics. And just because it is such a complex personal and social force, language creates fear. Very few people feel comfortable with their use of language in all social situations, just because language is such a powerful force.

As a student, you are not going to "learn" language—you already know it. Instead, you should concentrate your energy on understanding, exploiting, and expanding what you already know—get rid of the linguistic hang-ups that have probably plagued you for a long time.

One of the most important aids for expanding what you already know is practice. Like any other skill, writing and speaking with more control requires practice. The more conscious you are of the ways you already manipulate language, the easier it will be to practice. You might try keeping a journal. Write down anything that occurs to you—especially observations you have about language, how you use it and how others use it. You quickly become a skilled observer once you start looking and listening. There are a variety of exercises suggested in the following chapters which can give you a chance to experiment in writing with many different ideas. Try to pin down your feelings and observations. Sharpen your ideas. Force yourself to choose words more consciously. But, most important, enjoy the challenge. Don't get trapped by frustrations or fears. Get your ideas on paper without worrying about the finishing touches or what someone else will think. Those concerns can come later—and they will be much easier to deal with after you are really into your own language and enjoying it.

The purposes of this book, then, are to give you some background for thinking about language, to give you confidence by making you aware of how much you already know, and to suggest a variety of ways for further developing your awareness and skills.

1

language: some definitions

LANGUAGE IS ESSENTIALLY HUMAN

Have you ever thought about what language is? Is it communication? A way of making sense to ourselves and to others? A way of organizing reality and coping with our environment? Try to imagine yourself without language. You probably can't, because all our memories and imaginings come to us through words. Can you "think" without words? Can you be yourself without somehow translating that "you" into language? Think of the power of a word; let's start with your name.

For a normal human being, that name is a very powerful word. It's not just a name, but a concept, an identity. Just a few sounds, translated into letters, evoke a whole, extremely complex identity: YOU. Did you ever meet someone else with your name, even just your first name? It's a curious experience because so much of your identity and your feelings about yourself rest on just one or at most two or three little words. Do you remember feeling hurt in a social situation because someone forgot your name? Why did that bother you? What did that act of forgetting a word represent? To really explore the power of a name, try giving yourself a new one. Look into the mirror. Relax. Repeat your new name over and over. (You may feel silly, but try it anyway.) Now, describe your "new" self: Who are you? What are you like? What makes you tick? Let your imagination loose.

Such powerful attachment and response to names is a distinctly human characteristic. A dog can learn to respond to its own name. Fido, after all, will come when called to fetch the paper, to chew on a bone, or to attack one of your enemies if he has been trained to. But chances are pretty good that he can't—or doesn't—think about himself and attach a personality to his "handle." He responds to a name, but it is a much more direct, immediate sort of reaction. He can't look in a mirror and murmur curiously, "Fido." Language just doesn't mean the same to a dog as it does to us. Try another exercise. Observe an animal you know (or can arrange to meet). How does it respond to language? What kind of "language" does it use?

6

Language as we know it is uniquely human—we would not be ourselves without it. It's one of the few reliable humanizing forces that we can count on. Trained animals—chimpanzees, porpoises, even dogs—can learn the meaning of key words and phrases in any language and act on them. But they cannot manipulate language when they are out of each other's sight and hearing (they don't have writing systems), and they cannot teach another animal the language they themselves were taught. Fido can teach his pups a bark to show fear, but he never taught them their names or how to fetch his master's paper. As users of language, we not only communicate and act on meaningful words and phrases, but we also pass that knowledge along from generation to generation. That's one definition of culture, and without language, there would not be any.

Humans have evolved biologically to the point where, many experts believe, the newborn human child is equipped with an innate capacity both to learn language itself, whatever language his or her culture speaks, and to pass it on to others. Learning to speak is one of the most remarkable things a person ever accomplishes, and all of us, by the time we are three or four, have already learned most of what we need to know about language to communicate our needs and feelings. We thus all speak a language well suited to our needs, and we all understand the language around us. The language we speak and understand, however, is a complex collection of physical, mental, and social forces.

SOUND AND GESTURE

Spoken language is obviously sound. Whether English or French, Arabic, Spanish, or Swahili, all spoken language is sound. Some very different sounds, maybe, for different languages, but sound nonetheless. And the sounds any language uses are amazingly subtle. Try describing in very careful detail, for example, how you pronounce words like hat/hate or pitcher/picture? How do your mouth, throat, tongue, and other speech apparatus help make the sounds? What are the differences, if any, that signal the differences in meaning? Any one language only uses a portion of all the possible sounds the mechanisms of human speech can produce. And our spelling system doesn't even come close to describing the subtlety and accuracy of our pronunciation system. In English, for example, most of us have at least fourteen vowel sounds (not just five). Pronounce, if you need convincing, the following words: *beat*, *bit*, *bait*, *bet*, *bat*, *boo*, *book*, *bow* (the kind you tie), *bought*, *bomb*, *but*, *by*, *boy*, *bow* (what you take when everyone applauds).

Besides being a system of sounds, however, language can also be gesture. As we mentioned in the "Introduction," you communicate very different meanings by raising an eyebrow, frowning, or smiling. Even simple messages use a complex mixture of sound and gesture signals. For example, what if a cab driver cut you off at an intersection and beat you through a light? You might shake your fist at him, get red in the face, and spit out a string of words like, "What d'ya think you're doin'??!!" You have just communicated a very clear message—anger—using both sound and gesture. How have you learned to do that?

IMITATION AND ANALOGY

On one level, obviously, you learned by imitation. You drive in city traffic; you probably watched your parents (or other adults) drive in city traffic. You also learned at a very early age to express anger or hurt by shouts or crying. No one knows for sure yet exactly how children (or adults, for that matter) learn language, but some of it obviously stems from imitation, playing with sounds, even mimicking the style or tone of your parents' or others' speech. Can you think of any specific examples in your own speech that are recognizable imitations of the way your parents or others close to you speak—words, a special phrase, any slightly unique pronunciations?

Besides imitating speech, however, children also learn very early a sophisticated logical maneuver we call *analogy*. For example, until they are reminded a number of times, English-speaking children will instinctively say, "I singed a song yesterday." This is a perfectly reasonable sentence since they have already learned to say, "I played with the baby yesterday." We try to teach them that English uses *sang* as an irregular form to show the past performance of *sing*, but it is perfectly reasonable and quite perceptive of them to sense that since the -ed on *play* means "yesterday," it could work the same for *sing*. Irregular verbs are products of our language history, and the power of analogy has already forced some changes in modern English. For example, if you look up *leap* in the dictionary, you will find it gives you two past forms: *leaped* and *leapt*. *Leapt* is the traditional past form, but *leaped* is more and more commonly used. Can you think of any other examples of word forms like *singed* that children often use?

Children (and adults), to get back to our main point, learn by imitation and analogy, transferring what they learned in one situation to a new and different experience. That's one of the talents that accounts for our ability to produce sentences we never actually heard before. We all do it—it's another very significant mark of human intelligence—but how does it all work? What makes language tick? Perhaps the easiest way to find out is to ask the simplest question.

WHAT'S A WORD?

A word, at least on one level, is something you find in a dictionary; it's a collection of letters. The arrangements of those letters are governed by a variety of conventions which we needn't go into here. More important, you already know non-English letter combinations when you see them. You know, for example, that zhbti is not an English word, even though you've never seen it before. You know it by the same instinct that tells you "where go it did" is not an English sentence. Examine the "words" listed below; without using a dictionary, try to guess which are or aren't used in English.

through	etymology	elementary
mstor	ipqat	formidable
psychology	macintosh	teletype
Aeoui	llbrnj	zedrk

Words are units of language most of us take for granted. A child unable to hear or speak, however, develops a very different awareness of reality. Helen Keller was blind, deaf, and unable to speak. Read the following excerpt from her autobiography, and see if you have any better sense after you finish it of what a word is all about.

The most important day I remember in all my life is the one on which my teacher, Anne Mansfield Sullivan, came to me. I am filled with wonder when I consider the immeasurable contrasts between the two lives which it connects. It was the third of March, 1887, three months before I was seven years old.

On the afternoon of that eventful day, I stood on the porch, dumb, expectant. I guessed vaguely from my mother's signs and from the hurrying to and fro in the house that something unusual was about to happen, so I went to the door and waited on the steps. The afternoon sun penetrated the mass of honeysuckle that covered the porch, and fell on my upturned face. My fingers lingered almost unconsciously on the familiar leaves and blossoms which had just come forth to greet the sweet southern spring. I did not know what the future held of marvel or surprise for me. Anger and bitterness had preyed upon me continually for weeks and a deep languor had succeeded this passionate struggle.

Have you ever been at sea in a dense fog, when it seemed as if a tangible white darkness shut you in, and the great ship, tense and anxious, groped her way toward the shore with plummet and sounding-line, and you waited with beating heart for something to happen? I was like that ship before my education began, only I was without compass or sounding-line, and had no way of knowing how near the harbour was. "Light! give me light! was the wordless cry of my soul, and the light of love shone on me in that very hour.

I felt approaching footsteps. I stretched out my hand as I supposed to my mother. Some one took it, and I was caught up and held close in the arms of her who had come to reveal all things to me, and, more than all things else, to love me.

The morning after my teacher came she led me into her room and gave me a doll. . . . When I had played with it a little while, Miss Sullivan slowly spelled into my hand the word "d-o-l-l." I was at once interested in this finger play and tried to imitate it. When I finally succeeded in making the letters correctly I was flushed with childish pleasure and pride. Running downstairs to my mother I held up my hand and made the letters for doll. I did not know that I was spelling a word or even that words existed; I was simply making my fingers go in monkey-like imitation. In the days that followed I learned to spell in this uncomprehending way a great many

9

WHAT'S A WORD?

words, among them *pin, hat, cup* and a few verbs like *sit, stand* and *walk.* But my teacher had been with me several weeks before I understood that everything has a name.

One day, while I was playing with my new doll, Miss Sullivan put my big rag doll into my lap also, spelled "d-o-l-l" and tried to make me understand that "d-o-l-l" applied to both. Earlier in the day we had had a tussle over the words "m-u-g" and "w-a-t-e-r." Miss Sullivan had tried to impress it upon me that "m-u-g" is *mug* and that "w-a-t-e-r" is *water,* but I persisted in confounding the two. In despair she had dropped the subject for the time, only to renew it at the first opportunity. I became impatient at her repeated attempts and, seizing the new doll, I dashed it upon the floor. I was keenly delighted when I felt the fragments of the broken doll at my feet. Neither sorrow nor regret followed my passionate outburst. I had not loved the doll. In the still, dark world in which I lived there was no strong sentiment or tenderness. I felt my teacher sweep the fragments to one side of the hearth, and I had a sense of satisfaction that the cause of my discomfort was removed. She brought me my hat, and I knew I was going out into the warm sunshine. This thought, if a wordless sensation may be called a thought, made me hop and skip with pleasure.

We walked down the path to the well-house, attracted by the fragrance of the honeysuckle with which it was covered. Some one was drawing water and my teacher placed my hand under the spout. As the cool stream gushed over one hand she spelled into the other the word *water,* first slowly, then rapidly. I stood still, my whole attention fixed upon the motions of her fingers. Suddenly I felt a misty consciousness as of something forgotten—a thrill of returning thought; and somehow the mystery of language was revealed to me. I knew then that "w-a-t-e-r" meant the wonderful cool something that was flowing over my hand. That living word awakened my soul, gave it light, hope, joy, set it free! There were barriers still, it is true, but barriers that could in time be swept away.

I left the well-house eager to learn. Everything had a name, and each name gave birth to a new thought. As we returned to the house every object which I touched seemed to quiver with life. That was because I saw everything with the strange, new sight that had come to me. On entering the door I remembered the doll I had broken. I felt my way to the hearth and picked up the pieces. I tried vainly to put them together. Then my eyes filled with tears; for I realized what I had done, and for the first time I felt repentance and sorrow.

I learned a great many new words that day. I do not remember what they all were; but I do know that *mother, father, sister, teacher* were among them—words that were to make the world blossom for me, "like Aaron's rod, with flowers." It would have been difficult to find a happier child than I was as I lay in my crib at the close of that eventful day and lived over the joys it had brought me, and for the first time longed for a new day to come.

Helen Keller is a dramatic example of a person who grew to consciousness without language. By reading about her courageous experience, you can better imagine what it must be like to struggle through a haze of impressions to the clear and overpowering recognition of words. Things that are close to you often go unnoticed. It sometimes takes a jolt to make you see what you've walked past a hundred times and never paid attention to before. The power to symbolize, to use the symbols *w-a-t-e-r* to communicate to another in a desert where no water is present, is a gift most of you probably haven't thought much about. But here it is, "the living word," as Miss Keller describes it, the unique power that makes us human.

What is a word, then? It is a collection of sounds or a collection of letters representing sounds which *symbolize,* which stand in for something else, some object or experience. Most words are arbitrary symbols— there is little or no relationship between the actual word and what it represents. There are, of course, expressive words, like *whew* or *phew,* which sound like the sigh of relief they symbolize. But most words don't have much direct connection to what they symbolize and are therefore arbitrary symbols. We can use that as a working definition: **a word is an arbitrary symbol,** a group of sounds or letters representing sounds which stands for an object or experience, without needing to be in the presence of that object or experience. *W-a-t-e-r* means water—the clear, wet stuff— even to someone surrounded by desert.

THE POWER OF SYMBOLS

Symbols can also be gestures or objects, like a clenched fist salute or a cross. The first symbolizes a political stance, while the second represents a set of religious beliefs. Symbols can be very powerful. People are willing to die for them. They can alter lives or provide a common source of strength and understanding for the group of people who use them. Words as symbols can also be powerful—at times, even *iconic.* This means that the words themselves, not just what they symbolize, can be objects. In and of themselves, by their very sound and utterance, they can evoke fear, awe, or obedience. Among Orthodox Jews, for example, the word *God* is considered so powerful and so much identified with the powerful, awesome figure it symbolizes that it is considered blasphemous to use the word itself in ordinary conversation or even to write it out.

Swear words, obscene language, and taboo words are other powerful symbols which can provoke a person to rage, even violence. If you use such words in the wrong tone of voice on the wrong occasion, you can find yourself in a fight.

Words can hurt. Derogatory epithets like *kike, nigger, spic,* or *bitch* all have a history of hatred and bitter religious, racial, cultural, and sexual discrimination; they become tools which dominant cultures use to oppress minorities. Any child who has ever felt the sting of *nigger* or even *peanut* or *chicken* doesn't really believe that "sticks and stones can break your bones but names will never hurt you." Even a tough cop taunted with *pig* will react. Names can hurt. Words—symbols—are powerful weapons.

We use words to manipulate our environment—most of the time, obviously, not in such negative or dramatic ways. But without words to act as a kind of shorthand, we would be overwhelmed by the confusion of the world around us. Think for a moment about the word *chair.* We use it for high chairs, low chairs, chairs without arms, chairs with arms, chairs with or without legs, wooden chairs, plastic chairs, upholstered chairs, chairs to work in, to write at, to relax in, to eat in; we also use it for dining room chairs, kitchen chairs, desk chairs, rocking chairs, lounge chairs, armchairs, babies' highchairs, cheap chairs, plain chairs, fancy chairs. Without the word *chair,* we'd need at least twenty different references; with it, we summarize all these varied objects by one common denominator. We perceive that all these are something to sit in. (*In,* not *on*—that's a stool, right?) But what about a sofa? That's not a chair, is it? We'll need to refine our definition. Usually, unless someone is lap sitting, a chair is something only one person sits in at a time, so size also defines a chair.

Select a word for yourself and describe how it works. What class, or group of objects, does it represent? As we just did for *chair,* carefully define *all* the essential characteristics it includes and what it excludes. List some synonyms for your word which come close in meaning but have slightly different references (like *seat, sofa, recliner, bench, stool,* etc.).

Words slice up the world for us. Different cultures have different words and varied sets of vocabulary. For example, Eskimos have more words for snow than English speakers, but we have a lot more words for cars. Words are culturally determined by what they have to describe, but any language that has ever existed, to our knowledge, has had vocabulary adequate to the needs of its culture. That's an impressive record. If a culture needs a word for some new experience, discovery, or invention, it either borrows one from another language or makes it up. For instance, the English word *television* comes from the Greek root *tele-,* which means "at a distance or far off," and, obviously, from the English word *vision* (which, incidentally, comes from the Latin word *visio,* meaning sight). And there are always newly coined forms in a language like *televisionski,* a compromise sometimes used by Czech-Americans. Can you think of any other words in English which have been borrowed recently from other languages or newly coined?

EXPLOITING SYMBOL POWER

A word is an arbitrary symbol which slices up the world for us. Arbitrary symbols obviously have their limitations. How can the word *love,* for example, begin to define the complex emotions we attach to it? But that's where you come in. As a writer, as a person who is becoming more conscious of your language, you soon learn to refine your choice of words. For example, consider the following words: *skinny, thin, slender, lean, svelte, gaunt, puny, slim, scrawny, emaciated.* These all mean "not fat." But you will get a very different reaction if you call someone scrawny than if you call him or her svelte. The general definition, the common denominator, is obviously "not fat." This is what we call **denotation.** But the implications surrounding a word—the **connotation**—are very different for *scrawny* than they are for *svelte. Scrawny* implies "too thin or all skin and bones." That is obviously a negative (or "minus good") judgment. *Svelte,* on the other hand, implies "attractively thin or slender," a positive and complimentary judgment (or "plus good"). We can compile a table like the following one for all these words (and any others you want to add to the list), analyzing the words according to negative, neutral, or positive qualities:

minus good	neutral	plus good
skinny	thin	lean
gaunt	slim	svelte
puny		slender
scrawny		
emaciated		

These are generalized categories. Slim, at times, can fit in the "plus good" column (so can skinny, if you are trying desperately to lose weight); but for the most part, you should be able to agree on such connotations. Choosing words carefully gives you a lot more power.

Another source of word power is a trick experienced writers use all the time, one that is also a part of our everyday use of language. When *scrawny* isn't enough to describe someone's thinness, for instance, a person will add more details: "scrawny as a chicken" or "thin as a rail." These are common examples of a **simile,** a comparison of two or more things linked by the word *like* or *as.* **Metaphor,** a comparison implied without using *like* or *as,* has the same power. Both simile and metaphor are what are known as **figures of speech**—words used in combinations to extend their descriptive power. If the word *love* is limited, poets can extend its description with a simile: "My love is like a red, red rose." (Or they can use the New York metaphor, "There is a rose in Spanish Harlem. . . .") How is your love like a rose? Well, she (presumably "she," since we attach feminine characteristics to most flowers, curiously enough), she is soft, fragile, and delicate; she smells sweet; her cheeks and lips are blushed with the same beautiful shades of red; she is perhaps willowy and graceful, the way a rose blossoms on its stem; and, as some cynic once observed, "Yeah, she's probably got thorns too."

We all use similes as common figurative expressions in our everyday speech: nervous as a cat, dumb as a doornail, pretty as a picture, smart as a fox, quick like a bunny, sick as a dog, and so forth. Metaphors work the same, except they omit the *like* or *as* which similes usually use. Here are a few common metaphors: I'll be a monkey's uncle! I'm a nervous wreck! Romance can be a bad trip! Life is just a bowl of cherries! Describe some other examples you've heard or used yourself. (Graffiti and bumper stickers can be a rich source.)

More than just slang or timely humor, however, such direct or implied comparison is another way of extending the power of words. Consider the following passage, quoted from a student paper on sharks:

> A shark is every inch a lethal weapon, equipped better than any World War II tank. For example, huge, razor-edged teeth can deftly sever appendages and tear away twenty-pound chunks of flesh in one bite. In addition, the skin is coarser than any known sandpaper, rough as a rasp, and fantastic at flaying. Also, the tips of fins and edges of tails cut as expertly as the rapier of a musketeer. The body too is beautifully streamlined and capable of delivering fierce, rib-cracking bunts.

How has the writer manipulated simile and metaphor? Notice how much more effective her writing is because of it. You come away from reading the paragraph with a very vivid awareness of the shark's physical advantages.

STYLE

Exploiting language for its maximum effect is called **style**. Style in writing is like any other kind of style. Basically, it means using a variety of combinations (words, gestures, sounds, colors, shapes, etc.) to create certain desired effects. You have many different styles you use everyday. Consider clothes, for example. You are aware of the differences between formal dress (tuxedo and black tie or an evening gown); dress-up suit or ensemble; everyday neat casual styles; sloppy, around-the-house, blue-jeans comfortable; and a nightgown or pajamas. Each is a kind of style or dressing for the occasion. Perhaps your awareness of written style is not yet as sharp as the writer of the shark paragraph. (She is at the stage where she can exploit written language to create almost any effect she wants.) But just as we all have some sense of dressing for the occasion, we are all very skilled at a variety of spoken styles as well. You have already developed a remarkable ability to translate and generate varieties of words and sentences, as you saw earlier in this chapter, and you are also very adept at translating and creating different verbal styles.

Consider, if you will, the ritual of the morning greeting. There are at least five styles (and probably more) you might use before ever really getting down to work for the day. First, obviously, there is a kind of "language for self"—the broken, muttered patterns that run through our heads when the alarm first drags us awake. Mine go something like this: "Erouk. Groan. Yawn. Gees . . . cloudy . . . brrr . . . cold. (Glance in the mirror as I'm hauling myself out of bed.) Ugh. Should have washed hair last night." (Grumble. Stumble.) Then comes the first demand to be a social creature. You feel your way toward the kitchen where hopefully some loyal companion has made coffee: "(Grunt) Mornin' hon. Engh." You are dressed and on your way down the street when you meet a neighbor you know only casually: "Good morning, Missus Jones. Awful day, isn't it?" And you wait for her brief but very essential acknowledgment. (It's part of the little social games we all play. You have a "one or two stroke" relationship with Mrs. Jones, and if she didn't respond, it would ever so slightly but very noticeably set you off.) She nods and murmurs "sure is" and your casual, polite level of style has been reinforced. You arrive at work and greet a fellow worker you've known for six years but never met socially: "Morning, Luther. A lot of work for today? How's that report coming?" You have an informed, although usually formal relationship with many people you know at work. You are aware of some personal things about them, but there are many things you wouldn't tell them or share with them. Then your boss (who has just gotten back from a business trip) calls you into her office; you knock, walk in standing straight, with a composed smile, and greet her, "Good morning, Mrs. Arthur. I hope you had a pleasant trip."

You can fill in the other shifts in tone, posture, and gesture for yourself. They are all subtle, but with a little imagination, you should be able to translate them easily into your own individual styles. Think about it. You can come up with numerous situations where your style shifts ever so slightly, but very significantly. Once you've learned to look for the differences, you begin to see what a skilled language-making machine you really are.

EXERCISES

Language is essentially human

1. One definition of human beings is that we are "language-using animals." Can you think of any other characteristics that define being "human"? Could these other characteristics exist without some use of language?
2. Imagine yourself alone in another country where *nobody* speaks your language. How would you make yourself understood?
3. Describe one of your earliest childhood memories. Then talk about how language reinforces or distorts that recollection.

Sound and gesture

4. Pronounce the pairs of words listed below very carefully. Then, for each pair, isolate the sounds that change the meanings of the words. What vocal equipment do you use to pronounce the differences?

bit/pit	view/few
dip/tip	thy/thigh
girl/curl	zoo/sue

Based on your analysis of these pairs, can you make any generalizations about how some English consonant sounds are "organized"?

5. Notice a group of people together somewhere (waiting for a bus, waiting in line to register, standing around at a party where no one knows anyone else, etc.) What unspoken language patterns do they use? What gestures do they make—consciously or unconsciously—that communicate something about themselves?

6. Describe some habitual gestures you use to communicate.

Imitation and analogy

7. Observe some two- or three-year-old children and try to describe how they are learning language. What sounds do they make? What words do they already know? How do they begin to form sentences?

8. Can you remember any recent experiences where you imitated—intentionally or unintentionally—the behavior or speech of those around you?

9. **Dialect** is a term generally used to describe "local" language, that language we speak in common with those who live in the same geographical region or share similar ethnic or class identifications. A dialect shares not only obvious pronunciations which distinguish it from other dialects, but it also shares certain patterns of expression and distinctive vocabulary. Can you find any examples in your own dialect which distinguish it from other dialects you are aware of?

What's a word?

10. Make up a word that could be an English word but isn't, and provide your own definition for it.

11. Can you describe an experience you had where, like Helen Keller, you suddenly understood something in an entirely different way?

12. What's the difference between a sign and a symbol? Describe, for example, the difference between the boom and crash following lightning which is a sign of rain and the word *thunder.*

The power of symbols

13. What are the literal meanings of the following symbols: the dollar sign; the American flag; the Marlboro cowboy? Compare their literal meanings with any symbolic associations our culture attaches to them.

14. Ads sometimes use "status symbols" to sell products. Describe the meaning of the symbols used in the ad pictured on page 17.

15. Describe some other objects or gestures which have become symbols in our culture. What do they mean? How do they work? What effect do they have on us?

16. Analyze a derogatory racial, religious, ethnic, or sexual word which you have a particularly strong reaction to. What does it literally mean? Can you account for the effect it has on you?

17. We mentioned that Eskimos have more words for *snow* than we do, though we have more words for *car*. Can you think of any other objects dominant or important enough in our culture to require a variety of words to describe subtle differences? List them and discuss some of the differences.

Exploiting symbol power

18. Set up a table as we did on page 13 to show various connotations of some synonyms you compile. List them, give their denotative meaning, then analyze their connotations as we did for *thin, skinny,* and so forth. (If you get stuck, think about various synonyms for beauty, size, or feelings.)

19. Analyze the following prose passage and poems by Eldridge Cleaver, Langston Hughes, and Sylvia Plath. Pick out the metaphors or similes and explain their meanings.

When the guard has mail for me he stops at the cell door and calls my name, and I recite my number—A-29498—to verify that I am the right Cleaver. When I get my mail I avert my eyes so I can't see who it's from. Then I sit down on my bed and peep at it real slowly, like a poker player peeping at his cards. I can feel when I've got a letter from you, and when I peep up at your name on the envelope I let out a big yell. It's like having four aces. But if the letter is not from you, it's like having two deuces, a three, a four, and a five, all in scrambled suits. A bum kick. Nothing. What is worse is when the guard passes my door without pausing. I can hear his keys jingling. If he stops at my door the keys sound like Christmas bells ringing, but if he keeps going they just sound like—keys.

—ELDRIDGE CLEAVER

WHEN SUE WEARS RED

When Susanna Jones wears red
Her face is like an ancient cameo
Turned brown by the ages

Come with a blast of trumpets,
        Jesus!

When Susanna Jones wears red
A Queen from some time-dead Egyptian night
Walks once again.

Blow trumpets, Jesus!

And the beauty of Susanna Jones in red
Burns in my heart a love-fire sharp like pain.

Sweet silver trumpets,
        Jesus.

—LANGSTON HUGHES

BALLOONS

Since Christmas they have lived with us,
Guileless and clear,
Oval soul-animals,
Taking up half the space,
Moving and rubbing on the silk

Invisible air drifts,
Giving a shriek and pop
When attacked, then scooting to rest, barely trembling.
Yellow cathead, blue fish—
Such queer moons we live with

Instead of dead furniture!
Straw mats, white walls
And these travelling
Globes of thin air, red, green,
Delighting

The heart like wishes or free
Peacocks blessing
Old ground with a feather
Beaten in starry metals.
Your small

Brother is making
His balloon squeak like a cat.
Seeming to see
A funny pink world he might eat on the other side of it,
He bites,

Then sits
Back, fat jug
Contemplating a world clear as water,
A red
Shred in his little fist.

—SYLVIA PLATH

20. Try writing a short poem or a description of your own which uses similes
or metaphors to express an observation or a feeling.
21. Play a game called "Exaggeration." Have one person describe someone in
the class, using a metaphor. Have someone else exaggerate or contradict
the description with a simile. For example, one person says, "You're a
really cool chick." (metaphor) Someone else adds, "You're about as cool as
an ice-cube in hell!" (simile)

Style

22. In addition to our "local" dialects, we all use a rather private, intimate
language and style shared with just a few others. As one writer put it,
"Each intimate group must invent its own code." Describe some private
expressions or particular "codes" that you use only within your own family circle. Try to explain how they are used and what they mean. How
would you feel if a stranger in your home overheard and used some of the
"intimate" style?
23. Name some slang words you use or have heard used which have
specialized meanings only understood by a small distinct group of people.
Where did the words come from? What do they mean?
24. Describe several different situations where your style or speech changes
noticeably.
25. Since it is sometimes easier to see in others, describe the shifts someone
you know well goes through in a variety of different social situations.
26. Imagine yourself to be somebody famous—a movie actor, a politician,
someone whose voice and mannerisms you've listened to and seen. Close
your eyes and "hear" the person talking. Imitate his or her style. Write
down a sample—part of a speech, a dramatic scene, even ordinary
conversation—in the person's "voice."
27. Write two letters of complaint, one to a person you like and respect, one to
a person you despise.

28. Try writing the dialogue of a lovers' quarrel: one partner is very logical and refuses to get emotionally involved; the other is passionate and very emotional.

29. You have just witnessed a strange event: someone dressed in a white robe is standing on a street corner holding a Bible and screaming obscenities about man's sins and the end of this filthy world. A little old white-haired lady wearing sneakers and carrying a large black umbrella tiptoes up behind him and starts beating him over the head with her umbrella, shrieking, "I'll give you the end of the world!"

Provide an appropriate ending for the scene. Then, in at least two very different styles, describe what you saw. For example, one style might be the way you'd tell it to your best friend. Another style could be the way you'd report it to the police, if they were to ask.

Suggested Reader Selections

Stuart Baur, *First Message from the Planet of the Apes*
Martin Joos, *Too Many Clocks*
Benjamin Lee Whorf, *Languages and Logic*

Aldous Huxley, *The Arts of Selling*
Norman Mailer, *Ego*
Jessica Mitford, *The Story of Service*

2

a history of language conventions

WHAT'S CONVENTION?

One of the most important concepts to grasp in studying language is the notion of **convention**. Basically, it means "habit"—doing things the way others around us do. There are no laws written in stone that say, "i before e except after c." That's just a convenient rhyme that describes how standardized English spelling has evolved. It wasn't always that way, and it won't always be that way; but most educated users of the language follow that spelling rule today. The written symbol is actually two steps removed from the reality it symbolizes. The spoken word *water*, for example, is represented by those little squiggles on a page *w-a-t-e-r*. The written symbol *w-a-t-e-r* stands for the spoken symbol, which in turn stands for the clear, wet stuff. Since it's that far removed from reality, it's easy to see how writing is a cultural convention. Water, for example, was spelled *w-æ-t-e-r* in Old English and is spelled W-a-s-s-e-r in modern German.

"Proper" usage is much more an outcome of custom, historical accident, and cultural pressure than God-given commandments on grammars or spelling. You learn to spell "correctly" or use a standardized written dialect—what we call **Edited American English**—because that marks you as someone who has learned to play the game by the rules (the standards) which a dominant culture has consciously or unconsciously evolved for any formal social exchanges. Play by the rules, and you get a piece of the action. Misspell every other word you write, and you're branded. You can't get a better job, and the bureaucracy even sneers at your application for a driver's license. For better or for worse, it's always been like that: one group uses language to exclude others. Kids do it. Secret societies do it. Social cliques and street gangs do it. Even governments do it. In olden days, royalty and nobility did it—the royal court set the standards. Our culture is somewhat more democratic, but certain groups—the upper and middle classes who hold economic and political power—print the books and newspapers, pay for TV commercials, and usually serve on school boards. They therefore have the greatest influence on language rules. The whole issue of "standards" is a complex, sensitive area which needs a lot of thoughtful analysis.

We are all capable of linguistic prejudice. We regard anyone who speaks "different from us" with suspicion, and foreigners must prove they can adapt themselves to our language before they are accepted. That does not mean their native languages or dialects are lost. They usually aren't. History is filled with examples of one culture being dominated by another, but in the long run, overtaking the dominant culture's language or at least radically changing it. English today, for example, is an amazing composite of Italian, German, French, Spanish, Yiddish, Russian, Chinese, Arabic, and loan words from any other language you might name—all absorbed into and changing "English." But the powers of convention are strong. However flexible mainstream English may be in absorbing vocabulary and expressions from a variety of dialects and other languages, certain conventions or standards are still dominant, at least in more formal, "standard" English.

Linguists have argued vehemently in the last fifty years or so that the only "proper" study of language ought to be the study of all the different languages and dialects people in fact speak and write. However liberating that assumption may be for scholars, there are other stronger social realities which continue to judge us by appearances. Our dress and manners, and even more our speech and writing—how we pronounce, how we spell, and how we compose ourselves in writing—are often scrutinized. You can probably all describe a situation you've been in where it was obvious you were being judged by the language you spoke or wrote. The practical truth of the matter is that we are all linguistic chameleons: by the time we reach our teens, we have already learned several "languages" so well that we instinctively know when to change from one to another. And the more "languages" we can manipulate, the more powerful we become.

So that's what convention is all about: *arbitrary* standards. Arbitrary standards usually do not have very rational explanations other than "that's the way it's done." How do you explain *through/threw* or *to/too/ two*? You can't! That's just the way it's done. Without getting too frustrated, learn to recognize language conventions for what they are: fashionable "games" with some very arbitrary rules.

SOME HISTORICAL PERSPECTIVES

Let's begin with a bit of history to get some perspective on the "games." What's the difference between writing and speaking? Well, for starters, writing is a lot newer, maybe 5000 years old at most. Spoken language probably has been around in one form or another for over half a million years, although no one knows for sure. English is a member of the Indo-European "family" of languages, only one among many language

A HISTORY OF LANGUAGE CONVENTIONS

"families" in the world. We have very few remnants of the culture of the original Indo-Europeans. Linguists and anthropologists have reconstructed their language and bits of their culture by tracing common denominators in western Asian and European languages. They were a prehistoric people who had no written language. (That's what "prehistoric" means: history at least in one sense of the word didn't begin until writing developed.) We can only guess, therefore, they lived somewhere in the Middle East or southern Russia. Evidence indicates that sometime between 2500 and 1000 B.C., perhaps earlier, various descendants of the Indo-Europeans migrated. Their dialects gradually changed so much that the various branches, although still retaining many telltale traces of their common origins, grew unintolligible to each other.

Such changes are not that hard to understand. Think what it would be like, for example, if your grandmother had moved from the South, or from Germany, or from the mountains of Vermont when she was a girl. If she were to go back for a visit now, even though her immediate family has spoken the same dialect over the years, she would probably have a difficult time understanding relatives she left behind.

The tribes we presume to be the Indo-Europeans migrated, and by the time writing systems began to be developed, the languages were mutually unintelligible. Study the chart on pages 24–25 to get some sense of the complexity of the migrations.

English, as you can see, developed from the Germanic branch of the family. From about the fifth century B.C., there are records of Celtic tribes, another family branch, living in England, Wales, Scotland, and Ireland. (Celtic dialects are still spoken in Wales, parts of Ireland, and France.) After the first century A.D., the Romans, still another branch of the family, settled part of England. The territory became an outpost of the Roman Empire until the early fifth century, when the Roman Empire fell and the troops were withdrawn, leaving the native Celtic tribes in England floundering and open to attacks from neighboring regions. The Celts in England began feuding with the Scots to the north, and in 449 a Celtic chief named Vortigern is supposed to have paid some German soldiers to help fight off the Scottish invaders. The Germans—three closely related tribes called the Angles, the Saxons, and the Jutes—crossed the English Channel and apparently overstayed their welcome. They easily dominated the Celts, driving many back into northern England and Wales and enslaving countless others.

The country of the Celts now became Angle-land, the land of the Angles, or as we now know it, England. Anglo-Saxon, as their language has come to be known, continued to evolve away from the German dialects on the continent and began to develop dialects of its own. Many of the written records we have of this "Old English" have survived in the dialect of the West Saxon kingdom, the region that politically and culturally dominated the other Anglo-Saxon kingdoms during the latter half

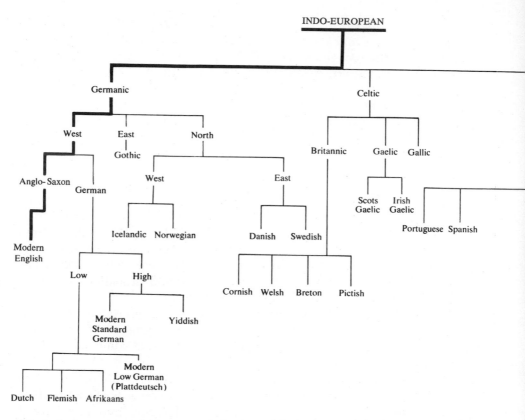

of the ninth century. Literary, political, and legal documents were written in the West Saxon dialect. Thus, even before other European countries developed standard literary and official languages, Anglo-Saxon (or Old English) had evolved into a prestigious, quite standardized written language which was widely understood. Enlightened West Saxon leaders like King Alfred (849-899) encouraged widespread literary development, and Alfred himself compiled and preserved an impressive library in addition to doing considerable writing and translating on his own. (We take basic literacy—even minimal reading and writing skills—so much for granted that it's hard to imagine civilization without them. But even as late as the ninth and tenth centuries, practically the only ones who knew how to both read and write were the clergy. Alfred, for example, taught himself to read when he was forty; the Emperor Charlemagne, who ruled most of Europe in the eighth century, learned to read but never quite got the hang of writing.) By the ninth century, Biblical and major Church texts were available in Anglo-Saxon as well as standard Church Latin, and all were laboriously copied and recopied by literate scribes who worked for the Church or nobility.

Although Alfred did much to stabilize English culture and politics, other invasions continued. During his reign, for example, the Danes (to-

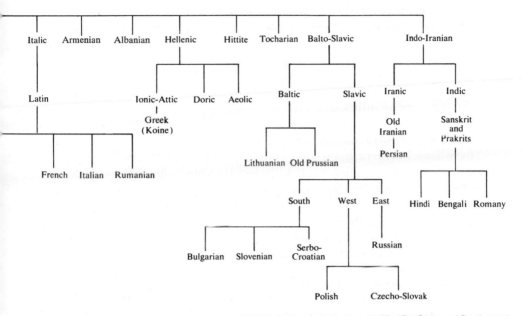

SOURCE: Slightly adapted from pp. 94-95 of *The Origins and Development of the English Language,* 2nd ed. by Thomas Pyles, copyright © 1964, 1971 by Harcourt Brace Jovanovich, Inc. and reproduced with their permission.

gether with the Swedes and the Norwegians, collectively called the Vikings) dominated considerable areas of the country and the Viking languages all gradually mingled with the Anglo-Saxon dialects. In 1066, however, a drastic event—the Norman invasion—changed the course of English history. The Normans were originally Vikings who had settled in France several hundred years earlier. For all intents and purposes, they had become French. Their invasion radically changed the linguistic development of English.

After about 1100, French became the language of the upper classes, and English, as one historian put it, "fell back completely onto its various dialects and became a language of peasants and laborers—and therefore, largely, unwritten." * William the Conqueror, the Norman king, ruled both England and the province of Normandy in France until 1204, when his successors lost the French territory. After the loss, the ruling Normans finally began to consider England as their home. English, then, gradually became more accepted as the "ordinary" form of speech; but in the years of assimilating Norman French with its Latin background, English had

*Morton W. Bloomfield, "A Brief History of the English Language," *The American Heritage Dictionary* (New York: Houghton Mifflin Co., 1969), p. xvi.

adopted a lot of French vocabulary as well as style, both written and spoken. "Middle English," as the language of the period from about 1100 to 1500 is called, is a mixture of Old English dialects, French (and through French and the Church, Latin), with smatterings of Scandinavian.

With acceptance by the Norman French "Anglos," English once again developed a standardized dialect—primarily that of London. By the end of the fifteenth century, English as it was spoken in London—by those in the royal courts, by government officials, and by university teachers and officials—became the recognizable ancestor of Modern English. Although there have been many influences and borrowings since then, Shakespeare's English (of the late sixteenth and early seventeenth centuries) is, with a little practice, quite understandable even today.

There have, however, been some major pronunciation shifts within the language—the contemporary English dialect that most closely resembles Shakespeare's English, for example, is a very heavy Scottish brogue—and these sound changes account for at least some of the confusion of Modern English spelling. The printing press was brought to England in the 1470s in the middle of a major sound change, now known as the "Great Vowel Shift." Many of the Middle English spelling forms were committed to print as their pronunciations were shifting. The vowel sound in Middle English *hous,* to take just one sample of the change, had been pronounced like the vowel in *who.* But Modern English *house*—pronounced as we do today— kept the same spelling even though the *ou* actually has many pronunciations today: compare the *ou* sound in *house* to the *ou* sounds in *through, rough,* and *though.* That's one reason why modern spelling can be so frustrating. But in spite of such pronunciation shifts without corresponding spelling shifts, English as we speak it and write it today is at least recognizable as a close relative of Shakespeare's.

Shakespeare's (or Modern) English, as we've said, is a blend of dialects and languages from other families. To get more of a sense of the relationship between English and the other major European language branches, study the following examples:

ENGLISH: hundred
LATIN: centum
FRENCH: cent
ITALIAN: cento
GERMAN: Hundert

ENGLISH: horn, house
ITALIAN: corno, casa

ENGLISH: man, will, must, house
GERMAN: Mann, wollen, müssen, Haus

As you can see, English is much closer to German, although it is obviously related to Latin, French, and Italian, and borrows vocabulary like the

French version *cent* (for our subdivision of the dollar).

Compare the following examples of English with German, Dutch, Danish, Swedish, and Icelandic (all Germanic languages):

ENGLISH:	Give us this day our daily bread.
GERMAN:	Gib uns heute unser täglich Brot.
DUTCH:	Geef ons heden ons dagelijksch brood.
DANISH:	Giv os i Dag vort daglige Brød.
SWEDISH:	Giv oss i dag vårt dagliga bröd.
ICELANDIC:	Gef oss i dag vort daglegt brauð.

How do they break down? Is English closer to Dutch or to Danish? Is Swedish closer to German or to Icelandic? Go back to the language tree on pages 24–25. Can you find any justification for the slight differences between English, German, and Dutch on the one hand, and Danish, Swedish, and Icelandic on the other?

WHAT'S STANDARD AMERICAN ENGLISH?

American English obviously came over with the settlers in the seventeenth century. Encountering many new experiences and objects, especially plants and wildlife, the new Americans had to develop their own words for things. But even after the Revolution, ties between America and England remained close; in fact, in today's age of instant mass communication these two major dialects have grown even closer.

Americans have always had something of an inferiority complex about their language. To some, at least, the British "accent" still represents a degree of sophistication not equaled on this side of the Atlantic. And it wasn't until the late nineteenth century that American writers really felt themselves to be part of a strong national literary tradition of their own. Many ethnic or minority writers—blacks Puerto Ricans, women, Indians, Jewish-Americans, to name only a few examples—have struggled for the last several decades to establish "identities" and relevant literary traditions, but this is nothing new. Earlier American writers went through similar struggles to establish a national identity apart from England's dominance. American literature as such wasn't even generally considered a subject worthy of in-depth study and a separate "discipline" until the first few decades of this century.

Current American English contains a remarkable record of our complex national heritage. There are hardly any languages you can think of that haven't found their way into English, but there are still ongoing and often bitter debates about the cultural oppression created by a standardized American English dialect. The history of any language, however, is the history of *changing* "standard" dialects, the shifting forces of cultural power.

One culture or power group within a culture attempts to dominate another—and this inevitably involves either the complete suppression or overruling control of the weaker culture's language or dialect. When African slaves were sold in America, to take an extreme example, they were often separated from their kin or mixed with others from different tribes so that they had no language in common. That was the only sure way to destroy their native culture and history, thus making them totally dependent on an alien culture and language, guaranteeing subservience, and preventing revolt. Total destruction of another culture's language, however, is not usually possible. Even the brutality of slavery could not entirely wipe out all traces of African dialects. Scholars have recently theorized that some current dialects of black English resemble certain West African languages: both have similar patterns of syntax, or word order within sentences. Words like *jazz* and *banjo* are also now presumed to be "Americanized" variations of African vocabulary.

Dialects are resilient. Even though most of the native African dialects were lost, distinct black variations of white English soon become common dialects for most slaves. When the Norman French dominated the Anglo-Saxons, the native dialects went underground for a while. Even though they were considerably altered after several hundred years and numerous "outside" influences, they eventually surfaced, and the London dialect actually became the standard English dialect. In New York City, in an area no larger than thirty city blocks, at least eleven mutually unintelligible languages and dialects survive—Czech, Hungarian, German, Spanish, Haitian, Armenian, Yiddish, Italian, Chinese, Jamaican—even Irish. Many of these dialects and languages have been Americanized and have drastically changed from their original forms. Spanish English, or "Spanglish," is just one interesting example—but distinct versions of each language or dialect thrive.

Because we all occupy such a relatively short time span of any language or dialect's life, it is hard for most of us to see any changes. Although we may acknowledge slight changes in vocabulary here and there, we assume our own dialects or languages—whether they're Boston Irish, New York Yiddish, black or Czech American English—to be constant and unchanging. We also tend to think of Standard American English as being even more rigid—about as flexible as the Statue of Liberty—to the point where it oppresses those born anything but middle-class WASP. Furthermore, our current technological world of instant print and rapid mass communications, with its well-paid performers and commentators speaking Standard American English, creates the illusion of widespread uniformity.

Even without drastic cultural upheavals like slavery, wars, or immigration, however, any language or dialect—standard or "nonstandard"—changes and changes noticeably over a period of even several generations. The mass media, for example, especially television, in addition to popularizing a standardized dialect, has also given us access to a much

28

larger range of nonstandard dialect groups. We can now *hear* each other for the first time in history. "The Waltons," "All in the Family," "Rhoda," "Sanford and Son," "Chico and the Man," "Kojak," "McCloud," and "Colombo"—all these are just a few of the prime-time programs that have broadcast a variety of nonstandard dialects for the last few years. Exposure to such a rich variety of dialects has and will inevitably continue to change the spoken and written styles of Standard American English as well as the dialects themselves. Can you think of any examples of dialect that have been absorbed into mainstream English? What changes have occurred in dialects you are familiar with? Obviously, once you understand how both standard and nonstandard dialects change, the whole issue of "standards" becomes a lot more ambiguous. Is there even such a single-minded phenomenon as Standard American English?

Our discussion of dialect variations and Standard American English conventions in fact only applies to a relatively superficial level of language—pronunciation, spelling, verb forms and tenses, a certain style and choice of vocabulary. All but pronunciation are the written conventions of Edited American English. So much of the bitter arguing about oppressive standard English, however, ignores a crucial fact: effective use of language is the same no matter which dialect or style you choose to speak or write. Interesting details, a variety of vocabulary, and an organized, clear development of ideas are common to all effective uses of language. Those qualities that make the so-called Standard American English dialect effective are the same qualities that make *any* dialect—spoken or written— effective.

To summarize, then, any discussion of conventions and standards must take account of all these historical and cultural forces affecting language. Language can be and frequently is used as a tool of oppression, exclusion, and manipulation. Those who control books, newspapers, and other media are those who often have the final say over what and who gets read and heard. But Standard American English is not so standard or uniform, rigid or unchanging as the label "standard" seems to suggest. Language, even a so-called standard dialect, changes. People—native and non-native speakers alike—use and invent language. Language users influence other language users. What is standard for one generation may not be so standard for the next. Dialects become part of the mainstream. The mainstream conventions influence dialects. Imitation is a basic fact of language learning. One of the advantages of learning to write more effectively is that the best writers are often those who *set* the current standards and influence conventions.

WRITING CONVENTIONS

The history of writing—symbols on a rock, in a cave, on parchment or a page—is another complex, very interesting phenomenon of language convention. Writing probably began when some of our primitive forbears scratched pictures on the walls of caves. The first writing was no doubt imitation or representation of the objects referred to. This earliest kind of writing is called **pictographic.** Reproduced here is a pictographic "letter," written in the nineteenth century by the chief of an American Indian totem (tribe or family) to the President of the United States.

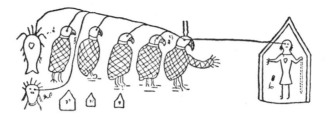

INTERPRETATION: A chief of the eagle totem who lives on the bank of a river, four of his warrior-kinsmen, a fifth warrior (of the catfish totem), and another chief, who is more powerful than the first leader, are all agreed in their views. They extend friendship to the president of the United States in the White House. Three of the eagle totem warriors have agreed to abandon their way of life and to settle in houses, thus adopting the white man's culture. It is hoped the president will understand the offer of friendship and return it.

Instead of using symbols like our alphabet letters to represent sounds which are heard, pictographic writing uses symbols to stand for ideas which can be pictured. Modern Chinese writing, although much further removed from direct, pictorial representations of objects or ideas, nonetheless still uses symbols to represent whole words or ideas. Linguists call written languages using characters like modern Chinese **ideographic** or **logographic** because the symbols are almost completely stylized, not recognizable pictures like the Indian pictogram. Reprinted below are six Chinese characters.

TREE   MOUTH   TONGUE

FOREST   WORDS   LANGUAGE

It is a major jump from ideographic writing to writing which uses symbols to represent **syllables**, or sound units. Instead of needing to know over 3000 different symbols to read or write Chinese, you need to learn only 85 symbols to read or write Cherokee, a **syllabary writing system**. In 1821 a Cherokee chief named Sequoya invented a writing system for his native language, making Cherokee the only American Indian language to have its own fully developed writing system. Although some of the symbols are borrowed from the English alphabet, the Cherokee system is a syllabary, not an alphabet.

The **alphabet** is unique. Instead of using symbols representing whole syllables or longer units of sound, our alphabet symbols represent sounds in a far more efficient system. Rather than having to learn eighty-five symbols in the Cherokee syllabary, for example, an English writer only needs to know twenty-six. One other feature of the alphabet that makes it stand out is the fact that it was invented only once. There have been a variety of independent developments and modifications of pictographic, ideographic, and syllabary writing systems. But the alphabet we know and all other ones are direct descendants of the first alphabet invented.

A Semitic culture, the ancestors of both modern-day Jews and Arabs, flourished in the Middle East before 2000 B.C. (Their language was a branch of the Afro-Asiatic language family that includes both Hebrew and Arabic*.) Phoenicia, a center of that Semitic culture, was a seafaring country of city-states which occupied parts of what is now Syria, Israel, and Lebanon. The Phoenicians developed a syllabary which, with modifications, is the basis of our alphabet. The Greeks borrowed the Phoenician syllabary system and used the symbols of the Phoenician syllabary to represent isolated sounds in their own language. Our English alphabet, named from the first two letters in the Greek alphabet, *alpha* and *beta* (*aleph* and *beth* in Hebrew), comes down from the Greeks through the Romans. To get a better sense of the efficiency of an alphabetic system, study the following list:

Notice that English uses only three symbols—*a*, *h*, and *n*—in several combinations; Cherokee uses five. Alphabet symbols are obviously more flexible and can be used in many more and varied combinations than can syllable symbols; you need far fewer to symbolize the minimal sound units

*Note that this is a different language family, not directly related to the Indo-European "family."

of any language, even though the actual words in a syllabary system may look shorter:

As you saw, pictographs and ideograms are even shorter (only one symbol, in most cases, for a word or idea), but you need a lot more of them. An alphabet system is much more efficient.

EXERCISES

What's convention?

1. Describe how conventions or standardized behavior operates in other areas besides language. Give specific examples from your own experience.
2. Can you think of a social situation you have observed where one individual or group was excluded by an "in" language?
3. List several examples of **homonyms**—words pronounced the same but spelled differently, like *threw/through*—and explain how each word is used differently.
4. Analyze the spelling and sounds of the following words: *tough, women, nation*. Based on the "rules" established in these three words, what should *ghoti* spell?
5. Can you find other illogical examples of "standard" English spelling?

Some historical perspectives

6. Below are three passages, all different versions of Matt. 6:9–13 ("The Lord's Prayer"). For *each* one, write out a literal translation (word for word in the same word order as the original) in Modern English.

> Fæder ure, þu þe eart on heofonum, Si þin nama gehalgod. To-becume þin rice. Gewurþe ðin willa on eor ðan, swa swa on heofonum. Urne gedæghwamlican hlaf syle us to dæg. And forgyf us urne gyltas, swa swa we forgyfað urum gyltendum. And ne gelæd þu us on costnunge, ac alys us of yfele. Soþlice.
>
> —FROM THE WEST SAXON GOSPELS, EARLY ELEVENTH CENTURY

> Oure fadir that are in heuenes, halewid be thi name; thi kyngdoom come to; be thi wille don in erthe as in heuene; ʒyue to vs this dai oure breed ouer othir substaunce; and for ʒyue to vs oure dettis, as we forʒ yuen to oure dettouris; and lede vs not in to temptacioun, but delyuere vs fro yuel. Amen.
>
> —FROM THE WYCLIF BIBLE, LATE FOURTEENTH CENTURY

> Our father which are in heauen, hallowed be thy name. Thy kingdome come. Thy will be done, in earth, as it is in heauen. Giue vs this day our daily bread. And forgive vs our debts, as we forgiue our debters. And lead vs not into temptation, but deliuer vs from euill: For thine is the kingdome, and the power, and the glory, for euer. Amen.
>
> —FROM THE KING JAMES BIBLE, 1611

7. After you've finished translating the passages in the preceding exercise go back and analyze them more carefully. Notice how much the "standard" conventions of spelling and word order have changed over a period of 900 years. Try and answer the following questions:

   a. What letter or letters in Modern English have replaced the Old English symbol æ?
   b. In Old English, the letters þ and ð were both used to represent the same sound. In Modern English, what combination of consonants is used for both?
   c. How is the Old English y written in Modern English?
   d. How is a modern v written in Old English? What vocal apparatus is involved in pronouncing the difference between the f and v sounds in Modern English?
   e. Can you make any observation about what happened to word order between Old and Middle English?
   f. What Modern English letter replaces the Middle English ȝ ?
   g. What two Modern English symbols are sometimes reversed in Middle English and seventeenth-century English?

8. Browsing through the dictionary, list at least five words which are modern versions of Old English words.
9. Again using the dictionary as a reference, list at least five words which are French or Latin in origin.
10. Can you find five different words that have been assimilated into English from five *different* languages other than the ones we've already discussed?

What's standard American English?

11. What are your reactions to this chapter's discussion of standards? Do you agree or disagree with the analysis? Do the historical changes of "standard" dialects make you see contemporary "standards" any differently? Why or why not?
12. Analyze one of the television shows currently running that uses dialect in the development of one of its main characters. Can you describe how pronunciation of some key words and use of vocabulary or idioms, gestures, and so forth differ from your own?
13. Dig around and find some examples of earlier American writing (at least two hundred years old). Analyze how conventions of spelling and word order, for example, were different then from current American English. Translate the passage you find into modern American usage.
14. Rewrite "The Lord's Prayer" in some modern dialect you are familiar with. Don't be afraid to use slang. (This exercise needn't be considered irreverent. Missionaries have always "translated" the Bible into local dialects.)

Writing conventions

15. Describe in your own words how the Indian pictograph on page 30 works: what symbols, for example, stand for what ideas?
16. Using the chart on page 35, translate the five Cherokee words listed below into their alphabetic equivalents.

GWY _____	Cherokee
bᴧˊⓌ _____	Sequoya
SɦZɹ _____	October, harvest month
OˈbɑᴘGˊ _____	instantly
Dₗ,ᴦ _____	war club

17. Like the verbal symbols we use as words, the symbols we use for sounds are very inclusive; that is, one symbol represents a variety of qualities. Letters are very arbitrary symbols. How many different sounds, for example, are spelled with the letter *a*? List as many words as you can that represent different sounds for *a* in your own dialect.
18. What would happen to our written language if we attempted to create a symbol for each separate sound? Try doing it for the words using *a* you just listed. Go back to your list and make up a different symbol of your own creation for each different sound, then rewrite your list using your "new" spelling. Change papers with someone and see if he or she can figure out your "system."
19. Below is an example of a reformed spelling system. What are the advantages or disadvantages of using it?

    Forskor and sevn yeerz agoe our faadherz braut forth
    on this kontinent a nue naeshon, konseevd in liberti,
    and dedikaeted to the propozishon that aul men ar kreaeted eequel.

20. Translate the above passage into conventional English spelling.

Suggested Reader Selections

Martin Joos, *Too Many Clocks*
McGraw-Hill Book Co., *Language and Equal Treatment of the Sexes*

Norman D. Hinton, *The Language of Jazz Musicians*
H. Jack Geiger, *All God's Dangers*
Norman Mailer, *Ego*
John McPhee, *The Capital of the Pines*

a	e	i	o	u	ʌ
D a	R e	T i	ꮼ o	Oʼ u	i ʌ
f ga	ge	gi	go	gu	E gʌ
ha	he	hi	ho	hu	hʌ
W la	le	li	lo	lu	lʌ
ma	me	mi	mo	mu	
θ na	ne	ni	no	nu	nʌ
I gwa	gwe	gwi	gwo	gwu	gwʌ
ꭿ sa	4 se	si	sɢ	su	sʌ
da	f de	di	do	du	dʌ
dla	L dlc	dli	dlo	dlu	dlʌ
dza	dze	dzi	K dzo	dzu	dzʌ
wa	we	wi	wo	wu	wʌ
ya	ye	yi	yo	yu	yʌ

symbol	value
ə	ka
	hna
G	nah
	s
W	ta
	ti
	tla
	te

Source: Adapted from p. 414 of *An Introduction to Descriptive Linguistics,* Revised Edition, by H. A. Gleason, Jr. Copyright © 1955, 1961 by Holt, Rinehart and Winston, Publishers. Reprinted by permission of Holt, Rinehart and Winston, Publishers.

3

effective writing

You already know how to write. You know the basic differences between effective, interesting writing and writing which is dull and boring. You might still have some trouble with spelling, or punctuation or verb endings, but those are relatively superficial aspects of language. Spelling, verb endings, punctuation, and not using fragments are mechanical conventions of Edited American English. The most important thing about writing is writing—using the common denominators of *all* languages and dialects, saying what you mean and meaning what you say. Put *yourself* on paper— your descriptions, your dreams and ideas. Communicate what you see and what you think in the clearest, most interesting, vivid way you can. Use all the colors in words, not just the blacks, grays, and whites. Turn your readers on. Anyone can do it. Learn to utilize what you already know.

USING SPECIFICS

Look at the following two phrases. Which is the more interesting description?

a dirty old wall
a grimy, soot-blackened, old red-brick wall, riddled with large holes in its mortar, sagging like an old mattress

Why is one phrase more interesting than the other? One key to any kind of effective writing is using specifics, including enough details to really get across what you are trying to say. Specifics, facts, visual details—all these are the essential ingredients, the substance of any writing. Without them, your writing is boring. With enough details, you can keep your readers hanging on and coming back for more.

To take another, more famous example, why do you think Muhammad Ali made such a hit a few years back when he predicted his famous victory by claiming he could "float like a butterfly, sting like a bee"? Those phrases are technically similes, but they are also very striking visual details. In that description, you can *see* the grace and precision which make Ali such a talented fighter. Try some exercises in description for yourself. For each of the following phrases, provide some more, very specific descriptive details:

an old shoe
a brand new dollar bill
your own hand
a broken mirror
an aching tooth

Try another exercise. Take a common household object with some detail to it—like a can opener, a stove, or a telephone. Pretend you've never seen it before. Without saying anything about how it works or what it is used for, simply describe what it looks like. See if others in the class can guess your object, simply on the basis of your careful description of its physical details.

Such visual details are the most basic kinds of specifics. We are a visual culture. Our eyes are probably the most highly developed of our sense organs. (If you don't believe that, try walking around blindfolded for a couple of hours.) We are the television generations, raised (or at least nurtured in our old age) with images in constant motion before our eyes. As a writer, however, you must teach yourself to see even more. Really look. Pay attention to the slightest details, and try to see what you've never noticed before. Focus, for example, on the following photograph and describe *everything* you see.

Try another exercise. The next time you go past a building you see every day, pay some attention to it. Check out the texture of the bricks or paint, any details around the door and window frames, the roof, eaves, and the chimney, any architectural subtleties in its design, and so forth. Look at it as if you've never seen it before.

One thing to keep in mind about making writing specific is the power of adjectives. It's the difference between a black and white photograph and one in color; it's the difference, for example, between "a dirty old wall" and "a grimy, soot-blackened, old red-brick wall, riddled with large holes in its mortar, sagging like an old mattress." Choose someone in your class and, without naming any names, describe your subject so others in the class can identify the person. Visual adjectives are essential. It obviously isn't much help to your listener or reader if you describe the person as the man or woman you'd most like to get to know outside class.

Besides visual details, details describing the other senses are also rich sources for specifics—hearing, for example. Pay more attention to listening. We all have certain habitual speech patterns or verbal quirks. Try describing someone else in class by imitating the way he or she speaks, or impersonate some famous person everyone else would know.

WHAT'S ORGANIZATION?

Try a writing exercise called **free association.** Start out with the words *wind, fury, purple, lull,* and see where they lead you. Relax. Say them over and over again, then let your imagination take off. What do the words—their sounds, their references, their associations—mean to you? Put down anything on paper that occurs to you. Write for at least half an hour.

After you've finished, read over what you wrote and try to account for the directions you took. There are no "rights" or "wrongs" here. Just see if you can describe how you proceeded. Can you explain what made you shift from one thought to another? Free-association writing develops its own kind of movement, and you can account for where you went in any way that makes sense of what you wrote. What you have just described is **organization**: the way something grows or evolves, the patterns you use to develop ideas or descriptions. Such patterns are the foundations that specifics build on. Without some kind of organization, your specifics make no sense.

We organize every time we look at things. The moment we move our attention from one thing to another, for example, we are in fact organizing. If you don't believe this, look around your classroom. Even as you look, you are organizing. Your brain is absorbing all sorts of stimuli at amazing rates of speed, yet you see defined objects—chairs, desks, walls, windows, other students, and so on. You don't just experience an over-whelming jumbled mass of sense impressions and details—colors, smells, or strange shapes, for example. Your brain sorts out and classifies. It shapes, defines, and relates the sense impressions to familiar patterns you have learned, so that you can say, "That is a chair and not a blackboard." Any use of language, even simply recognizing something as a "chair," involves a basic intuitive organization. To convince yourself just how much even the simplest perceptions are organized, try to blur the room. Squint or take off your glasses if you wear them. Try to put out of your mind definitions like chair, wall, and blackboard, and experience just the jumble of your senses. It can be mind-boggling if you really stretch your imagination

Virtually all things existing on this planet—all forms of plant and animal life, all rocks, soil, crystals, even forces like light—are organized. Did you ever look at a snowflake carefully or catch a ray of light reflecting off the edge of a piece of broken glass? The simplest amoeba and our own highly refined human bodies, which have had over 25 million years of evolution, are both organized with amazing efficiency and precision. Order underlies all forms of life. (The very word "form" implies shape or organization.) Think of our common origins—a fertilized human egg. From a microscopic egg and sperm, a fetus grows and evolves, methodi-cally and predictably, until it becomes a new life.

Every cell in our bodies is organized in various predictable combina-tions of different substances and arranged in such ways that the final product is the symmetrical whole we call the human body. Put both your hands together, palms up. Study them carefully. They are virtually the mirror images of each other. Look at your fingerprints. (Your thumb prints are the easiest to see.) They are uniquely yours and no one else's, but notice how one is a reverse image of the other. Describe how the rest of your body is organized, how all the pieces "fit" together.

Besides our physical organization, there is really very little human behavior that isn't organized in some way, even though the organization may not be apparent at first. Observe strangers waiting for something to happen. Even in what might seem like random behavior, you will proba-bly begin to notice certain patterns emerging, some kind of basic organi-zation. Someone, for example, may look at her watch every few minutes, then check down the street for the bus. After you have watched for a while, you will begin to see some patterns emerge.

And what about the private little rituals we perform every day? Analyze how you brush your teeth. Chances are you do it the same every time—the way you squeeze the toothpaste, where (left or right, top or bottom) you start brushing, the way you rinse out your mouth when you've finished. You are much more organized than you think you are. If that doesn't convince you, think about the way you habitually eat your food, or the way you take a shower, or the way you put on your shoes in the morning. Call them habits or quirks, they're still very organized patterns of behavior.

Obviously, there are degrees of organization. We all know people who are slobs or perfectionists. Most of us are a little of both. There are times when it's better to be more organized, and there are times when it's better to relax and not worry about it. To use a very homely analogy, when company's coming to dinner, when you want to impress someone, you put your house in order. Even if it's a superficial order (like kicking the dirty socks under the bed), you still straighten the cushions and get things in their right places. When you're entertaining old friends who know you pretty well, you probably aren't so fussy. You relax more and let it all hang out, but even that has a certain kind of organization, if you think about it. The point is that you already basically understand what organizing is, when and how and the variety of ways you do it. The trick is to become more aware of the possibilities of doing it effectively in writing.

Let's broadly define **organization** again. Quite simply, it is the *direction* you move in—the order in which you describe anything, the flow or development of your ideas. As we have seen, there is a certain logic inherent to any organization. No one style is "right" or "wrong"; it depends entirely on what you're doing. In your free-association exercise, for example, the logic of your organization depended on how your associations developed. Your details determined your choice of organization technique.

SOME TECHNIQUES OF ORGANIZATION

If you are describing something, like the photograph on page 37, for example, your organization will probably follow some physical order of the details you are describing—a spatial organization, if you want a classier word. If you were to describe your classroom, to take another example, the easiest way to do it would probably be to go around the room, pointing out different objects in the order they appear. This style of organization, which we can call simply **description**, takes its direction from the object or impressions you are describing.

You can also tell a story. That's called **narration,** or a **narrative organization.** If you were to write about yourself (something that happened to you as a child, for example), you would tell what happened, probably in the order that events occurred. Instead of describing a physical object or impression, you are moving through time. That's narration: "Once upon a time. . . ." A story. First this happened, then this happened, then something else happened. Predictions are a kind of future narrative: first this is going to happen, then this, then this, and so on.

If you were to give someone directions, your organization would inevitably depend on a tighter **"how to"** kind of logic—how to get where you are going. Try another exercise. Take two pieces of paper, any size, and write your name on each of them. Hide one someplace in the school, and on the other write directions describing how to find the hidden paper without naming any rooms. (It's cheating if you say that it's stuffed in the quarter slot of the third-floor phone booth.) To work, your directions will obviously need specifics (like "walk forty paces, then turn right where there is a large, four-foot zigzagged crack in the beige wall"), or your searcher won't have enough to go on. But without some organization, without giving your directions in an ordered series of steps, your searcher will end up in the basement before he or she ever gets to the phone booth. You will obviously know whether or not your organization and specific details "succeeded" if your paper is found.

Organization thus applies to all kinds of writing. How you organize, what style or techniques you use (the ones we've just discussed are only a few among many), depend on what you're writing about. So far we've pointed out four different techniques: free-association writing (the most loosely organized and idiosyncratic option), description, narration, and "how to" writing. But these are all labels, and, like any labels, they can be misleading. Narrative writing (any good story) has to have a lot of description to be effective. Many descriptions explain "how to" do something or help tell a story. But even though all these techniques overlap, such labels are useful because they make it easier for us to become aware of the variety of techniques we all use. Let's introduce another label, a larger category which, even though it is basically just another technique of organization, rates a section all to itself because it includes and expands on most of the effective writing techniques we've already described.

EXPOSITORY WRITING

You've already used **expository writing**—or, more technically, **exposition**—if you ever gave a speech or had an argument with someone. In an argument, for example, you may have tried to "expose" your opponent. Or you may have "analyzed" why the person who shares your house should also share the housework. In a speech you would have "explained" perhaps why you would make the best candidate for a school office.

Expository writing is simply a label given to that very common style of writing which concerns itself with explaining, analyzing, exposing, or convincing. Your "how to" exercise in giving directions was in fact a type of exposition. Expository writing is usually the kind of writing you find in textbooks (like this book), political speeches, how-to books, editorials, letters to the editor, term papers, and so forth. Remember any labels are inexact. The distinctions get fuzzy around the edges. Many kinds of writing you simply can't classify as expository or descriptive or narrative because effective writers use all these techniques and more. For purposes of analysis and discussion, however, let's assume there is a technique we can label "expository writing."

Suppose you were asked to describe your best friend's most annoying habits. If you just threw out a few generalizations about your friend (like "he's sloppy"), without getting down to any of the real dirt, the specific facts, you wouldn't be very convincing. If you wandered all over the place (if you talked about his unfortunate childhood and the poor guy's troubles with his job), instead of sticking to his bad habits, you would also not be very convincing. Moreover, you would end up frustrating your reader. Here your organization can be as simple as a straightforward recital of all your friend's annoying habits: he borrows money and never returns it, he always interrupts, he smokes cheap cigars, he is always clearing his throat, he doesn't change his socks often enough, he's rude to strangers, he sometimes forgets your name, he plays practical jokes all the time, and so forth. You can simply list all these annoying habits, or you can group your evidence for more powerful effect—his treatment of other people, his personal habits, his bad memory—being careful to itemize several specifics for each general complaint you mention.

As you are writing, you should ask yourself these questions: Will your readers be convinced? Have you given them enough facts, enough evidence to support your opinion? Is your evidence organized? The rest of this chapter will present several techniques which will help your writing to be convincing, well-supported, and well-organized.

Topic sentence and controlling idea

We organize most expository writing in **paragraphs**—indented units, usually about five to eight sentences long, although they can range from one sentence to a whole page. A convenient way of developing organization in a paragraph is to use a **topic sentence**, which is usually (but not always) the first sentence in the paragraph. The topic sentence sets up the **controlling idea,** the generalization that makes the rest of the paragraph much easier to read and write. The paragraph and the topic sentence are both conventions; they are traditionally accepted habits of good writing, used because they make both writing and reading easier to organize. All writers use the convention of an indented paragraph, but not all paragraphs have topic sentences as such. Experienced writers can manipulate their material in such a way that the organization is implicit, or under the surface. As a writer just starting to get into your own style, however, you should probably try to use topic sentences as much as possible because they help keep you on target.

"My best friend has some very annoying habits," is a topic sentence. The subject is your best friend, and the controlling idea is *annoying habits.* The key word here is *annoying.* Not just any habits, only the annoying ones. *Annoying* is a generalization, a "large" idea which you plan on explaining in more detail. Here the key word or generalization defines a fairly wide range of feeling. A generalization is the opposite of a specific. To be effective, good expository writing usually has *both* generalizations and specifics. Generalizations—controlling ideas—are the most common ways of organizing specifics in expository writing.

Being able to move from observation of specifics to a generalization about those specifics, finding a common denominator or underlying pattern, is a very fundamental type of thinking. Again, this skill is much more common than most people realize, but the trick is to improve your skill and make use of it in writing. Suppose, for example, you had noticed all of your best friend's habits for years. They bugged you, but you never put them all together and really thought about them before. Suddenly he interrupts you once too often; you get angry and start remembering. It all falls together. What word are you going to catch hold of to summarize the reason for all your frustration? *Annoying* works well. What about *maddening* or *boorish* or *rude* or *vulgar* or *troublesome*, even *piggy*. The point is to find just that right word, that striking generalization, which zeros in and hits your friend right on target. Just as writing interesting descriptions depends on the power of adjectives, setting up an effective controlling idea also demands finding just that right word to describe your idea. Search around until you locate the one that best sums up your feelings. That's what a controlling idea is all about—a key word or phrase, a generalization, which organizes and summarizes your specific evidence.

Fact and opinion

Any kind of observation or thought moves back and forth between generalizations and specifics. If you think of generalizations and specifics as being at opposite ends of a sliding scale, controlling ideas fall somewhere in between, depending on their degree of generality:

G ———————————————|——————————————— S
                 CI

Think about the scale in terms of the distinction between opinion and fact. Opinions ("I hated that movie," for example) almost always fall on the generalization side of the line, while facts ("Seventy-six people were killed in *Death's Revenge*") are at the opposite end. Opinions too far to the "left" on the scale are usually vague and ineffective as controlling ideas. If your controlling idea moves too far to the "right," however, there isn't much left to say. Specifics don't make good controlling ideas because they've said it all; they don't lead you anywhere. To produce a more effective controlling idea, you must narrow down an opinion without getting too specific. "I hated *Death's Revenge* because it was too violent" is a narrower generalization than the original, "I hated that movie." It is a little closer on the scale toward specifics, but without being too specific, it is still general enough to be useful for summarizing your evidence.

The trouble with opinions, however, even more specific ones, is that someone can always disagree. In this case, they can claim there *wasn't* too much violence. You then present specific evidence to support your opinion:

> I hated *Death's Revenge* because it was too violent. Seven people were shot to death, two were axed from behind, and one was stabbed twenty times. Two young lovers were pushed off a cliff. Not only that, but at least three innocent people were mangled on screen when they went through their car's windshield. A dog was run over by a speeding police car right in front of our eyes, and the heroine was blinded with acid.

You have now supported your opinion with very specific facts. While someone might argue with your opinion—your controlling idea—they could not really argue with your facts, providing your memory is accurate. They might be obstinate and claim that even all the facts you cited don't prove that *Death's Revenge* was *too* violent, but with such evidence, most readers would probably be persuaded that you proved your case. It's the specific, factual evidence supporting a well-defined opinion that makes expository writing effective.

Primary support

Besides providing the controlling idea, another use for generalizations or opinions within a paragraph is that they allow a more careful breakdown of your evidence. You can simply recite a list of complaints about your friend. Or, as we have already mentioned, you can group your evidence for more powerful effect—his treatment of other people, his personal habits, his bad memory, and so on. Generalizations like these are somewhat more narrowed down than just *annoying*, but they still need evidence to be convincing. They work within a paragraph as **primary support**; that is, they are the various categories into which you group the specific facts that back your controlling idea. If, for example, you are going to write a paragraph on the high cost of feeding a family, and you have prices for all sorts of food—potatoes, canned corn, pork chops, spinach, apple pie, and so on—how would you organize all the food into several categories of primary support? Organizing your evidence is really just plain common sense, using what facts you have to your own best advantage. In an argument with someone, for example, you're more likely to win—or at least score points—if you organize your evidence instead of just blurting out accusations at random. If you recall your most recent "lover's quarrel," you'd probably admit that you could have made a better case by being more organized (although admittedly organization is sometimes hard to achieve in the heat of emotion).

Analyze the primary support in the following paragraph:

> My best friend has some very annoying habits. For one thing, he is very forgetful. He will borrow money and never return it. He will always be late for any appointment. He even sometimes forgets his friends' names. He also tends to be inconsiderate of other people. For example, he interrupts frequently when someone else is talking. He is often very rude to strangers. And he plays practical jokes that aren't very funny. As if those weren't bad enough, he also has some remarkably bad personal habits. He is always clearing his throat. He never changes his socks often enough. He also smokes the cheapest cigars he can buy. All his annoying habits can really get to you. Nevertheless, he's still my best friend, although I often wonder why.

Primary support becomes very important when you are trying to organize larger amounts of information (for example, this chapter). If I had not used some sort of breakdown, some attempt to organize my thoughts into primary support categories, we would probably be wandering all over the place, and I would have lost you a long time ago (assuming you are still enthusiastically here). This section on primary support is itself a category of primary support for the larger discussion of expository writing. Finish reading the chapter, then figure out what the other areas of primary support are. Such analysis is obviously very useful in reading because it is a lot easier to absorb and remember manageable chunks of material than a page of solid print.

Transitions

The last effective writing technique we will deal with in this chapter is how to tie together all those generalizations and specific facts. Take a look at that paragraph about the friend's annoying habits. Can you point to any words or phrases which in fact don't really add much information as such but serve instead to connect one sentence or idea to another, to show the relationship between one thing said and the next thing mentioned? These are called **transition words** or **phrases**. The word *transition* literally means "movement from one place to another," as in *transit* or *transportation*. Transition devices in fact give your reader direction signals. Read the following version of the annoying habits paragraph with all transitions removed. You should be able to notice the loss. Not only does it read a lot "choppier," but the distinctions between primary support and specific evidence are also not that clear.

> My best friend has some very annoying habits. He is very forgetful. He will borrow money and never return it. He will always be late for any appointment. He forgets his friends' names. He tends to be inconsiderate of other people. He interrupts when someone else is talking. He is very rude to strangers. He plays practical jokes that

aren't very funny. He has some remarkably bad personal habits. He is always clearing his throat. He never changes his socks. He smokes the cheapest cigars he can buy. All his annoying habits get to you. He's still my best friend. I often wonder why.

Without going back to the original version of the paragraph, fill in your *own* transition words. Check out the list of transitions at the end of Appendix A. Most of them should be familiar. Get in the habit of using them more consciously in your own writing.

EXERCISES

Using specifics

1. For each of the following phrases, provide more, very specific details:

   a. an angry face
   b. a dirty frying pan
   c. a woman wearing too much make-up
   d. a worn-out sock
   e. a child's face, about to cry
   f. a dented fender
   g. the sidewalk on a rainy day
   h. a melting ice-cream cone
   i. a cat watching a bird

2. Translate the photographs on pages 48–49 into writing.
3. Describe the physical appearance of someone you are close to *without* referring to their clothes. Ask someone else to guess who it is from your description.
4. Describe the following different smells:

   a. a gas station
   b. the first warm day of spring
   c. a steak broiling
   d. your feet after a long, hot day
   e. an expensive perfume
   f. a cheap cigar

5. Describe your feelings after the following incidents:

   a. You just got an A on a quiz.
   b. Your best friend won an award you were hoping to get.
   c. The bus driver slammed the door in your face.
   d. You just hugged the neighbor's cat who has a bad case of fleas.
   e. It's two A.M. and you still haven't finished your paper due the next day.
   f. You just spilled ketchup on your new suit.

6. Describe someone or something you were afraid of as a child. (Be sure you use enough specifics to convey not only your fear, but also what it was about the person or thing that scared you.)

What's organization?

7. What organization do you see in the following series of numbers:
   10 7 1 13 7 4?
8. Arrange any numbers from 1 to 50 in at least five different patterns of organization and be able to explain the patterns (or give it to someone else and see if he or she can explain the patterns.)
9. Take the items listed below and organize them by categories in any way you can justify:

oysters	steak tartare	martini
eyeglasses	mink	hairdryer
motorcycle	sewing machine	necktie
orange juice	apples	refrigerator
roses	deer	water
light	thunder	air conditioner
zebra	oak	snow
sweater	dog	typewriter
button	milk	heat
scissors	shoes	layer cake
comb	bee	cow
baked ham	gardenias	wine
corn	maple	horse
daisies	perfume	dogwood
clouds	dictionary	shower
honey	trout	rake

10. Ask someone in the class who knows something about drumming to demonstrate different basic rhythms, syncopation, and so forth. Then analyze the organization of the beats.
11. Listen to a rock song on the radio and describe how it's organized. Pay attention to both the music and the lyrics.
12. Describe some personal habit or a private ritual you perform every day. Analyze its organization.
13. Young children frequently develop some organized patterns of play which might not seem apparent at first. Observe a child you know well and describe any patterns you can find.
14. Stare at the "still life" on page 52 and try to explain how it is organized. What is the relation of the different objects, shapes, or colors to other objects, shapes, or colors?
15. Notice the way you breathe. Describe the different things going on throughout your body every time you take a breath. Explain the order in which they occur.
16. Describe a dream you had and try to account for its "organization."
17. Write a poem beginning each line with "I wish . . ."

Some techniques of organization

18. Make up a bedtime story for a child you know.
19. Retell an old fairy tale you remember from your own childhood, but bring it up to date by using modern settings and language.

EFFECTIVE WRITING

20. Watch some thriller on TV and retell the story in your own words.
21. You have just witnessed an automobile accident and the police officer on the scene has asked for your eyewitness report. What happened?
22. Write a story which begins with the following first line: "An old man sat in the crowded, smoke-filled cafe."
23. Make a kid happy. Draw a complicated treasure map to show where you hid something special. Then translate the map into your own writing.
24. Describe how to build, make, or do something you're very familiar with such as sewing a dress, playing chess, baking a ham, cheating at poker, taking apart an engine, filling out an income tax return, etc.)
25. Describe the various techniques of organization you used in questions 18 to 24. (Remember labels can be misleading.)
26. Analyze the organization in the paragraph reprinted below. What do you think the writer is trying to communicate?

From the fire tower on Bear Swamp Hill, in Washington Township, Burlington County, New Jersey, the view usually extends about twelve miles. To the north, forest land reaches to the horizon. The trees are mainly oaks and pines, and the pines predominate. Occasionally, there are long, dark, serrated stands of Atlantic white cedars, so tall and so closely set that they seem to be spread against the sky on the ridges of hills, when in fact they grow along streams that flow through the forest. To the east, the view is similar, and few people who are not native to the region can discern essential differences from the high cabin of the fire tower, even though one difference is that huge areas out in this direction are covered with dwarf forests, where a man can stand among the trees and see for miles over their uppermost branches. To the south, the view is twice broken slightly—by a lake and by a cranberry bog—but otherwise it, too, goes to the horizon in forest. To the west, pines, oaks, and cedars continue all the way, and the western horizon includes the summit of another hill—Apple Pie Hill—and the outline of another fire tower, from which the view three hundred and sixty degrees around is virtually the same as the view from Bear Swamp Hill, where, in a moment's sweeping glance, a person can see hundreds of square miles of wilderness. The picture of New Jersey that most people hold in their minds is so different from this one that, considered beside it, the Pine Barrens, as they are called, become as incongruous as they are beautiful. West and north of the Pine Barrens is New Jersey's central transportation corridor, where traffic of freight and people is more concentrated than it is anywhere else in the world. The corridor is one great compression of industrial shapes, industrial sounds, industrial air, and thousands and thousands of houses webbing over the spaces between the factories. Railroads and magnificent highways traverse this crowded scene, and by 1985 New Jersey hopes to have added so many high-speed roads that the present New Jersey Turnpike will be quite closely neighbored by the equivalent of at least six other turnpikes, all going in the same direction. In and around the New Jersey corridor, towns indistinguishably abut one another. Of the great unbroken city that will one day reach at least from Boston to Richmond, this section is already built. New Jersey has nearly a thousand people per square mile—the greatest population density of any state in the Union. In parts of northern New Jersey, there are as many as forty thousand people per square mile. In the central area of the Pines Barrens—that forest land that is still so undeveloped that it can be called wilderness—there are only fifteen people per square mile. This area, which includes about six hundred and fifty thousand acres, is nearly as large as Yosemite National Park. It is almost identical in size with Grand Canyon National Park, and it is much larger than Sequoia National Park, Great Smoky Mountains National Park, or, for that matter, most of the national parks in the United States. The people who live in the Pine Barrens are concentrated mainly in small forest towns, so the region's uninhabited sections are quite large—twenty thousand acres here, thirty thousand acres there—and in one section of well over a hundred thousand acres there are only twenty-one people. The Pines Barrens are so close to New York that on a very clear night a bright light in the pines would be visible from the Empire State Building. A line ruled on a map from Boston to Richmond goes straight through the middle of the Pine Barrens. The halfway point between Boston and Richmond—the geographical epicenter of the developing megalopolis—is in the northern part of the woods, about twenty miles from Bear Swamp Hill.

—JOHN McPHEE

Expository writing: topic sentence and controlling idea

27. Underline the controlling ideas in each of the following topic sentences:

    a. People sometimes make stereotyped judgments when first meeting strangers.

    b. The weather in New Jersey can be depressing.

    c. Cats make interesting pets.

    d. Marlon Brando is a very versatile actor.

    e. Going to school full-time is usually an expensive experience.

    f. Motorcycles can be dangerous.

    g. Southern California has weather conducive to an outdoor life style.

    h. Written language has some pretty absurd conventions.

    i. The controlling idea is a useful device for effectively organizing a paragraph.

j. Studying language can give you some interesting insights into human behavior.

28. Which of the sentences below would make more effective topic sentences? Which would not? Why or why not?

   a. I hate to study English.
   b. Studying English can be very demanding.
   c. Temperatures in the Mojave Desert are grueling at any time of year.
   d. The Mojave Desert reaches temperatures of 150° in July.
   e. Muhammad Ali is a very flamboyant fighter.
   f. Muhammad Ali is a cool guy.
   g. The Middle East is a time bomb.
   h. Peace negotiations in the Middle East break down because each side feels it has ancient, time-honored rights to the land.
   i. Language dialects in America reflect the diversity of our cultural heritage.
   j. There are over 200 dialects of English spoken.

29. Fill in an appropriate adjective to make an effective controlling idea in each of the following topic sentences:

   a. Current fashion styles are very ————————— .

   b. Unemployment in this area is ————————— .

   c. Stereotypes can be very ————————— .

   d. My mother is a ————————— person.

   e. Childhood can be ————————— .

30. For each of the following groups of facts, provide a controlling idea which can effectively summarize all the information:

   a. (1) Sally Smith sued her boss who expected her to analyze stocks and manage client's portfolios but paid her only a secretary's salary.
      (2) She joined a local women's group and picketed a neighborhood bar which wouldn't admit women.
      (3) She helped form a day-care center so working mothers could leave their children with responsible adults.
      (4) She once shouted "Women!" when some local politician giving a speech kept referring to his campaign workers as "girls."

   CONTROLLING IDEA: ——————————————————————————————

   ——

   b. (1) Malcolm Martin would always take twice as long to finish a job as anyone else.

Pablo Picasso, *Fruit Dish,* 1908-09, winter. Museum of Modern Art, New York.

EFFECTIVE WRITING

(2) He frequently left out half the parts on anything he assembled.
(3) He always had a far-off look in his eyes.
(4) He would frequently hum a tuneless song or talk to himself.

CONTROLLING IDEA: _____

_____

c. (1) The Wonderwagon gets forty miles per gallon.
  (2) Its engine is air-cooled, so it never requires water or antifreeze.
  (3) It can go for 5000 miles without a tune-up.
  (4) Its body never dents or wears out.

CONTROLLING IDEA: _____

_____

d. (1) Current summer fashions feature a bathing suit using only 1/16 of a yard
       of material.
  (2) One dress style has no back and only half a front.
  (3) Short shorts are now "in" again and they average only about six inches
       from top to bottom.
  (4) One manufacturer is even making shoes with no soles.

CONTROLLING IDEA: _____

_____

Expository writing: fact and opinion

31. Label the following states F for Fact or O for Opinion:

   a. _____ Harry is a very gabby fellow.

   b. _____ Harry makes at least twenty phone calls a day.

   c. _____ Television sometimes assumes its viewers are children.

   d. _____ On a recent broadcast of "Changing World," the heroine looked di-
            rectly at the camera and said, "Oh, I am sad. I love my husband, and
            now he has left me. Oh how sad I am."

   e. _____ In the fall issue of Drive magazine, a woman dressed in a fur coat is
            driving a Porsche and smoking an imported French cigarette.

   f. _____ Ads often appeal to expensive tastes.

   g. _____ Rock superstars have some pretty weird acts.

h. ____ A rock singer once appeared on stage in rhinestone-studded army fatigues and proceeded to smash his guitar to bits.

i. ____ The CIA commissioned a millionaire to give a party for visiting Russian athletes.

j. ____ Government agencies sometimes spend money on questionable projects.

k. ____ Melvin Mews, a multimillionaire, put on a lavish spread for the visiting athletes.

l. ____ He served thousands of dollars of caviar, vodka worth $40 a bottle, eighty sides of barbequed beef, and a hundred pounds of lobster flown in from Maine.

32. List enough facts to prove each of the following opinions:

a. Goldfish make good pets. _____

_____

_____

b. Current fashions are very versatile. _____

_____

_____

c. My teacher is too demanding. _____

_____

_____

d. The weather can be very unpredictable. _____

_____

_____

e. Kids sometimes say the strangest things. _____

_____

_____

33. Well-defined opinion is obviously an important quality of effective writing, but even well-defined opinions left unsupported aren't very useful. Unsupported opinions or generalizations are all over the place, even though they aren't usually very convincing. Listen to your friends talk, watch television, or read a newspaper and see if you can list at least ten unsupported opinions or generalizations you run across.

34. Besides being too easily tossed around without facts to back them up, opinions can also sneak into writing posing as facts, and they can easily influence uncritical readers and manipulate their understanding. In extreme forms, this is propaganda. But disguised opinions occur much more frequently in milder forms, conveying the writer's point of view (or opinion) in place of the facts an unsuspecting reader *thinks* he or she is getting. Cut the opinions from the following statements and rewrite them as neutrally as you can. Explain the implied point of view of the original writer.

   a. The President of Silesia held a brief news conference this morning. When confronted with rumors of a budding romance with her handsome male secretary, she vigorously denied anything but an efficient working relationship.

   _____

   _____

   b. Last night's debut brought out the best and the worst of New York society; in a dismal downpour, lines twenty deep remained to see the glittering superstars slither into the theater.

   _____

   _____

   c. For the average worker, any economic slump can be devastating because there is the double-barreled threat of soaring inflation accompanying the spectre of unemployment.

   _____

   _____

   d. Helga Hotlips, that tawdry torch singer from Toledo, did her stuff for a standing room only crowd which wildly cheered every searing note out of her mouth.

   _____

   _____

e. The tense situation in the Middle East has worsened in recent months because of declining oil reserves in the West and skyrocketing costs of oil which the Arabs have exploited.

_____

_____

Expository writing: primary support

35. Arrange the following groups of sentences from the most general to the most specific:

a. (1) Food prices are soaring.
   (2) A can of peaches that used to cost 49 cents now costs 56 cents.
   (3) Canned goods are up over 20 percent.

b. (1) George Goodguy got into trouble when the police flagged him down.
   (2) He was arrested for driving without a current registration.
   (3) Driving someone else's car can be dangerous.

c. (1) Being a star has its drawbacks.
   (2) Movie star Mason Mod lost his toupee when a group of fans mobbed him coming out of the theatre.
   (3) Fans can sometimes get too enthusiastic.

d. (1) Traveling salesmen sometimes spend up to four months a year away from home, and they often get very lonely.
   (2) Absence makes the heart grow fonder.
   (3) A traveling salesman, Charles Smith, once called his wife three times in one night because he was so depressed.

e. (1) Minnie Haskins raises sheep, shears their wool, cleans, spins, dyes, and weaves it, then sells sweaters she knits for a living.
   (2) Minnie Haskins lives alone and is very self-sufficient.
   (3) Solitude breeds strength.

36. Go back to question 9 and rearrange the items so that you have at least two categories of primary support for each category you set up.

37. Analyze the following two paragraphs and underline all the primary support:

The soap opera "Changing World" deals with some
extremes of raw emotions. Hate, for example, is often
portrayed by both men and women. One male character
hated his wife so much that he threw a frying pan full
of Hotdog Helper at her. Besides hate, another

frequently dramatized emotion is excess agony. Elaine, a divorcee, cried so long after an unhappy affair with her married neighbor Alfred Union that she was hospitalized for dehydration. Worry is also shown to excess. One young mother was so concerned about her eight-year-old daughter's popularity that she forced the child to wear false eyelashes to school and bleached her blond braids even blonder. In spite of hate, agony, and worry, however, passionate romance still survives. Ursula Union is so in love with her husband, Alfred, that she wears a sheer lacy nightgown to greet him at the door. She hands him a double martini, then, without even waiting for him to take off his hat, she embraces him in a swoon.

The Wonderwagon is a very economical car to operate. For one thing, it uses very little gas. It has a specially constructed four-cylinder engine generated by a carburetor which just about runs on gas fumes. The car's weight is also balanced in such a way that going down hills, the motor idles, saving fuel for the acceleration needed at the bottom. It even has a catalytic converter which can transform pollution in the air into a combustible source of energy which supplements gas. Besides saving money on gas, the lucky Wonderwagon owner also saves on maintenance. The compact model, for example, can go over 5000 miles without needing any servicing. Fenders are dent-proof, and even the battery is guaranteed never to die because it automatically recharges itself from ultraviolet rays in the atmosphere. You also save on antifreeze and water because the engine is air-cooled, and it has no radiator. In addition to both fuel and maintenance economy, other operating costs are also minimal. Since the "Wag" is so tiny, it can always squeeze into the tightest spots, thus saving garage fees and even parking meter costs. It obviously qualifies for the lowest insurance rates since it is so small and cannot cruise above fifty-five miles an hour. Finally, besides all these advantages, the "Wag" even qualifies for a tax deduction because it is the only energy-<u>producing</u> car on the market: people always jump up and down, shout, and laugh whenever they see it drive by.

Expository writing: transitions

38. Go back over the two paragraphs in question 37 and circle any transition devices used.
39. Rewrite the following paragraphs, adding transition words or phrases wherever needed:

    Advertising creates needs. Most American families are convinced they cannot function without at least one or more cars. Those cars aren't usually the plain, stripped-down economy models. Air-conditioning, chrome trim, whitewall tires--whitewall radial tires--carpeted interiors, and a powerful engine are "necessities" of transportation encouraged by competitive automobile advertising. Family health is an area of "needs" generated by ads. Many studies have shown that Americans buy far more varieties of aspirin, sinus and cold cures, relief for stomach upset, pep remedies, children's vitamins, even diet aids than are necessary for good health and well-being. American families, thanks to advertising, spend billions of dollars annually on a variety of name-brand detergents, soaps,

and household cleaning products. Ads have made us
believe we smell in places we often don't. We "need"
personal colognes, mouthwashes, and an amazing
assortment of deodorants. Cars, health, and cleanliness
--all are obviously necessary--but thanks to
advertising, the average American family "needs" a lot
more than it used to.

A recent issue of <u>Fight</u> magazine, the controversial
new military weekly, described a heated debate over army
hair styles. The "Longs" feel they have a right to any
style they choose so long as it does not interfere with
their work. The "Shorts" claim any hair below the
collar is dangerous--it can get caught in rifles,
tangled in trees, or scalped by the enemy. Some "Longs"
are willing to compromise in war zones, but they see
the "Short" arguments as defenseless in peacetime. The
"Shorts" defend their style by claiming short hair
builds character. It presents an image of clean-cut
efficiency to the public. The "Longs" insist the public
isn't interested in seeing mowed heads. They prefer a
civilian look--which can be whatever the soldier chooses,
within the bounds of good taste. The "Longs" admit to
some disagreement about what determines "good taste."
Arguments on both sides have gotten pretty extreme. One
general was quoted as saying, "Any man with a single
strand of hair over one-half inch should be court-
martialed!" A mediator brought in by the Department of
Defense suggested a possible solution might be the
"Brass Bald," a fad among certain generals, which
completely eliminates any debates on length.

59

EXERCISES

Pablo Picasso,
Woman by a Window,
1956, Museum of
Modern Art, New York.

Expository writing: combining techniques

40. Select one of the general topics listed below which you have some opinion about. Narrow down and refine your opinion, so you can *prove* it in one paragraph. Write a topic sentence which defines your opinion in a clearly stated controlling idea, then write a paragraph at least eight to ten sentences long which develops your controlling idea with specific facts and uses primary support and transitions.

    a. professional athletics
    b. pop music
    c. cost of living
    d. current fashion
    e. smoking
    f. "open door" education
    g. economy cars
    h. advertising
    i. hair styles
    j. television programs

41. Write a paragraph comparing the two portraits above. Be sure you set up a topic sentence and use specifics to develop your comparison.

Thomas Gainsborough, *Mrs. Richard
Brinsley Sheridan,* c. 1785. National
Gallery of Art, Washington, D.C.
(Andrew Mellon Collection).

Suggested Reader Selections

John McPhee, *The Capital of the Pines*
Gay Talese, *New York*
Aldous Huxley, *The Arts of Selling*
Jack Shakely, *Sweet Charity*
Andrew Malcolm, *Chemists in Timber
Revolution*

Lewis Thomas, *On Societies as Organisms*
Jessica Mitford, *The Story of Service*

4
basic sentence conventions

Basic sentence conventions are the mechanics of Edited American English (or EAE as we shall refer to it from now on). EAE is all that "grammar" you never quite understood. You can communicate perfectly well without it, but in fact it is not that hard to learn. As a writer, you need the mechanics to polish your style, just as you need awareness of social customs and manners if you apply for a job, plan a wedding, or give a fancy dinner party. The mechanics, or conventions of writing, are really no more or less than "manners," generally accepted habits of communicating in a social group. Let's take a look at two of the basic conventions which form our modern English writing system: punctuation and sentences.

MARKING BEGINNINGS AND ENDS

Punctuation is a convention that we usually don't think about until we try to remember old comma rules, but punctuation makes a lot of sense when we begin to understand why and how it's used. What is it? Most basically, punctuation refers to those signs we use to mark off groups of words. One of the usual problems nervous writers encounter is where and how to use all the different punctuation marks there are. For now, we're going to consider only the problem of marking ends of sentences.

You probably have a general idea of what a sentence is, though most likely, you rarely speak in sentences. A sentence is a *writing* convention. Most of us *speak* in **fragments,** frequent exclamations liberally sprinkled with *ums* and *ahs.* (The only person I know who didn't learned English as a second language, and his use of complete sentences was so distracting that you seldom heard *what* he said.) In writing, however, sentences are a generally accepted—though fairly recent—way of communicating.

Use of consistent punctuation and capital letters to mark the beginnings of sentences is also a relatively recent custom. In some cases, it is rather arbitrary, which is why we can easily get frustrated with it. Most punctuation, however, is generally used quite consistently in EAE, and the rules for using it are only a few and not that complicated. Below is a short essay which explains more about the history of punctuation. All the punctuation marks at the ends of sentences have been omitted. Can you figure out where they go? Try reading out loud. Writing is, after all, basically a *formalized, arbitrary* version of spoken language. While none of us speak in complete sentences, end punctuation marks are a substitute for the way we conclude a message delivery in our speech. There is seldom any doubt when we end a sentence in speaking because our voice goes up or down or we use certain gestures and facial expressions. When you read the following paragraph, you should also be able to hear most of the breaks between these sentences. Don't forget to mark the **capital letters** beginning sentences.

punctuation and capitalization are fairly modern habits as early as the twelfth and thirteenth centuries they were hardly ever used very few people could read and write those who could were mostly clergymen or noblemen most of the things available in writing were biblical or literary manuscripts or documents of state these were copied over laboriously by men who were called scribes there was very little literature available to the average man very few knew how to read manuscripts were too valuable and difficult to obtain early manuscripts looked a lot like this paragraph they often did not even have breaks between words the printing press was invented in the fifteenth century punctuation only then became a more common thing even then it was not very standardized writers could put in dashes and commas or periods wherever they felt like it standards of punctuation were not really adopted until the eighteenth century newspapers became popular the average person had opportunities to learn to read a more standard system of punctuation became a must it developed obviously to make writing easier to read

WORD ORDER

Let's look closer at sentences. How can we talk more precisely about what a sentence "is"? Most of you probably punctuated sentences in that last exercise without too much trouble, so we can come up with the simplest working definition based on what we already know: a *sentence* is a written group of words, parts or pieces of speech which work together as a "unit" of some kind, marked at the beginning by a capital letter and at the end by a period (or question mark or exclamation point).

Look at the following two "sentences." Which comes closer to being an EAE sentence?

Increased the significantly cost of has living.
Angry purple money sits loudly.

English is very dependent on word order to communicate meaning. The first sentence obviously isn't EAE (or any other form of English, for that matter) because it's all jumbled. Unscramble it and you have, "The cost of living has significantly increased" or "The cost of living has increased significantly." Both of these are perfectly comprehensible English sentences. But out of order, the words make no sense. "Angry purple money sits loudly," however, does make a weird kind of sense, even though it sounds like a bad dream. Why? Well, obviously money isn't usually purple, nor is it angry, since it's inanimate and doesn't have feelings. Money doesn't usually sit (except in a bank vault) and nothing usually sits loudly, literally. But even though we can argue vigorously with the sentence's sense (or nonsense), it still has an eerie resemblance to an English sentence—more, certainly, than the first group of words does. Why? Because the right words are in the right places. You *can* put together sentences like these:

Angry white demonstrators shouted loudly.
That little old lady knits quickly.
Black rain clouds rumbled ominously.

Like these sentences, the nonsense sentence fits a pattern—something or somebody does or did something in some way.

Look at the following two sentences:

The man bit the dog.
The dog bit the man.

When we reverse the order of the sentence, we obviously change the meaning of the sentence. This is not the case in all languages. In Latin, for example, you can write "The dog bit the man" as:

Canis mordet hominem.
Hominem mordet canis.
Canis hominem mordet.

The order doesn't matter. The -em ending on *hominem* tells you that *hominem* (man) received the action. The *canis* (dog) *mordet* (bit) the man. We still have some of these endings in Modern English (they are called "inflections"), but there are not nearly as many as there used to be in Old English. Language seems to evolve to simpler forms, leaving traces of the old behind. For example, the -m ending still does remain on some pronouns:

The dog bit the man.
The dog bit *him*.

In English, however, most pronouns indicate what part they play in a sentence by changing *both* position and form, not just by changing endings:

They gave it to us.
We gave it to them.

Most native speakers of English would *not* say, "Them gave it to we," or "Us gave it to they." The form of the pronoun depends on its place in the sentence.

Another way of defining a **sentence** in English, then, is to say that it's a group of words *in a certain order*, begun with a capital letter and ended with a period (or ? or !). Word order, however, is rarely a problem; as a native speaker of English, you should be very confident of ordering words in a sentence because, at least in spoken language, you've been doing it quite adequately since you were two or three years old.

MAJOR BREAKS

Still another instinct you have but are probably not too aware of is a kind of second sense about where or how to "split up" any sentence. Suppose you were asked to divide our nonsense sentence into two parts:

Angry / purple money sits loudly.
Angry purple / money sits loudly.
Angry purple money / sits loudly.
Angry purple money sits / loudly.

The most instinctive break is the third one: "Angry purple money / sits loudly." Why? These two parts are the basic building blocks of any sentence: the first part tells us that something or somebody is doing or feeling or being something—what we traditionally call the **subject**. The second part of the sentence lets us know what's going on, some action or feeling or state of being that, in EAE at least, is a part of speech we label **verb**.* With few exceptions, the verb always marks time: past or present. Most sentences in English will have some verb that signals past or present and some basic subject. Most of you instinctively know which is which. Here is the nonsense sentence reduced to its barest bones:

Money / sits.
SUBJECT: *money*
VERB: *sits* (The *-s* indicates present time.)

Look at the following examples:

*If you are unsure of the labels used to describe parts of speech, check out Appendix A for a discussion of how to use such labels and why.

```
                    Joe  /  hates English.
      SUBJECT:      Joe (He's the one doing the hating.)
      VERB:         hates (The -s on hates tells you it's present.)

                    Joe  /  was here.
      SUBJECT:      Still Joe (He's the one who was here.)
      VERB:         was (This is the irregular past form of be.)
```

From the above, we can now give a more refined working definition of an
EAE sentence. Memorize it and keep it in mind: A **sentence** is a group of
words in a certain order beginning with a capital letter and ending with a
period (or ? or !) that usually has a subject and a verb which marks time.

So where do we go from here? The problem with "grammar," which is
what this is beginning to sound like, is that it never did much to help
anyone write better. It keeps some grammarians and teachers in business,
but in the past, at least, it has usually just made a lot of people bored,
frustrated, and insecure. What we'll be doing in the rest of this chapter,
however, is not "grammar" in the old, nasty sense of the word, but rather
description and analysis of EAE sentences. If you learn how to read the
recipe, it's a lot easier to bake a cake.

SUBJECTS

In English sentences, as we've seen, the subject is most often the word or
group of words coming *in front of* the verb:

```
          S   V
English is a Germanic language.

          S              V
English, a Germanic language, is closely related to Dutch.

          S              V
Most Western languages are Indo-European.
```

But not everything comes so nice and easy. There are also a lot of sentences in English that begin with words that are *not* part of the subject. We
frequently find words or groups of words coming at the beginning of a
sentence which are not part of the subject. You can move these words or
groups of words around. Move them to the end of the sentence, for example, and the sentence still makes sense:

```
                S V
Frequently, I like to sleep late.

S V
I like to sleep late frequently.

                S V
Occasionally, I work overtime.

S V
I work overtime occasionally.
```

We need to be aware of these words, called **adverbs**, because they are not part of the subject; we have to shift them, or move them out of the way, before we can check for subjects. Adverbs like *frequently* and *occasionally* tell us something about the verb, the action in the sentence; they let us know *when, where, why, how, how often, under what circumstances,* and so forth.

There are also groups of words that are not part of the subject. First there are those we traditionally call **prepositional phrases**—groups of words working together without combination subjects/verbs of their own and beginning with prepositions like *on, to, before, after, during, through, for,* and so on. You can identify these because they too can be shifted:

S V
Before the show, *I* want to get some popcorn.

S V
I want to get some popcorn before the show.

Circle the prepositional phrases in the following sentences and find the subjects:

Before lunch, I want to go to the store.
On my way home, I had an accident.
During the week, I have too much to do.
For lunch, I ate a carton of cottage cheese.

Another group of words sometimes confused with the subject is a **clause.** This is a group of words working together which has its own subject and verb. A very common kind of clause is an **adverb clause,** which hooks onto the main part of the sentence; it can begin with a variety of words—*because, although, even though, since, before,* and so on—all of which function like adverbs. Again it can be shifted:

S V
Because I was late, *the teacher* got mad.

S V
The teacher got mad because I was late.

Circle the adverb clauses in the following sentences and find the subjects:

Since he came, I haven't had a moment's peace.
Even though it's spring, the temperature is still cold.
Before we met, my life was dull and hopeless.
Now that we've met, every day is like a new beginning.

Notice that we have already established one simple rule for using commas in EAE: any group of words coming in front of the subject is usually set off by a comma. Single adverbs and very short phrases preceding the subject often don't need a comma, but longer phrases and clauses always do. Notice also that the comma is dropped when the phrase or clause moves to the end of the sentence:

Because I love you, I want to hold your hand.
I want to hold your hand because I love you.

You should now find it easier to locate subjects. Besides the joys of discovery and a handy comma rule, however, another reason for bothering to find subjects should be obvious. Without a subject, an EAE sentence is usually incomplete; it's considered a fragment, only a piece of a sentence. Fragments can be used for occasional effects. Unless they are *consciously* used for effect, however, fragments are usually considered rather careless violations of EAE (though, again, they are quite usual in ordinary speech).

The only other complication you might run into in your search for subjects is what is known as **you understood** or **commands:**

Shut the door.
Work until nine.
Please don't eat the daisies.

The subject in all commands is always an *implied* "you": (you) shut the door; (you) work until nine; please don't (you) eat the daisies.

That about covers subjects. Most subjects are usually nouns, pronouns, or other words or groups of words working like nouns. For now, it's enough if you can learn to find them.

VERBS

As a writer, you sometimes have problems with verbs because verb endings in many dialects of English are not pronounced. *Most* of us would say, "I hateteta leave thparty last night. . . ." But we're forced in EAE to write, "I *hated* to leave the party last night." Pronounce *d,* as in *hated.* Now pronounce *t,* as in *it.* Sound alike? The only difference is that *d* is what we call "voiced" and *t* is "voiceless"—that is, your vocal cords vibrate when you pronounce *d* but not when you pronounce *t.* Put your fingers on your throat and feel the diference. You can see how easy it is to drop or blend endings in speech, but in writing, you must remember to add the ending because in EAE it is frequently the only signal built into the verb which marks time:

I hate him.
I *hated* him. (But maybe I no longer do.)

That's an important distinction.

BASIC SENTENCE CONVENTIONS

Irregular forms

In general, it is usually easy to spot how verbs mark time in EAE: you simply look for the -ed that marks the past on most verbs. The real problem, however, comes with those **irregular verbs** that change spelling to mark the past.

There used to be many more irregular verbs in English (most English verbs whose origin is German still mark the past through various spelling changes), but as English developed through the Middle Ages and Renaissance, these irregular verbs rapidly changed to the simpler -ed markers and lost spelling changes (like leap/leaped instead of leap/leapt). Many people felt, however, that such a "normalization" took away much of the elegance they had cultivated in English—cheapened the language, so to speak—and they choose to protect their language from any further "erosion." In the eighteenth and nineteenth centuries, grammars were written in attempts to halt the changes, and these grammars set down what one "ought" to use.

Furthermore, with the rise of the middle class in both England and America, there was a great demand for grammar books, dictionaries, and books of etiquette which would explain how to speak and act "properly" to people who had only recently acquired social status and some wealth. Such books were (and still are) plentiful. They attempted to explain the subtleties of the "cultured" dialects to an insecure, newly successful middle class, even when the grammar they prescribed was actually at odds with the way cultured speakers "to the manner born" spoke or wrote.

Such gentlemanly grammars delayed a scientific study of language for more than a century. They not only succeeded in freezing the irregular (or "elegant") forms of many verbs and other spelling inconsistencies, but in writing grammars of the language, they also imposed a Latin grammar on what linguists later discovered was not a Latin language. English is a Germanic language, but Latin at that time was the only language close to English which already possessed a thoroughly analyzed grammar.

Imposing a Latin grammar on English is a little like trying to describe how a car works by using only words which label parts of a horse. A horse is a very remarkable system used by man for transportation; so is an automobile. And they do have some similarities—both run on fuel of sorts and travel over terrain on four extensions of a body. But the horse and the car are obviously different constructions. You can't get a very accurate picture of how an internal-combustion engine runs by talking about a heart and hooves. The same is true about languages. It is only in the last hundred years or so that linguists have been describing English as it is, not as it deviates from or fits into irrelevant descriptions of Latin. And it wasn't until the invention and popularization of the computer in the last few decades that more thorough, systematic models were developed which attempt to describe how the English we speak and write works, not how it "should."

Unfortunately, much of the insight that linguists and anthropologists have had into the way English dialects work has not yet filtered down to the "grammar" schools and high schools. Many colleges continue to teach traditional "Latinized" grammar. In this book, you may have noticed, we still use some labels borrowed from traditional grammar—like our parts of speech, for example—but we try to use those labels to describe how the language works, not to impose unchanging definitions.

But let's get back to verbs. All those irregular forms are still frozen in current EAE, although some are beginning to "thaw out." The simplest, least aggravating solution to the problem is to memorize the irregular spellings—photograph the spelling in your mind's eye whenever you run across an irregular verb—and make your own list of tricky ones. Review the irregular verbs listed in Appendix A, especially the complete breakdowns of the three worst ones, *be, have,* and *do.* A few irregular verbs like *cut, put, bet, let,* and *set* all use the same forms in past and present. These few are the exceptions to our definition of a verb "marking time." They, in fact, don't. Others, however, even though they are spelled similarly, *do* change forms to mark the past: *get/got, pet/petted.* There are no foolproof rules, so just memorize the differences.

Principal parts

If you're uncertain about the EAE past tense form of an irregular verb and your list isn't handy, you can turn to the dictionary. For example, suppose you need to know the past of *swim.* You would look the word up under the form *swim* (called the **infinitive** or "to" form)—not under what you think the past tense is. Under the entry for *swim,* you'll find *v.,* which identifies the word as a verb, then *swam/swum/swimming.* These are called the **principal parts** of the verb, the major spelling or inflection changes.

> *Swim* is the **infinitive** or **simple present.**
>
> I swim everyday.
>
> *Swam* is an irregular **simple past.**
>
> I swam yesterday.

Swum is an irregular **past participle**, most often used with *have, has,* or *had.*

> I have swum* laps for an hour.

Swimming is an irregular **present participle,** used with *am, are, is, were, was,* or (*has, have,* or *had*) *been.*

---

*If this form sounds somewhat awkward, it's probably because we're in the process of losing the *swum* form and we're more likely to use *swimming,* as in "I've been swimming."

I am swimming.
I was swimming.
I have been swimming.

Participle is a technical term for a verb that can't act alone as a verb. By itself, it does not "mark time," so it must "participate" with another verb which does mark time—some form of *have* or *be*.

There are the same number of principal parts for regular verbs as for irregular verbs. For example, the principal parts of the regular verb *work* are *work/worked/worked/working*. The dictionary does not list the principal parts of a regular verb because they are regular. You can figure them out for yourself: both the past and the past participle simply add -ed, and the present participle adds -ing.

These in summary, are the principal parts:

1. Infinitive or simple present
2. Simple past
3. Past participle
4. Present participle

Memorize the labels. They are useful handles. The parts they describe are the building blocks of the English tense system. For example, here are some common EAE tenses—the way time is marked—for the verb sing:

I *sing* everyday. (present, habitual)
I *sang* yesterday. (past; an action over and done with)
I *will sing* in the chorus next semester. (future; *will* is used with the infinitive)
I *have sung* in a chorus for two years. (an action begun in the past but recently completed or still going on)
I *had sung* that piece before it was popular. (an action completed in the past before another event described in the past)
I *am singing* now. (an action still going on; the -ing has a sense of action in progress which can be current or projected into the past or future)
I *was singing* when the dog began to howl. (an action taking place when another occurred)
I *have been singing* in a chorus ever since last year. (works like "I have sung," but communicates more of a sense of process or ongoing action)

You already use many of these basic forms in speech. In different English dialects, there are also several very consistent variations of these forms which mark different aspects of time. Learn to recognize the EAE forms and use them with all the written markers they need. For example, in speech, many of us would say, "I been goin' to school for two years now"; but, since been is a participle form, it does not mark time and so cannot stand alone. In writing EAE, therefore, you must indicate more:

I *have been going* (or I've *been going*) to school for two years.
I *had been going* (or I'd *been going*) to school for two years (before I was drafted).

71

We usually use the contracted form (*I've* or *I'd*) in speech. Since the contracted form is such a slight verbal marker, it gets lost easily when we translate it into writing.

Singular and plural forms

Besides forgetting irregular spellings and dropping contractions with participles, many writers have another major verb problem with the *-s* that marks singular present:

Joe hates English.

Use the *-s* or the *-s* form (*is, has, does*) to mark the present on all verbs that go with singular subjects other than I or you. EAE does *not* use a written *-s* on verbs with I or you, even though some spoken dialects consistently do:

Joe *hates* English.
I hate English.
You hate English.

Only Joe gets the *-s*.

What's so confusing is that the symbol *-s* marks singular on verbs, but oddly enough, it also marks plural (more than one) on nouns:

My cat *hates* children. (one cat)
My *cats* hate children. (more than one cat)

Notice that when you have an *-s* on the subject, you usually don't need it on the verb, but if you *don't* have an *-s* on the subject, you should check more carefully. You might need one on your verb if you are describing the present:

Cats hunt mice.
A cat *hunts* mice.

That leads us into the problem of agreement: subject and verb must agree in number, that is, a singular subject takes a singular verb marker, and a plural subject uses a plural verb (usually just the simple form of the verb without any marker in the present). In EAE, for example, you *don't* write:

The children *plays* handball in the street.
The children *is* noisy.

You *do* write:

The children *play* handball in the street.
The children *are* noisy.

Most of us have no trouble when the subject of a sentence is obviously singular or plural. There are a number of subjects, however, which look as though they might be plural but in fact are either deceptive spellings or what we call **collective forms**—words like *army, jury, gang,* and so forth. These all have plural forms *(armies, juries, gangs)* and in their singular forms, even though they are groups made up of more than one individual or thing, they take a singular verb marker:

The *jury* delivers its verdict today

Nouns like *toast, bread,* and *milk* are all considered singular unless they specify a quantity or a container:

The bread *is* stale.
The *pieces* of bread *are* stale.

Pronouns like *everyone, nobody, each* are also singular:

Everybody is finally here.
Each owes me ten dollars.

If you keep these few special cases in mind, you'll rarely have problems with agreement.

Passive and subjunctive

The only other "verb confusions" we'll need to discuss here are uses of what's called the passive and uses of the subjunctive. Concerning the first, consider the following two sentences:

The dog bit the man.
The man was bitten by the dog.

These both mean the same thing, except that the first emphasizes the action, the dog *biting,* and the second emphasizes receiving the action, the man being *bitten.* **Passive** (meaning literally "not active, unaggressive") is simply a description of the second emphasis—the subject receiving action, not delivering it. You all use these without much difficulty, but it's good to recognize the difference for two reasons. First, awareness helps you avoid written versions of dialect. "I *be hit* hard" must be written "I *have been hit* hard" to give it a time marker. (*Be* is simply the infinitive form and in EAE, it does not mark time by itself.) Second, learning to be aware of passive usage allows you more power and flexibility in manipulating your language. A child, for example, has already sensed a powerful difference if he or she says, "Mommy, the milk (is) spilled," instead of "Mommy, I spilled the milk." Switching the subject from *I* to the passive *milk* neatly shifts the blame.

Passive forms use a past participle with *am, are, is, was, were,* or *(has, have,* or *had) been:*

I *was hit* by a car.
They *were driven* crazy by the noise.
They *have been criticized* for their behavior.
I *am loved* by many.
He *is* always *attacked* for his beliefs.

73

VERBS

The passive always forces action back onto the subject.

The subjunctive is a form not used quite as much in EAE as it used to be, but it is still around and considered essential in many circles, so it's worth knowing. Can you hear the difference?

> If I was you, I'd hurry.
> If I *were* you, I'd hurry.

We recognize the second as a **subjunctive** because it substitutes the plural form *were* where you'd usually expect *was*, but it does this only in "if-y" situations: I'll never be you. But if I *were* . . . That's subjunctive:

> If I *were* rich, I'd give a lot of parties.
> If he *were* here, he'd congratulate you too.

EXERCISES

Marking beginnings and ends

1. Translate the following segment of a "manuscript" into Edited American English:

thehistoryofanylanguageisthehistoryofchangingstandards
languagechangesreflectthechangesofthepeoplespeakingthe
languageinademocraticsocietythelanguageofthebestwriters
andmostinfluentialleadersshouldideallysetthestandards
butitdoesnotalwaysworkthatwaytherearetoomanyotherforces
atworkonlanguageinamericanculturetherearepowerful
economicandpoliticalforceswhosesurvivaldependsonselling
theirproductstomillionsofpeopleweareurgentlypersuaded
tobuytheirproductswhetherdialsoapornationalsecurity
toofrequentlythesearetheforcesthatsetstandardsofour
language.

Word order

2. Unjumble the following "nonsense" sentences and rewrite them in conventional EAE word order:

   a. wind curious a whistled the in alligator.
   b. always twenty themselves cockroaches wash.
   c. argued the sweetly anteater hairy.

d. about worry can't fireflies sleeping you.
e. me harder electric my work typewriter to urges.
f. tears an orange cries gorilla crocodile angry.
g. urgently fire a crackling speaks.
h. balloon a hungry lollipops eats.
i. urgently happy smile daffodils.
j. preaches my sermons cat.

3. Unjumble the following "normal" sentences and rewrite them in conventional EAE word order:

a. you because madly you love I you're.
b. caused a to pollution our has environment threat serious.
c. me it to sock!
d. struggle our must we urge constantly to with destroy.
e. you I since forget I you forgive must can't.
f. be words can weapons as used.
g. thing I whole ate the.
h. order certain are sentences words in a subject.
i. marker a English all in sentences subject have a and time.
j. Mable marvelous mother my macaroni makes.

Major breaks

4. Split each sentence you unjumbled in exercise 2 into two major parts.
5. Split each of the following sentences into its two major parts:

a. My uncle Eddie eats apples.
b. The inside of any man's mind is more revealing than the outside.
c. My eighty-year-old grandmother wears sneakers.
d. Bennie, the neighborhood bookmaker, lays odds on anything moving.
e. The late afternoon sky is turning black.

Subjects

6. Circle any moveable words, phrases, or clauses in the following sentences. Then identify the main subject in each sentence. Check the list of prepositions and adverb clause words in Appendix A to help you recognize the moveable parts. Remember, you are looking for subjects in the *main* part of the sentence, not any subjects that might be part of a clause that can be shifted.

a. Once upon a time, there was a beautiful princess.
b. Even though she is shy, Mabel Markos speaks out publicly when she's angry.
c. Because he hates violence, Gregorio Martinez refuses to go into the kitchen when his wife is cooking.
d. Occasionally, spinach can be an interesting vegetable.
e. Although he's ticklish, Jamil Jamil earns his living by sitting on beds of nails.

75

EXERCISES

f. By the time I get to Phoenix, you'll be waiting.

g. Whenever I see her, I want to smile.

h. When the acorn grows, it becomes an oak.

i. Because she beat him at tennis, Martin Manly won't play with Matilda anymore.

j. If you get discouraged, remember the Alamo.

7. Subjects in the following sentences have all been omitted. Fill in an appropriate subject where it belongs.

a. Because I was late, got mad.

b. Sings in the shower.

c. Makes twenty copies at a time.

d. Before you joined us, had started to eat.

e. Have to coordinate their time well.

f. Is the common language which many European languages descend from.

g. Shrieked with delight.

h. Even though it snowed, continued their journey.

j. Slammed with a bang.

j. After work, stopped at a neighborhood bar.

8. After reading the following passage carefully, go back and identify the main subject in each sentence:

(a) The doctor kept me waiting in his outer office. (b) It gave me a chance to check out his style. (c) A sofa near the door was covered in shiny brown plastic. (d) Modern art hanging on the wall made the room look cold. (e) The glaring phosphorescent light gave the room an even more uninviting air. (f) On the table, the magazines and papers were precisely arranged. (g) The nurse worked away efficiently behind her desk. (h) When my turn came, a disembodied voice beckoned me over the monitor. (i) Hesitantly, I got up and went into the inner office.

Verbs

9. The following version of the passage in Exercise 8 omits some regular and irregular verb forms. Fill them in without referring back to the original.

(a) The doctor _____ me waiting in his outer offices. (b) It

_____ me a chance to check out his style. (c) A sofa near the door

_____ covered in shiny brown plastic. (d) Modern art hanging on the wall

_____ the room look cold. (e) The glaring phosphorescent lighting

_____ the room an even more uninviting air. (f) On the table, the

magazines and papers _____ precisely arranged. (g) The nurse

_____ away efficiently behind her desk. (h) When my turn came, a

disembodied voice _____ me over the monitor (i) Hesitantly, I

_____ up and _____ into the inner office.

Did you notice anything all these verbs have in common? An important technique to remember is *consistency*. Don't switch between past and present unless you have a reason for doing so.

10. Fill in the appropriate forms of the verbs in parentheses. (Check your dictionary or Appendix A for any you are unsure of.)

(a) I (bend) _____ the door yesterday when I (try) _____ to open it. (b) I had (lose) _____ my keys. (c) I (fall) _____ down as I was (get) _____ off the subway, and my keys (fly) _____ under the subway car. (d) I (cut) _____ my knee too, but some nice gentleman (hold) _____ my arm and (help) _____ me to my feet. (e) I (sit) _____ down on a bench and (struggle) _____ not to cry. (f) I (be) _____ very angry at myself for being so clumsy and (swear) _____ out loud. (g) People who were (run) _____ by (look) _____ at me as if I (be) _____ crazy. (h) I (say) _____ to myself that they would do the same thing. (i) I (put) _____ my chin in my hand, (tell) _____ myself to calm down, and then I (leave) _____. (j) The whole experience really (shake) _____ me up.

11. Below is a series of sentences using a variety of EAE tense distinctions. For each one, try to explain as specifically as you can exactly what "time" or aspects of "time" are being referred to.

77

a. I was working late when I heard a strange noise.
b. I want to become a doctor after I get out of the Army.
c. My grandfather had been in the Austrian Cavalry before he emigrated to America.
d. I have been trying to study for an exam all week, but it hasn't been easy.
e. Martin Manly refused to play tennis with his wife because he was afraid she would beat him.
f. He is never going to take another chance.
g. He had just started taking lessons when he challenged her to a game. She won.
h. Whenever you feel afraid, whistle.
i. I am going to buy a new car as soon as I can save enough money.
j. I have already saved $2000 dollars, but at the rate prices are going up, that won't pay for the fenders.

12. Write at least ten sentences describing some of your experiences as a student. Try using a variety of EAE time distinctions and be ready to explain what time or aspects of time are being referred to.

a. _____

_____

b. _____

_____

c. _____

_____

d. _____

_____

e. _____

_____

f. _____

_____

g. _____

_____

h. _____

_____

BASIC SENTENCE CONVENTIONS

i. _____

_____

j. _____

13. Many English dialects use a variety of different forms to show different aspects of the past, present, and future. Some black dialects, for example, make consistent distinctions between continuous, ongoing action and action of the moment: "He workin' when the boss come in" refers to work begun just to impress the boss. "He be workin' when the boss come in" refers to work that had already been going on when the boss showed up.

Analyze your own speech. Do you consistently use a variety of forms (not necessarily the same as EAE) to indicate differences in aspects of the past, present, or future? Write them down as you say them (without worrying whether they conform to EAE).

14. Write at least ten sentences by choosing one word from each column for each sentence. You may end up with some weird combinations, but be sure all the pieces "fit."

two	cat	wear	fast	apples
a	elephants	is	an	collars
some	order	eat	lace	games
those	children	chases	loud	rats
an	men	play	rotten	order

a. _____

_____

b. _____

_____

c. _____

_____

d. _____

_____

e. _____

_____

f. _____

_____

g. _____

_____

h. _____

_____

i. _____

_____

j. _____

_____

15. The following sentences use various dialect verb forms. Change them to EAE verb forms:

a. The terrified man in a gray suit look like he have seen a ghost.

b. Students hates English.

c. Everyone are here.

d. The jury were deliberating.

e. An army are composed of different kinds of people.

f. The milkman were late.

g. The lazy student done a very poor job of studying.

h. I be working hard.

i. An Italian neighbor down the street have his own grocery store.

j. My cats has fleas.

k. They was on their way home when it starts to rain.

l. Robert Redford and Paul Newman was a hit in *The Sting*.

m. Women's Lib be here to stay.

n. He think he gonna con me but I knows better.

o. We tries harder.

p. Joseph Brag just been fired from his job.

q. I wish I was slim, gorgeous, and rich.

16. Write as much as you can describing the first date you ever had. If you can't remember that far back, fake it. After you've finished, check over your writing for tense consistencies and EAE verb forms.

Suggested Reader Selections

Stuart Baur, *First Message from the Planet of the Apes*

Martin Joos, *Too Many Clocks*
Norman Mailer, *Ego*

Like customized cars and high-fashioned clothes, many English sentences are fancy variations on standard models. Once you learn to recognize the models, it is much more interesting to play around with variations.

Consider this sentence, which dramatically begins a chapter of *The Autobiography of Malcolm X:*

> Surrounding the house, brandishing their shotguns,
> the Klan riders shouted for my father to come out.

The author could have written:

> The Klan riders surrounded the house. They brandished
> their rifles. They shouted for my father to come out.

Somehow, the second version—three sentences instead of one, longer sentence—is not nearly as effective as the first. Why? By using -*ing* phrases, the writer focuses on the threat and terror of the action. The -*ing* phrases also give a more complicated rhythm to the sentence. The other version sounds flat, repetitive, and matter-of-fact by comparison—with none of the drama and build-up of the original.

The writer actually built on a very basic model:

> The Klan riders shouted.

This is usually called a "simple sentence," what we will label a **Type 1 sentence:** somebody or something does or did something. Here is another simple sentence, Type 1:

> Joe hates pickles.

There are a variety of techniques you can use to expand this simple sentence.

ADDING COMPOUND CLAUSES

One of the most common ways to expand a simple sentence is to "double" it. Just add more information. For example, Joe hates pickles, *and he never eats them*. *And he never eats them* is called a **compound** or **compounding clause** because it compounds or "adds to" another clause. We will label simple sentences expanded by compound clauses **Type 2 sentences.** There are several different ways of writing compound clauses:

> Joe hates pickles, and he never eats them.
> Joe hates pickles; he never eats them.
> Joe hates pickles; therefore, he never eats them.

Learn to recognize the difference between simple sentences (Type 1) and doubled or compounded sentences (Type 2). You use them all the time. Awareness of the difference not only gives you more variety to work with in writing, but it also gives you one more simple comma rule and a rule for using semicolons. The comma rule states that when *and, but, so, for,* and other conjunctions of this class are used to introduce an otherwise separate, independent clause, they are preceded by a comma. As for the semicolon, when you add an otherwise separate, independent clause without the conjunctions cited above, you must use a semi-colon because a comma by itself is too weak. The semicolon here functions as a conjunction and has the effect of fusing the two parts of the sentence. There is also another class of conjunctions—words like *however, therefore, moreover yet,* and so forth—which must take a semicolon preceding them (and sometimes a comma after them) when they introduce a compound clause. See Appendix A (page 134) for a more complete list of these and all other conjunctions discussed in this chapter.

The list below contains Type 2 sentences. Circle all the compound or Type 2 conjunctions (including semicolons working as conjunctions and commas or semicolons working with other conjunctions):

1. I want to come, but I can't.
2. We need more parking space; we also need more trees.
3. The sun is shining; however, it's raining.
4. The price of sugar has risen 80 percent since January, so the prices of candy have also gone up.
5. I saw the body, and then I fainted.
6. I saw the body; then I fainted.

The following sentences are either simple sentences (Type 1) or compound sentences (Type 2). Label them 1 or 2:

1. _____ I always work hard.

2. _____ My mother used to be an opera singer.

3. ____ We come to school every day, and we study hard.

4. ____ My uncle works in Brooklyn; he commutes by subway.

5. ____ I want to read; however, my children keep interrupting.

6. ____ Moving can be very upsetting.

7. ____ I hiked forty miles yesterday; as a consequence, I lost five pounds.

8. ____ Football fans can really be fanatics.

9. ____ Television is sometimes habit forming.

10. ____ Eating and drinking a lot in one night can put weight on you fast.

11. ____ Beer is especially fattening.

12. ____ People with beer bellies shouldn't drink so much.

13. ____ Mighty Mikhilovich, the Yugoslavian weight-lifting champion, is ticklish.

14. ____ Nellie Neville is a Senior Sister of the local chapter of the American Daughters of the West; she traces her heritage back to Buffalo Bill.

15. ____ Paul Pride, the all-American model, always gravitates to the nearest mirror.

ADDING ADVERB CLAUSES

Another technique for expanding the simple sentence adds an **adverb clause** introduced by an adverb conjunction like *because, although, even if, since, before, when, until, while,* and so forth. We call these **Type 3 sentences.** Unlike Type 2 conjunctions, which double the sentence by adding on another *equal* clause, these Type 3 conjunctions expand the sentence by adding *extra* information: how, when, why, where, and so forth. Both clauses in a Type 2 sentence are equal; there are two main subjects. In a Type 3 sentence, however, the adverb clause is subordinate, that is, less important and dependent on the other clause for its complete meaning, and the Type 3 sentence has only one main subject.

> Joe never eats pickles. He hates them. (1)
> Joe never eats pickles *because he hates them.* (3)
> *Because Joe hates pickles,* he never eats them. (3)

Notice the punctuation. In a Type 3 sentence, when the adverb clause is in the front, it is followed by a comma. But there is no comma when it comes at the end. The following sentences are all Type 3 sentences. Circle the Type 3 conjunctions:

1. Although it's late, I'm not in a hurry.
2. I haven't gotten an hour's sleep since exams began.
3. If the economy doesn't improve soon, we'll all be broke.
4. The bus won't leave until you arrive.
5. Prices will continue to go up whether or not our salaries do.
6. Even though I hate English, I love my English teacher.
7. Before you go, leave your money on the table.

The following sentences are either simple Type 1 sentences or have been expanded into Type 2 or Type 3 sentences. Label them 1, 2, or 3:

1. ____ Because it rained, the game was canceled.

2. ____ Whenever I get up late, I miss my train.

3. ____ You'll get fat if you don't stop eating.

4. ____ I like to eat, so it's easy for me to gain weight.

5. ____ Eating can be a very enjoyable hobby.

6. ____ There are always new foods to try.

7. ____ A good cook can sometimes spend eight hours in the kitchen for just one meal.

8. ____ Some foods demand courage.

9. ____ Steak tartare and broiled octopus aren't exactly the average American entrée.

10. ____ Fast-food chains are doing a booming business even though many feel the food is poor quality.

11. ____ We are always in such a hurry, so we often grab any food in easy reach.

12. ____ Although there are many food preparation regulations, a lot of sloppy processing slips by.

13. ____ A consumer once found three dead flies in a jar of strawberry jam.

14. ____ A test of the composition of one hot dog discovered pig's ears, insect parts, and other supposedly inedible matter.

15. ____ The text caused one researcher to throw up because he had just eaten a hot dog for lunch.

85

ADDING ADVERB CLAUSES

ADDING ADJECTIVE CLAUSES

Still another way of expanding a sentence is to add an **adjective clause,** a clause introduced by *who (whom* or *whose), which,* or *that.* This makes a **Type 4 sentence.** The adverb clause in a Type 3 sentence adds information about how, when, where, why, and so forth. An adjective clause, sometimes called a **relative clause,** adds information about who, which, or what. It builds up a noun or pronoun; the adverb clause builds up the verb. An adjective clause is also subordinate, that is, less important and dependent on the main clause for its complete meaning. Study the following sentences:

Joe hates pickles. He never eats them. (1)
Joe, *who hates pickles*, never eats them. (4)
Joe, *who never eats pickles*, hates them. (4)

I had a hot dog for lunch. It's not digesting. (1)
I had a hot dog for lunch *which is not digesting.* (4)
The hot dog *that I had for lunch* is not digesting. (4)

The baby boom is over. It began after World War II. (1)
The baby boom *that began after World War II* is over. (4)
The baby boom, which is over, began after World War II. (4)

Who is usually used to refer to a person. *Which* usually refers to animals or ideas. *That* can be substituted for either *who* or *which,* but it is usually alternated with *which.*

Notice the use of commas in the above sentences. If the *who, which,* or *that* clause is not necessary to the meaning of the sentence, you use commas as "handles" to show that the clause can be "lifted out." If the *who, which,* or *that* clause is necessary, however, you get rid of the commas. A *that* clause frequently has no commas around it. Note the difference between the following:

Ronald Ripoff, *who sells used cars*, is dishonest.
A man *that sells used cars* can't always be trusted.

Ronald Ripoff is dishonest no matter what he does. The fact that he sells used cars is incidental. Most people, however, wouldn't make such a sweeping generalization about any man. It's not just any man that can't be trusted; the writer is specifying a man that sells used cars. See the difference?

One other point that needs clarification is when to use *who, whom,* or *whose.* Although the *who/whom* distinction in spoken English is usually limited to more formal situations, EAE has adopted it as a convention. A simple way to remember the distinction is that *whom* is always followed by a whole Type 1 clause, while *who* is usually the subject of the adjective clause and is followed by a verb:

This is the man *whom I told you about.*
This is the man *who has to lead the march.*

You can avoid the problem by using *that* in either case:

This is the man *that I told you about.*
This is the man *that has to lead the march.*

Whose always signals ownership:

This is the man *whose store burned down.*

Don't confuse *whose*, the possessive, with *who's*, which is a contraction for *who is*:

This is the man *who's no longer working here.*
This is the man *whose job you filled.*

To determine which one to use, try substituting *who is* to see if it fits.

The following sentences are either simple, Type 1 clauses or have been expanded into Type 2, Type 3, or Type 4 clauses. Label them 1, 2, 3, or 4:

1. _____ My mother, who is an opera singer, practices in the shower.

2. _____ She doesn't sing very well any more because she is getting old.

3. _____ My dog complains a lot whenever he hears her.

4. _____ He doesn't like singing.

5. _____ The dog, who is a collie pup, screeches a lot himself.

6. _____ Mother used to sing opera in Milan.

7. _____ Now she just teaches opera to little rich children.

8. _____ She doesn't like her job because none of her students are really interested in learning.

9. _____ One little boy always sings the scales with his tongue stuck out at her.

10. _____ That little boy, who's really a monster, hates to take lessons.

11. _____ He comes because his mother insists.

12. _____ His mother, who wanted to be a singer herself, is trying to live through her child.

13. _____ That is always a dangerous thing to do.

14. _____ It confuses the child, who usually has enough problems to begin with.

ADDING ADJECTIVE CLAUSES

15. _____ It doesn't allow the child to have his own identity.

16. _____ My mother's job, which is really babysitting, is thus a lot of trouble at times.

17. _____ She does it because she has to earn a living.

18. _____ She is a widow, and she lives by herself.

19. _____ She is really seventy-eight years old although she looks like fifty.

20. _____ She has her own apartment in New York, and she likes to ride the subways.

21. _____ I always warn her to be careful, but she never listens.

22. _____ Someone once tried to hold her up; she talked him out of it.

23. _____ He ended up crying on her shoulder after she loaned him ten dollars.

24. _____ He paid her back the next week; in fact, he still comes to see her.

25. _____ Mother is a very unique old lady who is stubborn and always gets her own way.

COMBINING CLAUSES

Now that you've identified the basic clauses used to expand sentences, let's look at some combinations. Besides alternating Types 1, 2, 3, or 4 for variety, you can also use combinations of 2, 3, or 4 to expand the same sentence:

Joe, who hates pickles, never eats them because they make him sick. (4, 3)
Even though it's freezing, I'm not worried because I've got my love to keep me warm. (3, 3)
My mother, who was very health conscious, always warned me not to eat so much, but I didn't listen; as a consequence, I'm thirty pounds overweight. (4, 2, 2)
Because of the weather, the game which was scheduled for this afternoon was cancelled, and it will be replayed next week. (3, 4, 2)

Identify the following combinations of sentences:

1. _____ The optimist who claimed "life is just a bowl of cherries" didn't really understand all the implications; cherries have pits.

2. _____ Adolescence can be a trying time because many teen-agers who suffer identity crises take out their insecurities on those nearest to them.

EXPANDING THE BASIC SENTENCE

3. ____ Stanley Knowitall has to have something to say about everything; he'll offer advice on anything, and he'll presume to be an expert even if he knows nothing about it.

4. ____ He's a bachelor, but he once told a worried woman who was in her ninth month of pregnancy how to have a baby.

5. ____ The Wonderwagen is a remarkable car because it runs on very little fuel, and it almost never needs repairs.

6. ____ Cecelia Current will do anything to keep up with the latest fashions; she once appeared in a see-through blouse with a boa shawl, and she teetered around on shoes with five-inch platform soles.

ADDING ADJECTIVES AND ADVERBS

Besides combining clauses for variety, you can also build up basic parts of the sentence by adding modifiers—adjectives and adverbs—which expand your description:

My brother Joe hates pickles.
My *older* brother Joe hates pickles.
My *older* brother Joe *violently* hates pickles.
My *older* brother Joe *violently* hates *green* pickles.
My *older* brother Joe *violently* hates *green* pickles, *especially sweet pickles.*

Notice the comma before *especially sweet pickles.* This is an extra modifying phrase stuck on the end, so the "handles" rule applies: we set it off from the rest of the sentence with a comma, a "handle," to show it is an added piece of information, not essential to the main part of the sentence. The comma is a "handle" which you can use to remove the word or groups of words from the rest of the sentence:

Pickles, *especially sweet pickles*, are Joe's least favorite food.

Commas are also used between two or more adjectives, each modifying the same thing:

The *tired*, *angry* bus driver snarled at his passengers.
The *hot*, *crowded* bus crawled through traffic.

Adjectives modifying *other* adjectives, however, do *not* use any commas:

The *red hot* sun burned his eyes.
She was wearing a *light blue* dress.

Circle any adjective or adverb modifiers in the following sentences:

1. Several very strange people lived in that ugly, green house.
2. The tired, angry bus driver snarled at the noisy passengers.
3. The old man limped painfully down the littered street.
4. Depressed and exhausted, he could hardly move his withered arm.

5. Impatiently, he forced his stiff legs to move faster.
6. He finally gave up, and with a bitter look in his eyes, he slumped dejectedly to the curb.
7. His wrinkled, gnarled face reflected years of hard, grueling work.
8. Some screeching youngsters flew by on souped-up bicycles.
9. They hardly seemed to notice the old man who watched them through tired, bloodshot eyes.
10. Callous youth has a way of passing up old age, but old age inevitably takes its grim turn.

ADDING PREPOSITIONAL PHRASES

Besides using simple modifiers—adjectives and adverbs—to expand a sentence, you can also use prepositional phrases. Such phrases, beginning with words like *to, on, in,* and so forth, do not have subjects and verbs of their own:

Joe hates pickles.
Joe hates pickles *with a passion.*
Joe hates pickles *of any kind with a passion.*

The bus driver snarled.
The bus driver snarled *at the passengers in the back of the bus.*
The bus driver *with a bad temper* snarled *at the passengers in the back of the bus.*
In a hurry, the bus driver *with a bad temper* snarled *at all the passengers in the back of the bus.*

When you combine use of prepositional phrases with other adjective and adverb modifiers, you really expand your power of description:

In a hurry, the tired, angry bus driver with a bad temper bitterly snarled at the noisy passengers in the back of the crowded bus.

Circle any prepositional phrases which build up the following sentences:

1. That man in the gray flannel suit is a spy for the Internal Revenue Service.
2. The baton twirler at the head of the big brass band flashed a smile at her boyfriend on the curb.
3. In the movie *Diary of a Mad Housewife,* both the heroine's lover and her husband were blind to her needs.
4. On his journey toward success, Melvin Modern will stop at nothing.
5. He appeared one day with a ten-inch cigar in a pearl holder; he was wearing a monocle on a chain of rubies and emeralds and carrying a walking stick decorated with a carved ivory figure of himself.

ADDING INFINITIVE PHRASES

Another common technique used to build up sentences is the **infinitive phrase.** This consists of the preposition *to* plus the simple present of a verb,

90

usually working with another noun, pronoun, or adverb:

> *To impress his boss,* Melvin Modern will do almost anything.
> A student who is struggling *to attend school, to earn a living,* and *to raise a family* doesn't have much free time.

Such infinitive phrases are very common in English because so many verbs are paired up with *to*: try to, want to, need to, ought to, have to, plan to. You can add to the list yourself.

Infinitive phrases can also be used as subjects:

> *To know him* is to love him.

Circle any infinitive phrases in the following sentences:

1. In his struggle to become a famous actor, Tab Macho tried to marry a producer's daughter.
2. Abigail R. Tea once got excited enough to bite an artist when he refused to sell her one of his paintings.
3. To live happily, one must live wisely.
4. In order to earn enough money to travel across country, one enterprising student hired himself out as a "kitchen magician."
6. For one of his tricks, he tried to serve a flaming duck at an elegant dinner party, but he should have planned on a fire extinguisher because the tablecloth caught fire, and all the guests fled in panic.

ADDING PARTICIPLE PHRASES

We can add one more technique to our growing list of ways to expand a sentence: using **participles** or **participle phrases.** These are the -*ing* or -*ed* forms of the verb—unless they are irregular past participle forms like *written* or *sung*—and they are actually reduced forms of Type 4 clauses:

> The child, *who was shrieking loudly,* ran past the policeman. (4)
> The child, *shrieking loudly,* ran past the policeman. (participle phrase)

Our original example of effective sentence patterns, taken from *The Autobiography of Malcolm X,* uses -*ing* participles:

> *Surrounding the house, brandishing their shotguns,* the Klan riders shouted for my father to come out.

The -*ing* phrases have been built in to describe the main subject, *the Klan riders*. Participle phrases like these can either precede what they modify, like the example given, or they can follow what they modify:

> The Klan riders, *surrounding the house and brandishing their shotguns,* shouted for my father to come out.

Notice here too that the modifying phrases are surrounded by commas which work as "handles." They are extra pieces in the middle of the main sentence, and so they can be removed without destroying the meaning of the sentence.

Let's add some participle modifiers to Joe and his hatred of pickles:

My older brother Joe, *hating pickles,* never eats them.
Hating pickles, my older brother Joe never eats them.
Refusing to change his tastes, my older brother Joe hates pickles and never eats them.

Below are a few more sentences built up with participles and participle phrases. Circle all the participle modifiers:

1. Shrieking loudly, the child ran past the policeman.
2. The paper, beautifully written, deserved to be published.
3. Dressed in rhinestone-studded army fatigues and smashing their guitars, the teenage rock stars had their audience on its feet, screaming wildly.
4. His tie hanging limply from his collar, the old man waited impatiently on the unemployment line.
5. Surrounding the car and screaming, Malcolm's fans tried to get his autograph.
6. The defendent, claiming innocence, was still charged with horse thievery.
7. Pirouetting, the model tripped on her hem and fell on her face.
8. She stood up, blushing, and, pretending as though nothing had happened, gracefully made her exit.
9. Sniffing curiously, the dog tried to make friends with an angry skunk.
10. The getaway car made a fast turn, screeching as its wheels ran over the curb.

Like infinitive phrases, -ing participles and participle phrases can be used not just as modifiers but also as subjects. Circle any participles used as subjects in the following sentences:

1. Studying can be a drag.
2. Studying English can be even more of a drag.
3. Skating on thin ice is dangerous.
4. Applying make-up requires a great deal of skill and a steady hand.
5. Learning how to cook can produce some colossal failures.

Notice when an -ing participle or participle phrase is used as a subject, the verb is always singular. This is also true when an infinitive phrase is used as a subject.

USING REDUCED FORMS

A number of phrases and clauses which are used to expand a basic sentence have shortcut versions. You've just seen how an -ing participle phrase is in fact a reduced -ing form of the adjective clause. Similarly, a one-word participle is sometimes used as a simple adjective preceding a noun:

The *snarling* bus driver had an upset stomach.
The *singing* clown lost his trousers.

Another reduced form of the adjective clause can also produce an identifying phrase known as an **appositive:**

> My mother, who is an opera singer, practices in the shower.
> My mother, *an opera singer,* practices in the shower.
> *An opera singer,* my mother practices in the shower.

> Malcolm, who is a famous star, is always hounded by fans.
> Malcolm, *a famous star,* is always hounded by fans.

Notice here too the "handles" comma rule applies. The appositive is extra information, not essential to the sense of the sentence.

Some adjective clauses just drop the pronoun:

> The hot dog *which* I had for lunch is not digesting.
> The hot dog I had for lunch is not digesting.

> The money *that* I saved is spent.
> The money I saved is spent.

That used as a kind of conjunction (see Appendix A) can also be dropped:

> I saw *that* he didn't understand.
> I saw he didn't understand.

> The prisoner claimed *that* he was innocent.
> The prisoner claimed he was innocent.

You instinctively use both patterns, so there is no need to go into technical details describing why these variations occur. Just be aware of the differences. Sometimes the *that* is better used for the sake of clarity; other times, the sentence will read better without it.

Adverb clauses are also frequently used in reduced forms:

> Before the show started, we brought some popcorn.
> *Before the show,* we brought some popcorn.

> Because I love you, I can't eat.
> *Because of you,* I can't eat.
> *Loving you,* I can't eat.

Another common shortcut is rewriting prepositional phrases as possessive forms or simple adjective modifiers:

> The walls in this classroom are grimy.
> *The classroom's walls* are grimy.
> *The classroom walls* are grimy.

> The rear fender of the car fell off.
> *The car's rear fender* fell off.

In the following sentences, use alternate reduced forms where you can:

1. Hal Fellows, who was once governor of our state, loves to give long patriotic speeches on the Fourth of July.
2. The car that she drove was a quiz-show prize.
3. I heard that he started the fight.

4. Even though he is on a diet, Freddy Fats still eats candy.
5. The keys on my typewriter need cleaning.

SUMMARY

Below is a summary of all the techniques we've used to expand the basic sentence. Study it and then proceed to the exercises.

BASIC SENTENCE:	The bus driver snarled.
PREPOSITIONAL PHRASES:	*In a hurry,* the bus driver *with a temper* snarled *at all the passengers in the back of the bus.*
INFINITIVE PHRASES:	In a hurry *to get home,* the bus driver with a temper snarled at all the passengers in the back of the bus.
ADVERBS:	In a hurry to get home, the bus driver with a temper snarled *bitterly* at all the passengers in the back of the bus.
ADJECTIVES:	In a hurry to get home, the *tired, angry* bus driver with a *bad* temper snarled bitterly at the *noisy* passengers in the back of *hot, crowded* bus.
PARTICIPLE PHRASES:	*Frustrated by the heavy traffic, hating everyone he saw,* and in a hurry to get home, the tired, angry bus driver with a bad temper snarled bitterly at the noisy passengers in the back of the hot, crowded bus.
ADD A TYPE 3 CLAUSE:	Frustrated by the heavy traffic, hating everyone he saw, the tired, angry bus driver with a bad temper snarled bitterly at the noisy passengers in the back of the hot, crowded bus *because he was in a hurry to get home.*
ADD A TYPE 2 CLAUSE:	Frustrated by the heavy traffic, hating everyone he saw, the tired, angry bus driver with a bad temper snarled bitterly at the noisy passengers in the back of the hot, crowded bus because he was in a hurry to get home, *and he had an upset stomach.*
ADD A TYPE 4 CLAUSE:	Frustrated by the heavy traffic, hating everyone he saw, the tired, angry bus driver with a bad temper snarled bitterly at the noisy passengers in the back of the hot, crowded bus because he was in a hurry to get home, and he had an upset stomach *which was bothering him.*
REDUCED FORMS:	Frustrated by the heavy traffic, hating everyone he saw, the tired, angry, *bad-tempered* bus driver snarled bitterly at the noisy passengers in the back of the hot, crowded bus because he was in a hurry to get home, and he had an upset stomach *bothering him.*

EXERCISES

1. Combine each of the following pairs of sentences into one long sentence by making the second sentence in each pair a compound clause:

EXPANDING THE BASIC SENTENCE

a. Gregory Greed craves money. He will do anything to get it.

b. He once ripped someone's pants on a quiz show. He won $50,000.

c. The quiz show was called "Tell It Straight." It has gotten terrible reviews.

d. The game forces contestants to insult famous stars. The contestants get pretty nasty.

e. One enthusiastic player told movie star Mean Martin he had a brain the size of a BB pellet and a mouth like an alligator. Martin broke the contestant's arm, knocked out a tooth, and kicked him in the stomach.

f. Another contestant accused actress Susan Tragic of gross overacting. Ms. Tragic broke down in tears.

g. She sobbed bitterly. She claimed between sobs that she always tried for a restrained performance.

h. The master of ceremonies seems to love raw emotions. He encourages violence by egging on both the contestants and the stars.

i. Some television shows seem to exploit the viewer. "Tell It Straight" exploits everyone.

j. One contestant won a prize of $100,000 after proving the M.C. dyed his hair and wore a girdle. The government collected $75,000 in taxes.

2. Combine each of the following pairs of sentences into one long sentence by making either sentence in each pair an adverb clause:

a. Some men hate make-up on women. They prefer the natural look.

b. The cosmetics industry reaps high profits. It creates a line to sell the natural look.

c. I love you. I hate your dog.

d. Martin Manly is afraid of a woman beating him at anything. He despises women athletes.

e. I was waiting for a train. An old woman with four cats sat down next to me.

f. Being a driving instructor can be dangerous. New students sometimes panic.

g. Reggie Wheeler had to take a job as an instructor in the U-Can-Drive-It school. He couldn't find any other job.

h. On Reggie's first day on the job, a student lost control of the car. An angry cab driver edged up behind them and blew his horn.

i. The car jumped the curb, ran over a hydrant, and came to rest in a plate glass window. Reggie had been admiring an SKE Jaguar parked nearby.

j. Reggie grabbed for the controls. It was too late.

3. Combine each of the following pairs of sentences into one long sentence by making either sentence in each pair an adjective clause:

a. "Tell It Straight" is a new TV show. It has received terrible ratings.

b. Gregory Greed craves money. He will do anything to make it.

c. Reggie Wheeler used to be a racing car driver. He lost his nerve.

d. Reggie drove an Astra. His new model spun out of control during the 500 in France.

e. Reggie was badly injured in the race. He is now an instructor at the U-Can-Drive-It Driving Academy.

f. Professor Stanley Grinder teaches history at Ivory State College. He once made a study of the dating habits of students in his class.

g. Theodore Tastee is a famous gourmet cook. He has won many prizes for his recipes.

h. One recipe was called Teddy's Tasty Truffleburgers. It combines chopped sirloin, capers, garlic, truffles, and marshmallow with almond paste.

i. Tastee is a masterful chef. Many claim he is better than Egbert McMuffin.

j. Chef Tastee has been hired as a consultant. His job will be inventing new hamburger recipes for a famous fast-food chain.

4. Combine each of the following pairs of sentences into one long sentence in *three* different ways: first rewrite the second sentence in each pair as a compound clause; then rewrite either sentence as an adverb clause; finally, rewrite either sentence as an adjective clause:

EXAMPLE: Avid Car Rental advertises less. It does more business than Hurts.

COMPOUND CLAUSE: Avid Car Rental advertises less, but it does more business than Hurts.

ADVERB CLAUSE: Although Avid Car Rental advertises less, it does more business than Hurts.

ADJECTIVE CLAUSE: Avid Car Rental, which advertises less, does more business than Hurts.

a. The Wonderwagon is an economical car to operate. It runs on very little gas.

COMPOUND
CLAUSE: _____

_____

ADVERB
CLAUSE: _____

_____

ADJECTIVE
CLAUSE: _____

_____

b. Tillie Tyson is a Tibetan mountain climber. She loves the view from on top of the world.

COMPOUND
CLAUSE: _____

_____

ADVERB
CLAUSE: _____

_____

ADJECTIVE
CLAUSE: _____

_____

c. A new fabric on the market can lead to embarrassing experiences. It dissolves when wet.

COMPOUND
CLAUSE: _____

_____

ADVERB
CLAUSE: _____

_____

ADJECTIVE
CLAUSE: _____

_____

d. The Attic Discotheque just opened. It is in the basement.

COMPOUND
CLAUSE: _____

_____

ADVERB
CLAUSE: _____

_____

ADJECTIVE
CLAUSE: _____

_____

e. Duncan O. Pose is always looking for challenges. He has sold oil burners in Florida and freezers in Alaska.

COMPOUND
CLAUSE: _____

_____

ADVERB
CLAUSE: _____

_____

ADJECTIVE
CLAUSE: _____

_____

5. Below is a list of adjectives and adverbs. Add as many as you can to each of the following sentences:

blonde	energetic	dangerously	icy
loudly	orange	stunning	terrified
abstract	terrifying	impatient	overweight
bitterly	irately	gentle	Irish
carefully	talented	old	intently
beat up	gracefully	tiny	scrawny
dainty	enthusiastic	racing	stolen
skeptical	agitated	ancient	talented
angrily	green	shiny	endlessly

a. The woman screamed. _____

_____

b. An artist painted landscapes. _____

_____

c. The student struggled. _____

_____

d. The policeman directed traffic. _____

_____

e. A car skidded. _____

_____

f. The cat snarled. _____

_____

6. Below is a list of infinitive and prepositional phrases. Add as many as you can to each of the sentences you built up in exercise 5:

on the run	to earn a living	in the knick of time
to the show	out the window	to fend off attack
in the window	to make a point	in the right lane
at the passing cars	outside the door	at the children
in a hurry	to impress the neighbors	out of control
to win a prize	in the theater	over a fence
in order to get help	to a rock concert	to attract attention
under the umbrella	on the ice	to avoid an oncoming car
on the shore	in the rain	across the road
to understand the argument	in a tree	in a rage
in jeans	to a halt	

a. The woman screamed. _____

_____

_____

b. An artist painted landscapes. _____

_____

c. The student struggled. _____

_____

_____

d. The policeman directed traffic. _____

_____

_____

e. A car skidded. _____

_____

_____

f. The cat snarled. _____

_____

_____

7. Below is a list of participle phrases. Add as many as you can to each of the sentences you built up in exercises 5 and 6:

terrified of the dark	racing for the bus
struggling to get free	seeking his own style
resting in a tree	fearing the worst
laughing hysterically	hating her neighbors
aiming for perfection	reflecting the sun
loving attention	losing control
demonstrating a new technique	hypnotized by the magician
maintaining control	blowing a whistle
scratching his head	attracting a crowd
challenged by the elements	backed against the wall

a. The woman screamed. _____

_____

_____

b. An artist painted landscapes. _____

c. The student struggled. _____

_____

_____

d. The policeman directed traffic. _____

_____

_____

e. A car skidded. _____

_____

_____

f. The cat snarled. _____

_____

_____

8. Reverse the order of exercises 5, 6, and 7. Begin by building up the basic sentences with the participle phrases, then add the infinitive and prepositional phrases, and finally add the adverbs and adjectives wherever you can:

a. The woman screamed. _____

_____

_____

b. An artist painted landscapes. _____

_____

_____

c. The student struggled. _____

_____

_____

d. The policeman directed traffic. _____

_____

_____

e. A car skidded._____

_____

_____

f. The cat snarled._____

_____

_____

9. Rewrite each of the following sentences using alternate reduced forms wherever you can:

EXAMPLE: My mother, who is an opera singer, practices in the shower because she hates the blank walls of a rehearsal hall.

My mother, an opera singer, practices in the shower because she hates a rehearsal hall's blank walls.

Hating a rehearsal hall's blank walls, my mother, an opera singer, practices in the shower.

a. The fans who were surrounding Malcolm's car screamed and tried to grab the hat which he clutched tightly to his head.

_____

_____

b. Although he is usually suave and sophisticated, Malcolm, who is tall, muscular, and all-American, blew his cool when he started to shriek at the crowd that had started rocking his limousine.

_____

_____

c. Malcolm, who began spitting out of a broken window at a weeping fan, ordered his chauffeur to drive even if it meant running over the bodies of other young women who were hysterical and who were lying prostrate in the path of his car.

_____

_____

_____

d. Although Malcolm later apologized and claimed that he panicked, his chauffeur was given a ticket for hit-and-run driving, and Malcolm was still held in contempt of court for refusing to appear before the judge after he heard rumors that his fans, who were still enthusiastic, were ready to follow him to jail.

_____

_____

_____

10. Play a game called "Crazy Clauses." Go around the room and take turns building up each of the following sentences any way you can. Each person must repeat the entire sentence as it comes to him or her, and then add one new piece of information.

a. The man snored.
b. The child cried.
c. The cop frowned.
d. The baton twirler flashed a smile.
e. I heard a scream.

f. The tires squealed.
g. The stairs creaked.
h. The sun beat down.
i. The woman sighed.
j. The light changed.

11. Select five of the sentences in exercise 10 and expand each yourself by adding modifiers, phrases, and clauses. Use reduced forms for variety wherever you can. Experiment with a variety of patterns: try writing each sentences several different ways.

12. Using the clauses in columns A, B, and C, put together at least ten sentences. For each, select one clause from column A, one from column B, and one from column C. You can juggle the pieces around, and come up with weird combinations, but just make sure the mechanics work.

A	B
because Michael's mine	I love my dog
although it snowed	miracles can happen
after the ball is over	time flies
whenever Sammy sings	spring is just around the corner
unless you do as you're told	you're dead
since Malcolm arrived	work harder
if the Wonderwagon sells	capitalism will thrive
whether or not you pay	visit your mother-in-law
before the food arrives	love conquers all
while you're waiting	the rich get richer

103

EXERCISES

C

who would love to see you
that waits for no one
which we paid for
which is most important
which is a modern miracle
who is famous
that I told you about
who has laryngitis
which occurs annually
which we ordered

ACCEPTABLE: Although it snowed, I love my dog who has laryngitis.
UNACCEPTABLE: Unless you do as you're told, visit your mother-in-law which occurs annually.

a. _____

_____

b. _____

_____

c. _____

_____

d. _____

_____

e. _____

_____

f. _____

_____

g. _____

_____

h. _____

_____

i. _____

j. _____

_____

_____

13. Go back to each sentence you wrote in exercise 12, but add as many modifiers as you can from column *A* and column *B* below:

A	*B*
fuzzy	finally
debonair	last week
nagging	still
marvelous	powerfully
destructive	occasionally
efficient	yesterday
filthy	furiously
exotic	brilliantly
long-haired	promptly
elegant	sooner or later

14. Below are a jumbled list of modifiers, phrases, and clauses. From these spare parts, build at least ten long sentences. Again, you're free to try some weird variations, but just make sure what you end up with at least resembles EAE patterns.

gaunt	laughing hysterically
hoping to find gold	I have been aching
at the Mafia leader	who had betrayed her
the poodle gnawed and yapped	to learn grammar
dressed in orange	noisy
long-armed	that was eating spaghetti
chattering	jilted
when her husband asked her	eating a banana
the model paraded	Russian
for candy	the monkey resembled my
of the limousine	grandfather
the killer pointed his rifle	rotten
admiring	pet
thoughtlessly	whistling in the dark
struggling to get free	Italian
seductive	screeching loudly
who enlisted in the Marines	high-fashion
before the show began	the students revolted
to iron his underwear	down the aisle
because she was bored	from me
crying her heart out	by his trunks
diamond	when he was leaving
of coffee	who wanted them
aiming carefully	the children are clamoring
against their teachers	casting glances
confidently	dense
crowded	courageous

the waitress threw a pot whistling in the dark
on its leash high-powered
the housewife lost her temper nasty
by the fringe at the man
when the wrestler saw his opponent because he was so hairy
who are driving me crazy hired
in order to get away he grabbed the Olympic champion
to tell you about my ex-husband
at the audience with his family
worked to death at the window

a. _____

_____

b. _____

_____

c. _____

_____

d. _____

_____

e. _____

_____

f. _____

_____

g. _____

_____

h. _____

_____

i. _____

_____

j. _____

_____

15. Rewrite the following paragraph combining the sentences as many ways as you can. Try for variations and combinations of all the techniques you have learned. Experiment with reduced forms.

I was unable to sleep one night. I got out of bed. I dressed warmly. I started on a walk through the nearby woods. I was trying to clear my head. Many thoughts had been troubling me. I made my way through a path. The path was overgrown. I went toward a clearing. I had been there before. Suddenly I heard a scream. It was strange. It was muffled. It was shortly followed by a low growl. The growl was throaty. I was terrified. I whirled around. I was unable to see anything. The moon was hidden behind some clouds. I froze in my steps. I was afraid to move. My ears strained every sound. A bird fluttered idly. It stirred in its sleep. A few leaves rustled. They rustled against each other. A slight breeze brushed my cheek. A twig snapped. Suddenly the moon broke out. It broke out from behind the clouds. I could make out a strange shape. It was crumpled up against an old tree. The tree was oak. It was gnarled. I approached it cautiously. Again I heard the low, deep-throated growl. It was accompanied this time by a kind of whimpering. It seemed to have given up all reason. It conveyed utter despondency. It had given up all hope. I made my way carefully. I stood in the front of the crumpled shape. Suddenly it moved. I felt something tug at my ankle. I started kicking and screaming. Then I realized it was a small puppy. I tried to calm myself. I bent over the shape. I touched it gently. It stirred. I then saw what it was. A young child was dressed in a sheet. The child was nine or ten. He must have gotten lost in the woods. It was Halloween.

16. Do the same as you did in exercise 15.

    The most embarrassing thing that ever happened to
me was when I forgot my lines on stage at a school
concert. I was doing the narration part to the finale.
The audience was packed with parents, teachers, and
students. It was a concert where everyone came.
Suddenly the house lights went low. The heat from the
spotlights became overwhelming. My insides were burning
with such a sensation it seemed as if a torch had been
ignited. I stepped in front of the chorus. They began
to sing. I started beautifully, narrating the first
half. Then all of a sudden, I felt an intense heat come
over my body again. Beads of perspiration began forming
on my forehead. My hands were soaked with perspiration.
My legs began to give way from beneath my body. I was
scared. The chorus was singing; then the singing
tapered off to a mild harmonizing hum. I knew I had to
do the rest of the narrating. So I began. After taking
a deep breath, there was a tremble in my voice. The
words of the narration began flying past in my head. I
heard my voice echoing through the audience. The
audience's eyes seemed to be watching me earnestly.
Then my voice stopped. My mind became blank. I forgot
my lines. Everything in the place was quiet. One could
hear a pin drop. I felt as if I had been looking into a
lion's mouth, and he was staring back at me before he
attacked. I must have stood there for one minute of
complete silence which seemed like half an hour. Staring
at that lion, trying to remember, I couldn't. The
chorus began singing again. They tapered off to another
hum; then I knew it was the time for the prayer at the

end. I prayed to get that right. I started and finished; then I grew cold and trembled when the audience began to clap.

Suggested Reader Selections

Norman Mailer, *Ego*   Gay Talese, *New York*
John McPhee, *The Capital of the Pines*

6
editing

WHY EDIT?

Everything you see in print is not perfect. If you look carefully, you'll probably discover at least one "typo" and several lines mixed up on any page of a local newspaper. This book has been rewritten at least three or four times, some sections even more. An editor has critically read it and suggested changes. A copy editor has gone through it several times. Proofreaders have labored over the page proofs and galleys. Nevertheless, you will probably still find some confusing examples, a few exercises that don't work, and the inevitable sprinkling of spelling or typographical errors. With the exception perhaps of a new Rolls-Royce, very few human creations are perfect. The aim of this chapter—and to some extent, the aim of this book—is *not* to turn out model writers writing "perfect" copy. Much more important, we want to make you aware of the *process* of language *use*. Editing is a final stage in that process.

POINTS TO REMEMBER IN EDITING

As an editor, you should probably not expect perfection. You do try to spot as many slip-ups, misspellings, and rough spots as you can—the more experience you have and the longer you've been at it, the easier it gets—but you do so knowing that you never really "finish" writing anything. The great American novelist Ernest Hemingway is supposed to have repeatedly rewritten everything he wrote, only sending off a manuscript to be published when he needed money or was hounded by editors. Even then, he felt it wasn't finished. Mistakenly assuming that good writers effortlessly turn out perfect prose and ideal models of elegant style is one explanation for that fear which seems to plague so many inexperienced writers. Most of us have been raised in such awe of the printed word that we assume effective writing and editing are unattainable skills belonging to those few who get into print. You are handed a blank piece of paper, you are asked to write something, and you freeze. Every insecurity you have short-circuits your creative energy. Why? Impossible standards. The "I'll never get it right" syndrome. What's the cure? "I'll never get it right, but so what, who cares?" No. That's also obviously self-defeating.

The solution, if there is any simple solution to such a widespread cultural hang-up, is perspective. That's a handy word. It means, on one level, seeing things in relationship to each other. It means not missing the forest because you only see trees. Keep your writing "in perspective." If, for example, you have worked through any of the exercises in the first chapters of this book and enjoyed them or shared them with others, if you've been working out some thoughts and observations in your journal that have given you some insight into yourself, then you are already an experienced writer even if you feel you still need practice. That's one sense of perspective. Another is understanding perspective as "point of view." The way things are or seem to be depends on who's doing the looking. You are the writer—not some hypothetical English teacher; therefore, you are ultimately the one who decides on the quality of your writing. How?

Be your own editor. After happily overcoming the initial fear and panic of the "perfectly blank page" syndrome, many writers swing too easily into the opposite trap of "Ah, it's mine, my innermost me, and no matter what anybody else sez, I ain't gonna change a word." That's perhaps a necessary attitude while you're just beginning to have confidence in your abilities to write, but it's a dangerous perspective if you want to experiment and grow. No matter how famous or well-published, a writer who stops experimenting and growing is dead. And boring. An essential perspective for all writers is being critical. Look at what you've written and frown. Experiment. Change words around. Substitute other words. Cut. In short, edit. It's not easy. As a matter of fact, it can be very frustrating and painful, drawing ugly red lines and scribbles through some of your own creations. But that's what editing is all about: looking at what you've written with a critical eye; not crumpling up your paper in disgust and tossing it in the nearest trash can, but seeing the strengths and weaknesses, the good and bad. It's very seldom all one or the other. Take a look at the following paper and point out both its strong and weak points.

Living in the city requires as much skill as playing a hand of cards, because survival is the key to whether one is as being qualified.

In order to maintain city status one must not overlook the significance of the corner and what it means to most Americans in cities. It is a meeting place, and sometimes a place to do nothing. When people meet on corners, the importance of the person is dictated, by his position occupied. People that gather on corners, always give the appearance of having rights

POINTS TO REMEMBER IN EDITING

to that area. Also those that are walking down the
street, will relinguish their right to the sidewalk by
walking conspicuously around those hanging out on the
corner. If you are standing with you back to the wall
or directly to the corner building, this put you in the
position of leadership. Since drinking is the biggest
single activity that occurs, a spontaneous gathering or
pooling the money is important. After which the corner
becomes alive with conversation and hero stories, and
the passing of the bottle around.

    Second in importance is the bar which is usually
very crowded. One must know the rules here, such as
ordering drinks, requiring seats or approaching people,
trying not to invade the space of those sitting standing
or dancing. In actuality the proprietor does not
allocate this space, its just the way it is, and always
will be. A person walking in a bar will position
himself several seats away from the others. Most people
assume direct control of the area in front of them. No
one will intrude in this area without permission. And
as the bar becomes crowded, the space becomes less, and
progressively less controled, yet privacy is not
destroyed.

    As boring as it may seem, activity is very much in
abundance in the city; theres always the barbershop and
the stoop. Usually eating, drinking, playing cards and
engaging in idle conversation is practiced and a
masculine concept is present. On the stoop, teenage
males will position themselves in a standing position
along side the stoop in the manner of sentry. While
the kids take the bottom steps, adults handle the middle
steps, allowing privacy and freedom to talk about sex

and speak openly about any and everything in the neighborhood. However the barbershops offer a little different kind of male oriented concept. The rules does not perpetuate the same concept inside as they seem to be outside. Receiving a haircut, one is not required to get involved in conversation, while the barber is experting his advice on sports and other events. Drinking is limited to a selected few of the barber's friends and regular customers. And it is done where a person takes turns disappearing to the men's room. If a person sticks to the rules, city life can be safe and enjoyable.

As you discuss the pros and cons of the above essay, develop your own critical check lists for effective editing. The one reprinted below was put together by several students.

A CHECK LIST FOR STYLE

—Do I capture my reader's interest right away?
—Do I keep my reader's interest?
—Are there enough specifics to get across a point or to describe an impression?
—Can I use more examples to illustrate my points?
—Do I use enough attention-getting adjectives and active verbs?
—Could I have experimented more with vocabulary?
—Do I use analogy or metaphor or simile to make a point clearer?
—Are my descriptions or discussions organized?
—Is the technique of organization clear?
—Do I use enough topic sentences?
—Is my controlling idea in a paragraph clear?
—If I'm discussing something complicated, do I organize my ideas into different areas of primary support?
—Again, do I have enough evidence to prove my points?
—Does all my evidence "fit" and support my controlling ideas or what I'm describing?
—Do I wander off any of my main points?
—Did I edit enough and get rid of anything that doesn't fit?
—Does one idea lead into another?
—Do I use enough transition words?

113

—Do I have some kind of conclusion or summary?
—Do I use enough variety in my sentence patterns?
—Can I build up sentences with more phrases or modifiers?
—What's the overall impression my reader might have of me when he or she is finished reading? Boring? Exciting? Informative? Really knows the stuff? Unsure? Uptight? Confident?

EDITING FOR MECHANICS

What about EAE mechanics? There are really not that many written conventions you don't already know about. You can easily overcome even the wildest absurdities of English spelling and some of the more elegant EAE verb forms by cultivating your skepticism If there's even the slightest twinge of doubt about spelling, roam around in your dictionary until you find the word, and add it to a list you keep of words you often misspell. I've also found it useful to write a list on the inside covers of my dictionary—it saves thumbing. In addition to keeping lists, try "photographing" a troublesome word. Get a picture of the correctly spelled version in your mind and "snap" it. You may never learn to be a perfect speller, but you should be able, without too much trouble, to develop a "second sense," a twinge or awareness that warns you when something is slightly off.

As for other mechanical problems, it's simply a matter of editing: learn to spot something that needs a slight adjustment. Very few writers turn out anything close to flawless EAE on a first draft. The more practice you have and the more aware you are of written forms as you read and write, the easier it gets. But for all good writers, it's always the editing that formalizes their style. One very important fact to remember is that there are only a few basic EAE conventions which probably account for about 90 percent of EAE violations. If you learn to spot unwanted fragments, for example, you can probably wipe out half the troubles you're having with EAE sentence structure and punctuation. We'll briefly discuss fragments and a few other basic bloopers, then put together a checklist for mechanics.

Fragments

A **fragment,** as we've been using the term, means literally a piece of a sentence, or a group of words that can't work together without some props. If you've been on your toes, you've noticed I've occasionally used fragments. To make a point. Intentionally. But fragments can be annoying when they're not intended—even sometimes when they are. A complete EAE sentence needs a subject and some verb which (implicitly or explicitly) marks time.

Using a participle phrase as an independent sentence without a subject or some other verb to work with it is a violation of EAE, even though it's quite common in some spoken dialects. A participle or a participle phrase is a perfectly respectable EAE construction when it serves as a subject or expands a sentence. It just can't be used as the main verb in an independent EAE sentence. Thus, The man going home" is a fragment. "The man going home is my father" is an independent sentence because the participle phrase is used as the subject of a complete sentence. "The man is going home" is also an independent sentence because the -ing form has been used with a verb that marks time.

Translate the following fragments into EAE:

1. He working too hard.
2. I drawn the drapes.
3. The man singing too loud.
4. My wife always worrying.
5. We spending too much money.
6. The coach yelling too loud.
7. He seen the murder.
8. Ali been a good fighter.
9. You done the wrong thing.
10. The painting selling for too much money.

Another dialect form which persists in writing is the use of be to indicate consistently occurring or future events. In EAE, this is considered a fragment and the am, are, is, was, were, or have (has or had) been forms are substituted.

Translate the following forms into EAE:

1. I be working late tonight.
2. The manager be setting up a sale.
3. He be always making a mess of things.
4. They be coming in on the train tonight.
5. The bus usually be late.

Still another very common fragment results from misusing an adverb clause. "Because I love you" is a fragment, even though "I love you" is a perfectly adequate EAE (Type 1) sentence. When you add a because, you've got an adverb clause—a fragment unless you hook it onto another independent clause and make a Type 3 sentence:

> Because I love you, I want to hold your hand.
> I want to hold your hand because I love you.

Adverb conjunctions like because, although, even though, or before all make whatever follows them **dependent**— that is, they have to hook onto other sentences. Adverb clauses can not stand alone: you can't just say "Because you're mean," unless you are answering a question already asked. You haven't given enough information. Your reader has been set up to expect more. Because tells your readers you are about to give them both a reason for something and a consequence. If you say, "Because you're mean, I hate you" or "I hate you because you're mean," you've given them both.

Another similar problem results from using a "who" or a "which" adjective clause by itself: "This is the man." "Who is here." The second is a fragment. You have to write, "This is the man who is here," a Type 4 sentence. The "who" clause can't work by itself unless you are asking a question: "Who is here?"

Translate the following fragments into EAE:

1. Since he punched me.
2. After I got there.
3. Which I saw.
4. Because he's mine.
5. Who saw the movie.
6. Unless you do it.
7. Which are waiting.
8. Whether or not I do it.
9. Whenever I try to study.
10. Who was leaving.

Other common problems

Besides the fragment, two other very common lapses of EAE are the **comma-splice** and the **run-on** sentence. Quite simply, these are each two separate sentences which have been strung together with a comma or simply run together:

RUN-ON: Joe hates English he never studies.

COMMA-SPLICE: Joe hates English, he never studies.

They need to be marked separately (with a period and capital) or joined with some kind of conjunction or a semicolon, *not* just a comma, and certainly not just run together with no recognition of the break between them. You can write:

TYPE 1: Joe hates English. He never studies.

TYPE 2: Joe hates English, and he never studies.
Joe hates English; he never studies.
Joe hates English; therefore, he never studies.

TYPE 3: Because Joe hates English, he never studies.
Joe never studies because he hates English.
Joe hates English because he never studies.

TYPE 4: Joe, who hates English, never studies.
Joe, who never studies, hates English.

A comma is too weak to hold two independent sentences together. It can only hold together independent sentences in a series of three or more items. In this case, the items are strung together with commas and a comma and conjunction between the last two items:

Joe hates English, he never studies, *and* he's failing.

The team got the ball in the final minute of the game, the audience roared with approval, *and* the coaches leapt to their feet.

Sometimes you'll see that final comma omitted, but since it's consistent with our Type 2 clause rule—which always requires the comma before *and*, *but*, *for*, and so forth—it's easier to remember to use it. Without the "*, and*" you'd use two or more semicolons:

> Joe hates English; he never studies; he's failing.
> I came; I saw; I conquered.
> I want you; I need you; I love you.

Other common EAE blunders can be caught with careful editing. One frequent goof results from carelessly using reduced forms or **misplacing modifiers:**

> *Playing* the piano, *my dog* howled.

Obviously most dogs don't play the piano. Here you need more information than the reduced clause provides:

> *While I was* playing the piano, my dog howled.

What about this one?

> She wore a yellow ribbon around her *neck which* was tied in a bow.

Hopefully, her neck isn't tied in a bow. The adjective clause should stick close to what it modifies:

> She wore a *yellow ribbon which* was tied in a bow around her neck.
> Around her neck, she wore a *yellow ribbon tied* in a bow.

Straighten out any mix-ups in the following sentences:

1. The child ran past the policeman, shrieking loudly.
2. Beautifully written, the student turned in an *A* paper.
3. Because her diapers were wet, the mother changed the baby.
4. While running for the bus, the light changed.
5. Dripping in the sink, he was awake all night.

Another slip results from **faulty parallel construction.** Don't, for example, mix together infinitive and participle phrases:

> To get drunk and passing out isn't my idea of a good time.

Change both to either infinitives or participle phrases:

> *Getting drunk and passing out* isn't my idea of a good time.
> *To get drunk and pass out* isn't my idea of a good time.

Remember, the marriage vow reads "to have and to hold," not "to have and holding."

Other slips are the result of **screwy logic** or **ambiguity:**

> It was snowing because he braked and the car skidded.

This should be written:

> It was snowing, and because he braked, the car skidded.
> Because it was snowing, when he braked, the car skidded.

Ambiguity also results when the same word or phrase reads several different ways within a sentence. The following headline once appeared in *The New York Times:*

RUTGERS PAPER BACKS ARMING GUARDS

Can you spot the ambiguities in these sentences?

> Visiting in-laws can be hard on a marriage.
> I have three hangnails and a pimple on my chin.

These items describe most of the common slip-ups to watch for in editing EAE. Below is another check list which illustrates most of them, as well as others we haven't discussed here, but which should be self-evident. Add to it any others you notice for yourself.

A CHECK LIST FOR EAE MECHANICS

Editing Verbs

--Watch for the -s on singular present verbs when it's needed:

The boy sit~*s* here.

--Don't use *be* instead of the other forms of the verb:

I be~*am* late.

--Don't use the -ing form as the main verb:

I ~*am* working hard.

--Keep the same tense when you are referring to the same time:

He came to a spotlight and goes~*went* through it.

--Be sure you have past tense markers:

I work~*ed* hard yesterday.

--Check for misspelled irregular verbs:

I singed~*sang* a song

--Check for subject/verb agreement:

Everyone work *s* hard.

We ~~was~~ *were* late.

People ~~is~~ *are* always greedy.

Editing nouns and pronouns

-- Check for pronoun/reference agreement:

I like people who tell you what ~~he~~ *they* thinks.

--Check for noun/reference agreement:

Some people have no love in their heart*s*.

--Check for articles (use *an* before a noun beginning in a vowel sound):

~~a~~ *an* accident   ~~a~~ *an* error   ~~a~~ *an* incident   ~~a~~ *an* hour

--Check for misspelled pronoun forms:

hi~~s~~self *him*   them~~self~~ *selves*

Editing punctuation

--Check for run-ons and comma splices:

I came, *and* he left. I came, *and* he left.

--Check for commas punctuating Type 3 clauses:

Because I was late, I missed class.

I missed class, because I was late.

--Check for "handle" commas at *both* ends of a Type 4 clause or appositive:

My mother, who is an opera singer, weighs 225 pounds.

My mother, an opera singer, weighs 225 pounds.

--Don't stick in commas where they don't belong (especially between subjects and verbs):

Marriage, is a wretched institution.

119

EDITING FOR MECHANICS

Editing faulty constructions

--Check for fragments (frequently made by not recognizing the adverb conjunction):

Because I was late, ~~;~~ *I missed the bus.*

--Check for misplaced modifiers:

the faucet kept him
Dripping in the sink, ∧ ~~he was~~ awake all night.

She wore a yellow ribbon ✓ around her neck (which was tied in a bow.)

--Check for screwy logic:

and
It was snowing ∧ because he braked ∧ ~~and~~ the car skidded.

--Check for ambiguity:

NEWS:
RUTGERS ∧ PAPER BACKS ARMED GUARDS

--Check faulty parallels:

to
To have and ∧ holding...

Editing spelling

--Check your dictionary!
--Straighten out "problem pairs":

there/their/they're	weather/whether
its/it's	quiet/quite
to/too/two	where/wear/were/wore
our/are/hour	then/than
whose/who's	since/sense/cents
right/write	though/thought/through/threw
know/no/now	weight/wait
whole/hole	

--Watch for two frequent elisions:

have
could ~~of~~ use ∧ to
d

EXERCISES

1. Edit any violations of EAE forms you find in the following sentences:

a. He were late for class.

b. My mother yell at me a lot.

c. My daughter love cats.

d. He done a lousy job.

e. Ann always pick up stray dogs.

f. I be working too hard.

g. I has too much work to do.

h. The sun are not shining.

i. My cat do hate strangers.

j. Everyone were whistling.

k. Summer are almost here.

l. I has a hard job learning English.

m. We does try to study.

n. He were going to be late.

o. I have did a good job.

p. I gone home late last night.

q. I catched a big fish yesterday.

r. My uncle who is a farmer growed a big crop of tomatoes.

s. I have ate too much.

t. My telephone has rang too often.

u. We tryed harder.

v. I seen a ghost.

w. The jury were deliberating.

x. An army are composed of different kinds of people.

y. He be working when the boss come in.

2. Edit any fragments, run-ons, or comma splices you find in the following sentences:
   a. Advertising tries to brainwash us even though we use common sense we are still vulnerable.
   b. David Ogilvy wrote a book about advertising, it is called *Confessions of an Advertising Man.*
   c. He is a successful writer, he is also a successful ad man.
   d. He exposing the gimmicks of advertising.
   e. In one ad, a sexy woman is gambling she is smoking Benson & Hedges.
   f. This is an example of image making the ad is saying that if you smoke Benson & Hedges you will have a lot of money and look like the woman in the ad.
   g. You be easily persuaded.
   h. *Free* and *new* are the most powerful selling words, they have a lot of emotional power over us.
   i. Because we all want something for nothing.
   j. We are also susceptible to words like *miracle, quick, easy, sensational,* they misrepresent reality.
   k. After you think about it.
   l. Words can be promises advertising promises us anything we want.
   m. Advertising is really like fairy tales for adults we believe in happy endings for beer drinkers and cigarette smokers.
   n. Advertising appeals to our seven deadly sins it especially aims at lust, vanity, and greed.
   o. Advertising is getting scientific for example they now do research studies on what colors affect us most.
   p. Reds and greens.
   q. Advertising also uses sounds to make you remember the product two examples are "Please don't squeeze the Charmin" and "Coffee and Kents."
   r. These both use rhymes you remember the product because of the rhymes.
   s. This kind of communication deadly.
   t. Sometimes music keeps on echoing in your head it's a real invasion of privacy.
   u. Such misuse of influence dangerous.
   v. Because it affects us when we don't know it.
   w. And because it controls our interests and makes them very material.
   x. We are more concerned with buying the latest brand of fancy whiskey than we are with our fellow man, that's a very dangerous thing for society.
   y. Debasing language and the people who use it.

3. Edit any violations of EAE forms you find in the following sentences:

   a. Their was bad whether at see.

   b. While doing the laundry, my cat got run over by a truck.

   c. To get a job is one thing; holding on to it is something else.

   d. A person ought to be more considerate of their neighbors.

e. I just witnessed a awful accident.

f. Joe told hisself to get up and get going.

g. When I was on my way home from school I stopped and had a hamburger.

h. Its a girl!

i. The too Corleone brothers tried to hard too get ahead.

j. Their going too be late.

4. Edit the following paragraph:

   The child was standing in what looked like a culver
as I cam nearer to this area, I notice that there wasn't
any sounds to be heard.   This made my mind very uneasy
I did not want to belive what my eyes had seen.   But my
mind told me, that there must have been a very terrible
accident.   My first thought was to see about that little
child, that I had seen standing near the culver.   As I
approach were the child was standing, I heard a strange
sound.   A sound of someone that was in very bad pain.
Without thinking, I reached out a picked up the child,
the child was not crying she look like she were in a
state of shock.   I layed her down, and then placed my
coat over her, to keep her warm.   As I was doing that,
that sound came rushing into my ears again.   I jerked
myself around to see which direction the sound was
coming from.   But night skys was dark, and the only
light their was, was coming from the headlights from my
car.   I hurryed over to the car and opened the door to
put my high beams on this would give me more light to
see by.   Then I saw what look to be a body.   I must have
been about twenty five feet from where I layed the child
down at.   I ran as fast as I can.   I came upon a old man
he looked to be about seventy five years old about four

feet to his right, there was a women, that looked about
the same age. I didn't have to tell you want my eyes
were looking at.

5. Here's what one student's edited paper looked like, but he still missed a few
slip-ups. Try to find some more:

The child was standing in what looked like a culver*t*.
~~As~~ I cam*e* nearer to this area, I notice*d* that there ~~wasn't~~ *weren't*
any sounds to be heard. This made my mind very uneasy
I did not want to beli*e*ve what my eyes had seen. But my
mind told me*,* that there must have been a very terrible
accident. My first thought was to see about that little
child*,* that I had seen standing near the culver*t*. As I
approach*ed* were the child was standing, I heard a strange
sound. A sound of someone that was in very bad pain.
Without thinking, I reached out *and* picked up the child;
the child was not crying she look*ed* like she ~~were~~ *was* in a
state of shock. I ~~layed~~ *laid* her down*,* and then placed my
coat over her*,* to keep her warm. As I was doing that,
that sound came rushing into my ears again. I jerked
myself around to see which direction the sound was
coming from. But night sky*s* was dark, and the only
light ~~their~~ *there* was*,* ~~was coming~~ *came* from the headlights from my
car. I hurr*i*ed over to the car and opened the door to
put my high beams on. *T*his would give me more light to
see by. Then I saw what look*ed* to be a body. . I must have
been about twenty five feet from where I ~~layed~~ *laid* the child
down ~~at?~~ I ran as fast as I ~~can~~ *could*. I came upon *an* old man
~~he~~ *who* looked to be about seventy five years old. *A*bout four
feet to his right, there was a women*,* that looked about
the same age. I didn't have to tell you ~~want~~ *what* my eyes
were looking at.

124

6. Below are two sample student paragraphs. Edit each of them and discuss their strengths and weaknesses. Which is more effective and why?

Anything goes in today's far-out fashions. You can choose any style you feel like wearing. You doesn't have to follow freaky fashion trends any more. Some cutthroat designers are just trying to make a bundle by switching hemlines anyway. You have the freedom to choose whatever weird style makes you feel good. Your nosey old grandmother ain't got no right to nag that your skirts is shocking short or your hair too long & sloppy. If you want to wear old torn jeans to class or work, its your business, brother. And jist because you wears a groovy old army jacket don't make you a draft-dodger either.

Anything goes in today's unisex fashion world. Whether your a man or a woman, you can have the freedom to get together any look you want--tough or frivolous, slick, sedate, or sloppy. For the aggressive, tough look, you can wear heavy, laced boots with thick wool bell bottoms topped off by a studded leather belt. Or you can choose a frilly shirt with ruffles at the neck or a lace see-through shirt. On the other hand, if you prefer the slick look, try a suit made of rust colored cordoroy with stove-pipe pants and a down-to-the-knee military cut jacket, topped off with a crushed cordoroy cap. For the more sedate man or woman, however, their's always the standard three or four button tweed suit with lapels and tailored trousers, perhaps finish off by a subdued silk scarf or tie. Last but not least, their's always the old standby, our casual look. A guy or a gal can don a comfortable well-worn pair of jeans decorated with flower patches or an army insignia. Whatever the look, the only things predictable is individuality, man or woman, you wear the mood you feel.

125

7. Edit the following student paper:

A crowd has gathered. There has just been a
accident. A cab is smashed into the side of a
limousine. The cabbie has gotten out of his cab, and,
red in the face, he is bellowing at the chauffer. The
chauffer gets out of the limousine, tosses his cap back
inside, and walks slowly toward the cabbie. I see that
the front lights on the cab are broken, and the front
fender is hanging off. I see not only that the cab man
face is red; his mouth is shaped as through he is going
to spit. The chauffers face is dark-skinned, and he has
long black wavey hair that seems to shine as the sun
beats on it; he is wearing a blue suit, blue shirt with
white shoes. The crowd is waiting as though they are
waiting to see Hank Aaron break the home run record. I
can heard the cab man saying, "Look at what you've done
to my cab. You've ruined it." The chauffer looks at
him with a crooked smile and said, "Who do you think you
talking to you beat-up old side buster. You are the one
who went through the red light and struck my car."
     The police is beginning to arrive on the scene.
Two cops get out of the car. One has a pregnant belly.
The other one is tall; he has a gray strike in his hair,
and his eyes are the color of the sky. They began to
push through the crowd. The tall cop ask the cab man
what happen. The cab man say "This man ran through the
light and hit me." The cop ask him his name. The cab man
said; "My name is John Smith. I live at 333 West Street."
     The chauffer say; "He's lying. Ask anyone in the
crowd. They saw him go through the red light and ram
into my Cadillac. My boss will be in an uproar when he
sees this. I might even lose my job."

126

"Who cares," says the cab man.   "You don't know how to drive anyway."

The crowd has growed bigger; it's beginning to look like a Saturday night on Times Square.   The pregnant cop is asking the chauffer who's car he is driving.   The chauffer is telling him the owners name and address. The tall handsome cop is taking down all of the information that they need for both partys.   The police is telling the crowd, "Go home the side show is over with."   The crowd is beginning to break up like the balls on a pooltable when they have been hit each goes in their own direction.   The police gave the cab driver back his license and the chauffer back his.   Each get back into his own car and drove off.   Each in his own direction.

8. Edit the following paragraph:

A stapler is a very strange but useful device.   It look like a baby alligator without any teeth.   If you never seen one used.   You would never guess what it for. It have two jaws which opens up into a large V, a slot for dropping in miniature wires, and a long slinky spring that keep the wires moving forward when its in use.   Whenever its pressed together with pieces of paper in the middle, it lock a tiny wire through the papers, clamping them together in a more or less permanent bond. It can also staple together two papers or twenty.   If its a heavy duty stapler.   It can even hold together a book.   Opened up, it also staple things on bulletin boards, on walls, or even puts up ceilings. Although it can leave two little holes in a careless finger.   It have an amazing variety of uses for such a weird-looking little machine.

9. The essay in this chapter about city social patterns is an interesting and well-documented example of some of the nonverbal "language" and social organization discussed in Chapters 1 and 3. Go back and edit the essay for both style and mechanics. How is it organized? Rewrite it expanding the introduction and conclusion; if possible, add more details to those the author describes.

10. Using the rewritten essay as a model, write another essay describing the "unwritten rules" that govern other aspects of social habits and behavior you are familiar with (for example, a family dinner, commuting, people at a sports event, teen-age dating rituals, or the "singles" scene).

Suggested Reader Selections

Andrew Malcolm, *Chemists in Timber Revolution on Verge of Test-tube Trees.*

What are "parts of speech"? Huh? Awww! *Those* are "parts" of speech, literally, "chunks" of the language which we look at and try to describe. *Huh* and *awww* are called **interjections** in traditional grammar. They are exclamations which are "stuck in" or interjected into a stream of speech, and they usually express some sort of direct emotional response.

Why bother with the labels? In the stream of noise we call language, we hear not just an uninterrupted flow, but a series of "chunks," smaller units all working together.* Sometimes how they work is not too clear, or at least so it seems when we try to analyze their working. How can we come up with a clear description of these "chunks"?

Well, how do we describe anything? Usually, we begin by trying to figure out what something "does," or what it looks like, or what it sounds like or smells like. If, for example, you were trying to explain to someone how an automobile engine worked so he or she could drive a car more efficiently, chances are you would label the parts. Even if you didn't call something a piston, it would probably at least end up as "one of the whatchamacallits that goes up and down in a cylinder (another label) and moves the drive shaft (still another label)." You are labeling something by what it does, how it functions in the overall design of the machine. It is more elegant, not to mention easier, to call the "whatchamacallit" a "piston," assuming both you and the person you are talking to understand what the label refers to. That's what labels are all about—often arbitrary references, mutually agreed on by those who use them, that describe or at least refer to what a thing is or how it functions.

What is the difference between the following two phrases?

the White House keeper
the white housekeeper

There are several ways you can talk about the differences. In writing, for example, the difference is obvious because of the capital letters in the first and the compound word *housekeeper* in the second. What if you just heard the expressions, however? How would you describe the differences? You *could* point out the differences in pronunciation. When you say the first,

the White House keeper

the heaviest (or primary) stress hits *White* and the next heaviest (or secondary) stress hits *keep*. In saying the second phrase,

the white housekeeper

*Compare spoken English with any spoken foreign language you don't understand: the foreign language *does* sound like an "uninterrupted flow," but your ear "breaks up" the stream of English into words.

the primary stress is on *house*, with a secondary stress on *white* and *keep*. We also pause between *white* and *house* in the second phrase whereas we pause between *house* and *keeper* in the first one. Sound out the differences for yourself.

We use labels like primary or secondary stress to describe the differences in pronunciation. Now suppose you were asked to describe how else the words in each phrase relate to each other, not just how they are pronounced. How does *white* function in relationship to *house* and *keeper* in the first phrase compared to the second? In order to describe it, you need labels, labels that we can all understand. That's where **parts of speech** come in. These are not just fancy words for fancy's sake but convenient labels that make it easier to describe how the engine—the language—works (or doesn't work).

In the first phrase *White House* working as a unit describes *keeper*: the the keeper of the White House, who is usually a guard, a military attaché, or what have you. *White House* here is thus functioning as an **adjective,** the label that identifies a word or group of words which have the function of describing something about another word. *White House* can also be a **noun,** the label traditionally defined as "a person, place or thing." But here it is an adjective. Confusing? The essential fact to recognize is that parts of speech, like many other labels our culture uses, do not work all the time in all ways for all things. They simply describe the way a word or group of words works or functions in relationship to other words in a particular sentence. To take another example, a woman can be a daughter, sister, wife, mother, student, police officer, member of the school board, valentine, or compassionate friend. All these are labels. They define a woman in different roles. If they are overused (like *wife*) they distort a woman's complexity. But used to describe a particular role assumed, they make it easier to describe that role. For example, when an undercover, female police officer in her line of duty must make an arrest, it is handy and obviously necessary that she announces she is a police officer. A label defines a function in a particular role.

It is the same with language. *White House* is a noun, the home of the President of the United States. In our first example, however, it also works as an adjective, describing the noun *keeper*. In the second phrase, *housekeeper* is the noun. How do we decide that? Well, we could say it is a person, hence a noun, but it is safer to define it by how it works in the sentence: it is what's being described. He or she is *white*, an adjective which presumably describes the housekeeper's race. *White*, elsewhere, can also work as a noun. For example, "Whites and blacks working together have successfully integrated this school." In *White House*, *White* can also be described as an adjective (the White House by historical convention is painted white), but the White House (where the President lives) is not the same as the white house down the street. We can argue that the *White* in the Washington White House functions differently from the *white* in any white house which is not a black house. It's the same difference that distinguishes a greenhouse where you grow flowers from a house that happens to be painted green. For our purposes, we can say that the President's *White House* and a florist's *greenhouse* both work as a compound noun. The label defines the function of the word or words in the sentence.

So what's a **noun**? A person, place, or thing? That gets a litle fuzzy around the edges. Pick out the nouns in the following sentences and see if you can determine why you picked them:

> The boobles ate the mumrows.
> A bangler struck his zooney.
> All whocheys whistle.
> My smidlows gerbled.
> That chingiest madlin is an ardrack.

There are clues that point out nouns. Frequently, they follow those "little" words labeled **articles:** *an, a, the.* They can be doubled (or made plural) by adding an *-s* (as in *one whochey, two whocheys*). They can be described, as in *the chingiest madlin* (the madlin with the most ching!). Our definition of noun would have to include all those characteristics. Begin to see where we are headed? Parts of speech are simply convenient labels we give to words which work in similar ways within a sentence.

We've sorted out nouns, adjectives, and articles. Now what about the others? Which words work as verbs in the following sentences?

> My gnut swarks twice a day.
> The macraws smidely sugged some choocks.
> Angrabs are bibling their knorts.
> Mach up!

Verbs, traditionally defined as words conveying action or state of being, are easier to label if you see them working in a sentence. Basically, they are the words which usually mark time by telling whether something going on is past or present. What is the difference between "My gnut swarks twice a day" and "My gnut swarked twice a day"? Most verbs are words which can add an *-ing* and pair up with *am, are, is, was,* or *were* (also verbs):

> Angrabs are bibling.
> The angrab is bibling.
> The angrabs were bibling.

You know *mach* is a verb because it fills the slot _____ up! (It is like "shut up!" "Wash up!" and "Put up your hands!") Remember, however, labels can change. The *-ed* form of the verb *mach* can also work like an adjective: "That man looks mached." Here, *mached* describes the noun *man.* An *-ing* form can also be an adjective; "The bibling angrabs lost their knorts." *Bibling* here describes something about the noun *angrabs.*

Adverbs are words which often do for verbs what adjectives do for nouns—describe, by adding more information. Adverbs answer the questions how, how much, where, when, and why. How did those *macraws* *sug? Smidely! Smidely* works here as an adverb, describing *how* the macraws sugged. The *-ly* ending frequently marks an adverb:

He's been very depressed late*ly*.
They quick*ly* flipped through the book.
The baby shrieked hysterica*lly*.

Adverbs also function to describe more about adjectives. In the following two phrases, which *pretty* works as an adverb?

a pretty hot day
a pretty, hot day

If you guessed the first, you have a good idea of what adverbs are and have hit upon another conventional comma rule.

What about **prepositions**? These are easy to spot—they usually work as pointers in a sentence, giving directions: *up, down, under, over, in, inside, into, through, to, next to, near, on,* and so forth. They very often team up with verbs: *team up, look after, sit down.* Or they introduce phrases:

He walked *up the street,* and then he went *into the house.*
He climbed *up the stairs* and put his wallet *on the dresser.*

One way of recognizing prepositions is to add to the following list of verb-preposition combinations: *throw out, throw up, sit down, sit on, sit in, take out, put up.* You won't have to look far—they are all over the place.

Conjunctions, another part of speech, work several ways. First there are the *and* variety. These simply work to tie together two or more words, phrases, or clauses. *And* is the most common:

Joe *and* I
Joe, Mabel, *and* I
I went to work, to school, *and* to sleep.
I came, I saw, *and* I conquered.

The semicolon also works as a conjunction:

I came; I saw; I conquered.

There are also other words, most of them usually adverbs, which work as conjunctions when they are teamed up with a semicolon:

I came; *however*, he had already left.
I overslept; *therefore*, I missed my class.

These conjunctions "conjoin"; that is, they tie two equal parts together. There are other kinds of conjunctions, however, which also tie phrases or clauses together, but not as equals. They create dependency, forcing whatever follows them to hook on to another main sentence:

I was late *because* I missed my bus.
I was late *because* of the weather.
Because you're here, I'm happy again.

132

APPENDIX A

What about all those other words—words like *him, my, I, hers, that, these, who, whose, what,* and so on? Study how they work in the following sentences:

My smidlows berbled.
Whose angrabs are *these*?
Your bangler loves *mine*.
That is *mine*.

They all function either to indicate possession or to replace a noun's function within a sentence. Hence they are called **pronouns.** Some of them are the only words left in English which change form depending on where they are in the sentence:

My angrabs bibled at *him*.
His angrabs bibled at *me*.

Nouns, verbs, adjectives, adverbs, pronouns, conjunctions, articles, interjections—these are the labels we use to describe parts of speech and how they function. They aren't always accurate, and their use is still very imperfectly understood, even by the experts. The same word can fall into more than one of these categories, depending on how it is used. *That*, for example, has at least five different functions:

1. As a pronoun having reference to something preceding it: "*That* is correct."
2. As a pronoun used to introduce an adjective clause: "This is the gnat *that* bit the cat *that* ate the rat *that* lived in the house that Jack built."
3. As an adverb: "Is it *that* hard?"
4. As an adjective with a noun: "*That* man is my father."
5. As a kind of conjunction: "I saw *that* he didn't understand."

The point is that not all labels work all the time. We use labels where we need them to explain how a sentence works (or doesn't work), or we use them when we want to play around with a sentence and take it apart just to see how it does work.

In one sense at least, that's what grammar is all about—inventing labels we can use to describe the engine and how it runs. Many people claim you can drive just as efficiently without knowing how the engine works, and they may well be right. But learning how language in general (and your language in particular) works, analyzing how so many pieces seem to fit so neatly and predictably together, listening carefully to a child just learning how to speak—all these can be challenging and rewarding explorations.

In the rest of this Appendix, you'll find lists of some of the most commonly used—and most commonly confused—parts of speech, grouped according to their different functions. Notice that some words appear on several lists.

PREPOSITIONS

about	by	outside	according to
above	down	over	as for
across	except	past	as to
after	for	since	because of
against	from	through	by means of
around	in	throughout	by reason of
at	inside	till	by way of
before	into	to	for the sake of
behind	like	under	in keeping with
below	near	until	in regard to
beneath	of	up	in spite of
beside	off	upon	instead of
between	on	with	on account of
beyond	out	without	out of

COMPOUND (TYPE 2) CONJUNCTIONS

and	yet	
and yet	accordingly	nevertheless
but	as a consequence	nonetheless
for	consequently	otherwise
nor	furthermore	then
or	however	therefore
so	moreover	thus

ADVERB (TYPE 3) CONJUNCTIONS

after	if	when
although	like	whenever
as	since	where
as if	so that	wherever
because	that	whether
before	though	whether or not
even if	unless	while
even though	until	

PRONOUNS

Used to introduce adjective clauses **(Type 4)**:

who (whom, whose)	whoever (whomever, whosever)
which	whichever
that	whatever
what	

134

Used to introduce questions.

who	what
whom	whoever
whose	whatever
which	

Used to refer to a noun *or show* possession:

I	we	
you	you	(used in *subject* position:
he, she, it	they	"*He* came in late.")
me	us	
you	you	(used in *object* position:
him, her, it	them	"You can give *it* to *him*.")
my	our	
your	your	(used to show *possession with*
hls, her, its	their	*a noun*: "This is *his* coat.")
mine	ours	
yours	yours	(used to show *possession without*
his, hers, its	theirs	*a noun:* "This is *hers,* not *yours.*")
myself	ourselves	
yourself	yourselves	(used *reflexively:*
himself, herself, itself	themselves	"They can do it *themselves.*")
this	these	(used to point out or *demonstrate:*
that	those	"*These* are better than *those.*")

IRREGULAR VERBS—PRINCIPAL PARTS

TO BE

PRESENT		PAST	
I am	we are	I was	we were
you are	you are	you were	you were
he, she, it is	they are	he, she, it was	they were

PRESENT PARTICIPLE: being
PAST PARTICIPLE: been

TO HAVE

I have	we have	I had	we had
you have	you have	you had	you had
he, she, it has	they have	he, she, it had	they had

PRESENT PARTICIPLE: having
PAST PARTICIPLE: had

LABELING PARTS OF SPEECH

TO DO

I do	we do	I did	we did
you do	you do	you did	you did
he, she, it does	they do	he, she, it did	they did

PRESENT PARTICIPLE: doing
PAST PARTICIPLE: done

THE PRINCIPAL PARTS OF OTHER IRREGULAR VERBS

arise/arose/arisen
awake/awoke (awakened)/awoke (awakened)
bear/bore/born
beat/beat/beaten
become/became/become
begin/began/begun
bend/bent/bent
bet/bet/bet
bid/bid/bid
bind/bound/bound
bite/bit/bitten
bleed/bled/bled
break/broke/broken
breed/bred/bred
bring/brought/brought
build/built/built
buy/bought/bought
catch/caught/caught
choose/chose/chosen
cling/clung/clung
come/came/come
creep/crept/crept
cut/cut/cut
deal/dealt/dealt
dig/dug/dug
dive/dove (dived)/dove (dived)
draw/drew/drawn
drink/drank/drunk
eat/ate/eaten
fall/fell/fallen
feed/fed/fed
feel/felt/felt
fight/fought/fought
find/found/found
fly/flew/flown
forget/forgot/forgotten
freeze/froze/frozen
get/got/gotten

lead/led/led
leave/left/left
lend/lent/lent
let/let/let
lie/lay/lain (to recline)
light/lit/lit
lose/lost/lost
make/made/made
mean/meant/meant
meet/met/met
pay/paid/paid
put/put/put
quit/quit/quit
read/read/read
ride/rode/ridden
ring/rang/rung
rise/rose/risen
say/said/said
see/saw/seen
sell/sold/sold
send/sent/sent
set/set/set
shake/shook/shaken
shine/shone (shined)/shone (shined)
shoot/shot/shot
shrink/shrank/shrunk
shut/shut/shut
sing/sang/sung
sit/sat/sat
sleep/slept/slept
speak/spoke/spoken
stand/stood/stood
steal/stole/stolen
stick/stuck/stuck
stink/stank/stunk
swear/swore/sworn
swim/swam/swum
take/took/taken

go/went/gone
grow/grew/grown
hang/hung/hung
hear/heard/heard
hide/hid/hidden
hit/hit/hit
hold/held/held
hurt/hurt/hurt
keep/kept/kept
know/knew/known
lay/laid/laid

teach/taught/taught
tear/tore/torn
tell/told/told
think/thought/thought
throw/threw/thrown
understand/understood/understood
wake/woke (waked)/woken (waked)
wear/wore/worn
win/won/won
wring/wrung/wrung
write/wrote/written

TRANSITIONS

Notice that most of the following are words or phrases which function as adverbs or conjunctions to mark logical shifts within or between sentences.

With examples:

e.g.
for example
for instance
i.e.
incidentally

indeed
in fact
in other words
in particular
namely

particularly
specifically
that is
thus

With additions:

again
also
and
and then
besides
equally important
even

first
further
furthermore
in addition (to)
likewise
moreover

next
second
similarly
subsequently
third
too

In comparisons:

in the same way
likewise
similarly

In contrasts:

after all
although
and yet
but, or, nor
conversely
despite

even though
however
in contrast (to)
in spite (of)
instead (of)
nevertheless

notwithstanding
on the contrary
on the other hand
still
while
yet

Showing cause and effect:

accordingly
as a result
because
consequently
for

hence
if . . . then
necessarily
since
so

so that
then
thereby
therefore
thus

Showing passage of time:

after a while	presently	since then
afterward	recently	temporarily
at last	shortly	then
lately	since	

With hypothetical conditions:

as if
as though
even though
if

With conclusions or summaries:

accordingly	in conclusion	then
and so	in other words	therefore
as a result	in short	thus
consequently	in summary	to conclude
finally	on the whole	to summarize
in brief	so	

With concessions:

after all	at the same time	of course
although true	granted	perhaps
and yet	naturally	though

appendix b
punctuation review

ENDING SENTENCES:	period	.
	question mark	?
	exclamation point	!
	comma	,
	semicolon	;
MARKING BREAKS	colon	:
WITHIN SENTENCES:	dash	—
	parentheses	( )
	brackets	[ ]
LINKING WORDS TOGETHER:	hypen	-
MARKING MATERIAL OMITTED:	ellipsis	. . .
SHOWING DIRECT SPEECH OR THE EXACT WRITTEN WORDS OF SOMEONE ELSE:	quotation marks	" "
	single quotation marks	' '
SHOWING OWNERSHIP OR MARKING CONTRACTION:	apostrophe	'

ENDING SENTENCES

Using periods, question marks, or exclamation points obviously demands knowing what a sentence is. If you have any doubts, review Chapter 4.

Please shut the door.
Will you please shut the door?
Shut the door!

THE CRITICAL COMMA

1. Use in a series (three or more words, phrases, or clauses):

   I enjoy *sleeping*, *drinking*, and *loafing*.
   Students *going to school*, *earning a living*, and *keeping house* don't have much free time.
   I want to succeed, *I want to love wisely*, and *I want to die rich and happy*.

2. Use after any phrase or clause preceding the main subject:

   Although I hate you, I also love you.
   Racing down the street, he tripped and fell.

3. Use before conjunctions joining two otherwise independent sentences:

   I hate you, *but* I also love you.

4. Use before a modifying phrase at the end of a sentence:

> She ran quickly, *breathless with anticipation.*

5. Use to separate modifiers when each independently describes something about the word it modifies:

> It was a *long, tedious, poorly played* game.

6. Use as "handles" before and after an "unnecessary" adjective clause:

> My mother, *who is an opera singer,* practices in the shower.

7. Use as "handles" before and after words or phrases "embedded" in the sentence: appositives, transitions, participle phrases, words of direct address, and so forth:

> My mother, *an opera singer,* practices in the shower.
> Our dog, *however,* howls whenever he hears her.
> The Klan riders, *surrounding the house,* shouted for my father to come out.
> I swear to you, *honey,* that I haven't lied.

8. Use between direct speech or quoted material and tag phrases:

> The cop muttered, *"Move on!"*
> "Move on," *muttered the cop,* "or I'll arrest you!"

THE SEMICOLON

1. Use as a conjunction to join two otherwise independent sentences:

> *You made me love you; I didn't want to do it.*

2. Use with conjunctions like *however, moreover,* and *likewise* (see Appendix A) to join two otherwise independent sentences:

> It's raining; *however,* the game will go on.

3. Use with a compound conjunction *only* in a longer sentence containing a lot of other commas:

> The child, hungry and tired, whined constantly, screaming frequently; but the mother, even though sympathetic, could do nothing to make him feel better.

THE COLON

Use to signal an explanation, a series, or a list to come:

> All her efforts point to one motive: hate.
> In order to survive, true love must have two basic qualities: honesty and humor.
> Truffle burgers are made from a combination of strange ingredients: chopped sirloin, truffles, capers, garlic, anchovies, and marshmallows in almond paste.

THE DASH

1. Use to insert or interject material within or at the end of a sentence. It works like an intensified comma. It sets off—and calls attention to—the word, phrase, or clause that has been added:

   Joe despises pickles—*especially sweet pickles*—and he never eats them.

2. Use to dramatically change directions within a sentence. It breaks normal word order and "shifts gears";

   Stale bread, a few scraps of overripe cheese, and some sour milk—this was all the food the survivors had managed to save.

PARENTHESES

Use parentheses to insert additional material into a sentence. Parentheses are used like "handle" commas and dashes, but they make whatever they enclose even more of an "aside":

The majority of our population (*71 percent to be exact*) favors tax reform.

BRACKETS

Use brackets to insert your own information or clarification into something you are quoting:

The lawyer shouted, "You are making a mockery of justice by accusing this man [*Senator Bradford J. Waterdam*] of conspiring with common criminals!"

THE HYPHEN

1. Use the hyphen to separate words running off the end of a line. The word is broken between syllables (which you can find in any dictionary):

   John hated any overt show of emotion, especially frustration or anger.

2. Use the hyphen to show relationship between two or more modifiers:

   a *red-haired* man
   a *long-neglected* ghetto
   a *blue-eyed* blonde
   a *slow-moving* line
   an *I-don't-give-a-damn* attitude

3. Use the hyphen with certain prefixes and compounds:

   ex-wife
   all-purpose
   self-supporting
   mother-in-law
   mayor-elect

THE ELLIPSIS

Use the ellipsis (. . .) to indicate material omitted:

The President asked, "How are we ever going to finish this . . . thing?"

QUOTES

1. Use quotes to mark direct speech. Notice all end punctuation and commas fall *before* the final quote mark (only the semicolon and colon go outside). Begin a new paragraph for each change of speaker:

   An old lady came to the door. She opened it slowly and asked, "May I help you?"

   "Yes," I said. "I brought your lost grandson home." As I turned around to look for Johnny, I noticed he was gone.

   "Come in," the old lady said. "Sit down. I'm not John's grandmother. I'm his mother. John has been dead for thirty years, and every year, someone comes to the house as you have saying they are bringing him home."

Notice the difference between direct quotes and indirect quoting:

DIRECT: I asked him, "Where do you live and what is your name?"
INDIRECT: I asked him where he lived and what his name was.

In a direct quote, the speaker's words are given *exactly* as he or she spoke them, even though you are reporting what you heard after the fact. In an indirect quote, the tense changes to past to indicate the past happening. Don't make the mistake of translating a direct quote into an indirect statement without changing the syntax or word order.

UN-EAE: I asked him where did he live and what was his name.
EAE: I asked him where he lived and what his name was.
        I asked him, "Where do you live and what is your name?"

2. Use quotes to mark the *exact* words someone else wrote:

   Anthony Able, a famous columnist, once wrote, "Whatever you do, do it well." Able's famous quote, "Whatever you do, do it well," has influenced a lot of people.
   My mother always told me that it was "in bad taste" for people to chew gum.

3. Use quotes to warn your reader that a word or phrase is used in a special way (WARNING: do not overuse):

   Commas sometimes act as "handles": they can be used to "lift out" a word or phrase if it isn't necessary.

4. Use quotes to indicate the titles of short stories and poems, essays, articles, chapters, or radio and TV programs:

   The first chapter of this book is titled "Language: Some Definitions."

Do not use quotes with titles of longer works: books, magazines, newspapers, plays, long poems, or any separately published material (published within its own covers). Instead, use an underline, which in print becomes italics. All major words of any title, quoted or underlined, are begun with capital letters:

> The second chapter of *Writing in Context* is called "A History of Language Conventions."

5. Do not use quotes for emphasis or for foreign words. These too are underlined (or converted to italics in print):

> You should *not* go.
> That dress is *très chic.*

THE APOSTROPHE

1. Use the apostrophe to mark contractions:

don't (do not)	you're (you are)	It's (it is)
can't (cannot)	he's (he is)	you'd (you had)
won't (will not)	I'm (I am)	I've (I have)
isn't (is not)	we're (we are)	he's (he, is *or* has)

2. Use the apostrophe to mark possession on nouns:

Mary's husband	the children's toys
Mary's husband's cousin	the worker's rights
Mr. Jones' house	the workers' rights

Notice that when a noun already ends in -s (like *Jones*), you only have to add an apostrophe. To mark plural forms like *children,* add 's. Otherwise, the following forms apply:

> 's = singular possession
> s' = plural possession

appendix c
organizing a
longer paper

Once you have mastered the techniques of writing a paragraph, a longer paper shouldn't seem so formidable. The same basic techniques apply: you use topic sentences, primary support, and specifics. You have more room to expand, so you can explore a larger area of your topic. You have more specifics, so instead of writing everything in one paragraph, you organize your information into several paragraphs. Just as there are different kinds of paragraph development, there are also obviously a variety of techniques for organizing a long paper. All the organization techniques discussed in Chapter 3 also apply to the longer paper. There is no "one way" to write anything. There are, however, several basic guidelines which most college writing usually follows.

INTRODUCTION

The first paragraph of a longer paper is almost always an introduction. It can very effectively do two things at once: first, it gets your reader's attention; second, it summarizes the main argument or direction of the paper. This main argument or direction is called a **thesis statement.** In one or two sentences, you briefly set up and define your thesis—you let your reader know where you are headed. What are you going to discuss? What are some of the main points you are going to hit? This introduction simply whets your reader's appetite, so it need not get too specific. Until you are more comfortable writing longer papers, however, you can most effectively use your introduction to keep yourself on target. Set up your thesis statement in your introduction, then stick to it.

DEVELOPMENT

Your development paragraphs are written like any other expository paragraphs: each has its own topic sentence and specific facts. If they are longer paragraphs, you will also use primary support to organize them. Each development paragraph of a longer paper takes one aspect of your thesis, presents it in a topic sentence, and develops it in detail. The only refinements you need to be aware of in a longer paper are careful transitions *between* paragraphs and some kind of logical sequence. If you are discussing the changes in fashion from the forties to the seventies, for example, it would probably make sense to discuss each decade's fashions in order. Or if you prefer organizing around styles, discuss hemlines, pants styles, and accessories, but just be sure one paragraph logically leads into the next. Your organization should be apparent to your reader after one quick reading. Besides organization, the same principles of specific evidence also apply: facts convince; unsupported opinions do not.

CONCLUSION

The final paragraph of any longer paper should be some kind of conclusion. This can be a dramatic finale, driving home every major point you've made, or it can be a more gentle "easing off," leaving your reader with the "flavor" of your argument. How you conclude is more a matter of style than necessity, but keep in mind that the last words are often the ones that echo longest. A conclusion can be a unique opportunity to lift your readers out of their seats. You prove that you have done what you set out to do.

All these techniques for writing a longer paper—introduction, development, and conclusion—are just sound common sense. If you ever tried to give a speech or write a report, you have probably come up with most of them for yourself. If you rewrote the essay on city social habits in Chapter 6, you have already been using most of these techniques. Your control of organization and your mastery of specific facts function for a longer paper the same way they function for a paragraph: they make your writing effective. Besides these, however, two other techniques useful in writing a longer paper need to be discussed.

OUTLINING

An outline is a tool to use if it helps you. As a writer, I prefer a very rough outline form—notes to myself, really—so I don't forget any important points. A rough outline sketches the skeleton of a paper. The convention of alternating Roman and Arabic numbers with capital and small letters is simply an easy way to distinguish between large generalizations, primary support, and specifics. It helps you see how all the pieces fit together. Learning to use an outline can also give you two other advantages: it easily shows you when things need rearranging (just as an x-ray reveals broken bones), and it also gives you a handy tool for taking notes as you read or analyzing someone else's writing.

As a writer, you can outline either before or after you write. If you outline before writing, sketch the main idea you plan to develop and some of the specific support you want to include. Then write from your outline and refer to it as you develop your paper. To outline after writing, first put down your thoughts on paper, then go back and rearrange them. After you've moved the pieces around, write an outline to check your organization. Either way works. Experiment with both. Below is a rough outline of a student paper on changes in pop music.

ORGANIZING A LONGER PAPER

THESIS: Important changes took place in pop music during the fifties and sixties

I. The fifties

   A. Bill Haley

      1. Added beat to rhythm

   B. Elvis Presley

      1. Body movements

      2. Mixed blues, country, jazz

         a. "Blue Suede Shoes"

         b. "Heartbreak Hotel"

II. Early sixties

   A. Bob Dylan

      1. Folk style

      2. Message

   B. Beatles

      1. Electronics

      2. Irony

      3. Message

   C. Johnny Cash

      1. True-to-life ballads

      2. The "hard" experience

   D. Aretha Franklin

      1. Blended gospel and jazz

III. Late sixties

   A. Blood, Sweat, and Tears

      1. Blended jazz and rock

   B. The Band

      1. Blended folk with rock

      2. Experimented with "new" instruments

CONCLUSION: Pop music is not a stationary art form

The writer could develop this outline into one long paragraph or, if he had enough specifics, expand it to anywhere from five to ten paragraphs. The writer used the outline to get a sense of how all the parts fit together. He wasn't consistent in filling in all the facts (he only has two specifics listed—I *a* and *b*), but the outline has served its purpose.

PARAPHRASING

Specifics can sometimes be a problem in writing a paper—where do you find them and how do you use them? So long as you can write about things you have firsthand knowledge of, facts aren't really a problem, but when you begin to explore new things that interest you, that you might want to write about, you then need to search for specifics beyond your own experience. Newspapers, weekly news magazines, television, or even asking a lot of questions can all turn up facts on any number of different subjects and supplement your own information without involving you in writing a research paper. The trick is to use those facts effectively in your own writing. If you find an interesting article in a magazine, for example, you can't just "lift" the information and use it wholesale; you have to **paraphrase**—translate your source completely into your own words—or quote it exactly, within quotation marks. Too much quoting is boring to read, so except for an occasional line to give your argument the weight of authority, stick to paraphrasing. Study the following example to see how it's done:

ORIGINAL PASSAGE: "The Forest Service which presides over about one-quarter of the country's forest land, estimates that when Columbus landed, there were about one billion total acres of forests here."

PARAPHRASE: The U.S. Forest Service, according to an article in *The New York Times,* reports approximately one billion acres of woodland covered America 500 years ago.

Now, practice paraphrasing by translating into your own words various passages from the sample paper included in this Appendix. Next, try outlining the paper to see how it is put together.

Below is another check list, which you can add to as you become more aware of other techniques in preparing a longer paper. Use it to analyze the sample paper that follows.

CHECK LIST FOR A LONGER PAPER

—Is the introduction in a separate paragraph?
—Is the thesis statement clearly defined?
—Does the introduction catch the reader's interest?

—Do all the development paragraphs have their own topic sentences?

—Are the topic sentences easy to find?

—Does the topic sentence of each development paragraph clearly refer back to and develop an aspect of the thesis?

—Does each development paragraph have enough specifics in it to be convincing?

—Are there clear transitions *within* paragraphs?

—Are there clear transitions *between* paragraphs?

—Can you follow the development of the thesis from paragraph to paragraph?

—Is there a separate concluding paragraph?

—Does it summarize the rest of the paper?

—Does it leave the reader with a clear sense that the writer has done what he or she set out to do?

A SAMPLE PAPER

A SAMPLE PAPER

An encounter with a shark in the sea or on a magazine page will whet an appetite of fear. Be it great white, blue, mako, hammerhead, nurse, tiger, or bull, these majestic killers are surely worthy of their universal reputation. In fact, even a peripheral study of the species--its physical attributes and its behavior patterns--will strengthen the sense of awe and the feeling of fearful respect that shroud this marauder of the deep.

One of the first gruesome realizations of such a study is the grim observation that a shark is every inch a lethal weapon, equipped better than any World War II tank. For example, huge, razor-edged teeth can deftly sever appendages and tear away twenty-pound chunks of flesh in one bite. In addition, the skin is coarser than any known sandpaper, rough as a rasp, and fantastic at flaying. Also, tips of fins and edges of tails cut as expertly as the rapier of a musketeer. The body too

is beautifully streamlined and capable of delivering
fierce, rib-cracking bunts.

Next, and equally important, is the masterful
efficiency of this enigmatic ruler of the sea. There
is, for instance, the noteworthy feat of perfectly
executing ninety-degree turns with a mere flick of the
tail. Despite the often considerable length and weight
of the body, which can be as much as twenty feet and
well over two thousand pounds, a shark can smoothly and
effortlessly spear through the water at a cool twenty
knots. Interesting also is the fact that the monster's
formidable mouth can replace lost teeth within twenty-
four hours. Moreover, a shark can jut his jaw forward,
actually dislocate it to assist in the certainty of one
clean bite. He can also slam his jaw shut, applying up
to eighteen tons of pressure per square inch, depending,
of course, on his size. And a final tidbit of true
efficiency is the existence of pressure centers within
the shark's body. These nifty little vibration
detectors, running up and down the entire body length,
are actually sophisticated homing devices that direct a
shark to its prey by sound.

Another awesome characteristic of a shark is his
tendency to be an opportunist. Although in the past,
scientists have maintained that sharks attacked solely
for food, evidence is being compiled indicating that a
shark deliberately and frequently stalks the weak or
crippled, be they fish or human. This is dramatically
supported by the number of merciless devourings of
wounded from shipwrecks and airplane crashes. Likewise,
a distressed and floundering swimmer has more than once
been too tempting a morsel for a shark to by-pass.

Still another awesome feature about this species is

ORGANIZING A LONGER PAPER

its endurance. Sharks have existed on earth for over one hundred and forty million years, and have undergone few changes in that time. Somehow, these predators have survived the varying water levels and water temperatures during those millions of years. Also they have managed to endure and survive bites of their own species and the terror of their eating frenzies. For some reason yet unlearned, the shark is one of the few sea creatures not severely hampered by man and his pollutants.

In spite of all such documented characteristics of the creature, however, there is no definite set of rules yet established for their behavior patterns. Uncertainty still clouds the species and test runs at the Lerner Marine Laboratories on Bimini failed to prove when or under what circumstances a shark would or would not attack. Tests held at Marine Land, Florida, for similar reasons and equally unsuccessful, moved one of the researchers, Clifford Townsend, to comment, "The only thing predictable about a shark is its unpredictability. Never trust a shark." Given the species' indecisive behavior patterns, it is easy to understand the panic one feels when a gray fin slits the surface of the sea.

A final and timely item of interest concerning sharks is the possible key they hold to scientific and medical discoveries. Presently, scientists are interested in the "cancer shield" most sharks seem to possess. Drs. David Hall and Richard Adamson of the federal government's National Cancer Institute are experimenting with the method by which sharks detoxify cancer-producing agents in their bodies. Scientists are also attempting to discover why sharks' hearts give their owners so little trouble. Likewise, Dr. Igor Klatzo of the National Institute of Health is

investigating why it is that sharks show less reaction
to brain injury than mammals.

A brief look into the world of the shark--his
structure, his techniques, and his "life style"--leaves
one with a final impression that is best summed up by
Phillipe Cousteau, son of the famed ocean scientist
Jacques Cousteau, when he said, "When their formidable
silhouette glides along the populated coral cliffs, fish
do not panic, they quietly clear the lord's path and
keep a wary eye on him and so should man."

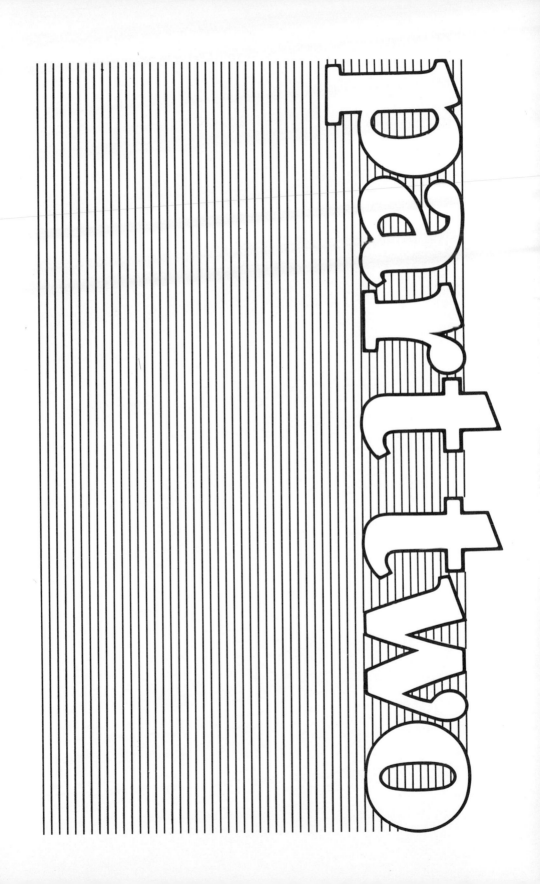

part two

STUART BAUR

first message
from the
planet of the apes

The following article describes in detail how a Columbia psychology professor, Herbert Terrace, is trying to teach a chimpanzee Ameslan, the American Sign Language of the deaf. Dr. Terrace considers his work potentially revolutionary. As you are reading, see if you come to the same conclusion. Specifically, you might tackle the question, "If animals can talk, what is so distinctive about human beings?"

I met Herb Terrace for the first time on Columbus day up at Columbia, where he is a professor of psychology. . . .

Terrace was genial as we shook hands; but underneath the geniality there was a trace of a habitual anti-anti-intellectualism. He knew that he was on the verge of an enormous intellectual gamble, perhaps a life's work, perhaps the sort of scientific revolution with religious consequences that occurs once every few hundred years. He agreed it was time to be written about, but he was clearly leery of being trivialized in print.

"I hear," I said, "that you and a squad of specially trained magicians are teaching a chimp to talk. . . ."

Terrace winced, told his secretary not to accept any calls for the next hour, and closed the door to his office. We sat down and he told me about Nim, the infant male ape upon whom so much depended.

Terrace said that Nim was being taught a vocabulary of *signs* as defined by the conventions of Ameslan, the American Sign Language, the gestural language of the deaf.

"As Nim masters more and more signs," he said, "I plan to determine whether he can combine them according to simple syntactical [EAE] rules. When he has attained a vocabulary of 30 signs I want to find out to what extent this new vocabulary will influence his mental development." He and a colleague at Columbia, Thomas Bever, a psycholinguist, planned to test this relation between Nim's linguistic and mental development.

In the future, added Terrace, he planned to demonstrate and to record communication between two or more Ameslan-equipped chimps. Further ahead, he intended to train a signing chimp to teach a naïve one how to sign. And still further ahead, he said he wanted to breed two signing

155

chimps and see whether, of their own volition, one or both of them would teach their offspring the American Sign Language.

But sometime in the nearer future, Terrace would be able to study the cognitive processes of the chimpanzee: a man proficient in Ameslan would ask a chimpanzee proficient in Ameslan questions about the chimp's memories, moods, dreams, simmering resentments, nightmares, and sexual urges, and, presuming the chimp were curious enough, would answer any questions the chimp had—man and chimp conversing in a sign language.

This epochal conversation, consisting only of an exchange of elegantly precise gesticulations, would be recorded and preserved on video tape.

With this and other evidence, said Terrace, he would have nailed to the wall proof that a subhuman primate can acquire a syntactical competence that at least overlaps with that of man. And once he had proved syntactical overlap, the age-old distinctions concerning man's uniqueness would no longer hold. Anyone still intent on preserving man's nobility in the hierarchy of nature would have to come up with subtler distinctions than the clincher that is usually advanced: man has language, animals don't.

It was pretty heady stuff, and Terrace, who is operating on a shoestring budget until he can secure adequate grant support, was well on his way. He had a nearly year-old chimp, and the chimp was picking up signs at a steady rate.

The assumption underlying Terrace's gamble is that the evolutionary gap between man and chimp is small enough to ensure that chimps have at least a primitive form of the neural mechanism needed to generate sentences.

"Mind you," he said, "I'm not the only one trying to teach a chimp a sign language. There are others . . . but I hope to be the one who is going to do it right."

• • •

A week after our wary first meeting on Columbus Day, Terrace, no longer fretting visibly about being trivialized in print, talked freely about himself. He was born in 1936 in Brooklyn to a Polish immigrant working-class family. He got into Cornell on a scholarship after graduating from Stuyvesant, a high school in Manhattan which, for over half a century, had been to the greater New York area roughly what the *Ecole Normale Supérieure* was to France—the most academically rigorous specialized public school of its time. Terrace graduated in the top 4 per cent of his class.

"In my senior year at Cornell," he told me, "I decided, against my parents' wishes, not to follow in the footsteps of my sister, who had become a doctor. I wasn't sure just what I wanted to do, but I stayed on at Cornell for another year and got my master's in psychology. Then I went up to Harvard to the Department of Psychology for my doctorate. For the first time I felt challenged to fight for my intellectual life. I performed my initial experi-

STUART BAUR

ment in behavioral research on errorless learning with pigeons while I was taking a course given by B. F. Skinner. This was before he had published *Beyond Freedom and Dignity*. Before he was that widely famous. He saw the importance of the experiment and encouraged me. That's where it all began. . . ."

He received his doctorate in 1961, and after two years as an instructor in the psychology department at Columbia, Terrace began his serendipitous rise: he became an assistant professor in 1963; three years later an associate professor; two years after that a full professor at the age of 31. Along the way he has been a Josiah Macy Foundation fellow, a predoctoral fellow with the U.S. Public Health Service, and a Guggenheim fellow. In 1973 he was elected president of the Society for the Experimental Analysis of Behavior.

In addition to his interest in learning theory, Terrace became interested in language acquisition during a seminar held by B. F. Skinner in 1960, and since then has lectured at Columbia on language acquisition as viewed from various points of view, including the Skinnerian behaviorist position. This maintains that language is just another form of behavior and develops from scratch as a series of responses to stimuli from the external world, and that vocabulary and syntactical competence are reinforced by conditioning just like any other kind of behavior.

During his years at Columbia, Terrace kept tabs on experiments conducted with chimpanzees to investigate their learning processes and linguistic abilities. He found that since the early thirties, in the United States and Russia, there had been various attempts to teach chimpanzees the native language of the experimenters, but that there was virtually no evidence from the chimpanzees of an active vocabulary.

By 1965 it was pretty widely accepted that chimpanzees were phonologically inept: their vocal apparatus was simply incapable of producing anything more than a few very primitive utterances. Noam Chomsky [a linguist] concluded: "Anyone concerned with the study of human nature and human capacity must somehow come to grips with the fact that all normal human beings acquire language, whereas acquisition of even its barest rudiments is quite beyond the capacities of an otherwise intelligent ape."

Then one night in 1966 in Reno, Allen and Beatrice Gardner—a husband-and-wife team of psychologists at the University of Nevada—saw something the entire behavioral community had missed. They were watching a film made by Catherine and Keith Hayes which showed the result of their six-year attempt to get a female chimpanzee called Vicki to speak. The film was considered a classic of its kind, for of all the chimps experimented with since the early thirties, Vicki alone could manage *four words*, if encouraged. The encouragement took the form of swatting her on the neck, breastbone, chest, or stomach until she screeched out her chimp version of the appropriate word. The film was not shown as an experimental psychologist's triumph, but as proof that the very best a chimp could do with language acquisition after six grueling years of training was a mere four words that had to be pummeled out of her.

The Gardners, however, noticed that Vicki accompanied her meager set of utterances with hand gestures, and it occurred to them that although all speech is language, not all language is speech. Watching Vicki's hand movements they wondered whether it might not be possible to side-step a chimp's phonological difficulties with a sign language. A nonvocal, sign, or gestural language—it seems so obvious today.

The Gardners knew that there was a gestural language already available: Ameslan, in which a word is signified by a gesture made with the hand or the hands. They knew that Ameslan had a grammar of its own that organized gestures into sentences, and that it was the primary means of communication among the deaf.

In June of 1966, the Gardners acquired an approximately year-old wild female chimpanzee that had been captured in Africa. They named her Washoe, after the county in Nevada where they lived. With a few minor exceptions, the only language used in her presence was the American Sign Language.

At first the Gardners taught Washoe by rewarding her when she made more and more suitable approximations of the sign to be learned. But after the first year, another method, called *guidance* or *molding*, in which the experimenter actually formed the chimp's hands into the appropriate sign, proved to be more effective.

In a preliminary 1969 report of their Project Washoe, the Gardners listed 85 signs that satisfied their criteria. And by the time Washoe was approximately six years old, when she became too unruly to handle and was sent to the Institute for Primate Studies at the University of Oklahoma, she had an active vocabulary of 132 signs as defined by the conventions of the gestural language of the deaf.

Aside from their initial stroke of brilliance in trying a gestural rather than a vocal language, the real importance of Project Washoe was the Gardners' analysis of Washoe's multisign sequences.

Washoe made her first two multisign sequences (*gimme-sweet* and *come-open*) when she was no more than two years old, around the time that human children utter their first two-word sentences. Between April, 1967, and June, 1969, 294 different two-sign combinations were reliably observed. Of these, 240 contained at least one of these signs: *come-gimmee, you, me, more, please, go, hurry, in, out, food, open, up*. With the exceptions of *me* and *you*, the signs most used in combination with the 120 others in Washoe's active vocabulary were those that included appeals, locations, and actions.

The Gardners' 1971 report on Project Washoe concluded that the signs really did serve constructive functions, and that based on a recognized

STUART BAUR

system for describing acquisition of language in children, a subhuman primate had generated sentences for the first time in history!

There really had been nothing quite like it since 1908, when Freud murdered traditional philosophy with his theories of the instinctual nature of man and the unconscious. And now what remained—man's unique capacity for language and therefore for conceptual thought—had been challenged by a tongue-tied chimp using the gestural language of the deaf.

The American behavioral archipelago realized what had happened, and gave the Gardners credit for using a gestural language. But the psycholinguists with a stake in the acquisition of language as studied in children—Eric Lenneberg, Ursula Bellugi-Klima, and Roger Brown—balked at the Gardners' conclusion: were the multisign combinations of a chimp similar to the multiword utterances of a child? Brown argued that the crucial tip-off to syntactical competence in a child's multiword utterances is word order.

For instance, if a chimp signs come-gimmee tickle as frequently as he signs tickle come-gimmee, it may simply be cranking out the signs appropriate for the incentive of being tickled, which is not the same as generating a sentence. And, Brown argued, since word order is "as natural to a child as nut-gathering is to a squirrel," unless one had frequency data for appropriate and inappropriate word order, Washoe's "semantic intentions" would remain a matter of guesswork.

Unfortunately, the Gardners had not bothered to assemble frequency data on word order. They still haven't published any, and Washoe has become known as the ape that almost, but not quite, made it into the hall of language.

Herb Terrace acquired his first chimpanzee, a young male called Bruno, early in 1968.

Terrace had casually mentioned to the Gardners in 1967 that he too hoped to try his luck with a chimp someday. A few months later, to his surprise, he got a call from Dr. W. B. Lemmon, the director of the Institute for Primate Studies at the University of Oklahoma, who wanted to know if he would like a newborn male chimp.

"I wasn't really ready for a chimp; the timing was all wrong. But when I mentioned Lemmon's offer to a former undergraduate student of mine, Mrs. Stephanie Lee, she volunteered the use of her apartment on West End Avenue. So, on March 5, 1968, I flew out to Oklahoma and brought Bruno in his diaper, all bundled up in blankets, back to New York."

"It seemed instantly and completely natural to us to treat Bruno exactly as one would a human infant," wrote Mrs. Lee in the progress report she kept between March 6, 1968, and May 25, 1969. "At the time we wouldn't have known how to do otherwise, since we had only our experience as parents to rely on."

Terrace and Mrs. Lee did not attempt to teach their first chimp any

Ameslan. He was really part of an experiment, a dry run from which they hoped to gain invaluable practical experience as to how an infant ape adjusted to the household of a New York family. What intrigued everyone was the bond that developed between Bruno and Joshua, Stephanie's four-year-old son. "They were siblings in every sense of the word," wrote Mrs. Lee. "Theirs was a very intense relationship made more intense by the amount of physical contact they maintained."

After Terrace returned Bruno to Oklahoma in May of 1969, he left the country on a sabbatical at the University of Sussex, in England. Midway through the sabbatical he made a quick trip to Africa to see Jane Goodall, the young Englishwoman who had become expert on, among other things, the hoot-and-cry "alarm system" used by chimpanzees. Terrace was curious to know if Goodall had seen any signs of a gestural language in use among wild chimps. She hadn't.

"It didn't matter," said Terrace. "The fact that there is no indication of a gestural language in the wild should not be taken as evidence that chimps can't do so in a properly modified environment."

Terrace came back from his sabbatical convinced that he could pull it off. But three years slipped by before he got his second chimp, by which time two experimental psychologists, Premack and Rumbaugh, had published impressive papers on their work with caged chimps. Premack had used a token language; Rumbaugh, a computer-monitored lexigram language; but neither had provided overwhelming proof of syntactical competence. The time was ripe for Terrace to make his move.

He acquired his second chimp, the one he hopes to make history with, on December 4, 1973. Stephanie flew out to Norman, Oklahoma, to the Institute for Primate Studies, and brought Nim back to New York herself, to a three-floor town house on West 78th Street. Stephanie, recently remarried, was now Mrs. Stephanie LaFarge and the mother of seven children: three from her first marriage, four more from playwright Wer LaFarge's previous marriage. Nim was only two weeks old when he moved in with the nine LaFarges, Merika, a friend of the family, and a gentle, bewildered-looking police dog called Trudge. It was . . . a complete family.

Terrace and Stephanie were sure that Nim's exposure to a human home environment almost immediately after his birth would provide them with the best opportunity to teach him a gestural language and observe his linguistic responses. Washoe, the Gardners' chimp, had been kept in a trailer in their back yard, and became very spoiled. Terrace was sure that his emphasis on intense socialization, including strong discipline when necessary, would enable him to work with Nim at least until Nim reached intellectual maturity, an age estimated by Jane Goodall to be about sixteen. Washoe had become unmanageable by the age of six.

While Nim was being settled in at the LaFarge town house, Terrace arranged for his medical needs. Dr. Steve Lerman agreed to serve as Nim's pediatrician. For unusual emergencies, Professor Thomas Blumenfeld of the College of Physicians and Surgeons of Columbia University agreed to act as a consultant. Blumenfeld had wide experience with primates; he is the "pediatrician" for infant gorillas at the Bronx Zoo.

Next, Terrace contacted the people who had expressed an eagerness to be volunteer teachers in his project and informed them that he had acquired his chimp at last and that they should prepare themselves to sacrifice part of their vacations in the summer of '74 to go to special classes at N.Y.U. to learn Ameslan. He further stipulated that each volunteer would have to pledge at least five hours a week to Nim at the LaFarge town house and later at a special classroom-lab constructed for Nim in Schermerhorn Hall at Columbia. All the volunteers agreed to hold themselves in readiness.

Some of the members of the LaFarge household, plus Terrace himself, planned to attend the Ameslan classes at N.Y.U. This way, Nim would have about a dozen teachers. Terrace wanted to provide for him a stimulation greater than that provided for a human infant.

Although Terrace knew that the signs Nim would acquire would be determined by the chimp's proclivities and the varying abilities of his volunteer teachers, he drew up an initial target list: *up, hug, tickle, more, come-gimmee, drink, listen, look, hurt, sorry, out, red, green, yellow, blue, white, black, book, key, Nim, me, apple, banana, who, shoe, on, in, below, above, you, go, baby, blanket, ball, flower, food, three, bottle, cat, toothbrush, smell, what, hurry, please, quiet, dirty, hammer, bird, where, dog,* plus all the names of Nim's companions.

The volunteers would have to write a short summary of their observations for that day. But once Nim started to sign regularly, video-taping equipment would be used. Terrace intended to video-tape as many sessions as possible. If no signing occurred, the tape would be erased. The signs that had been recorded, however, would be edited and stored in a permanent file that could be examined by *any interested party*, not just those who were present at the time. Ultimately, Terrace planned to invite deaf volunteers into the project to act as evaluators of this taped evidence of signing. Once Nim had acquired a vocabulary, Terrace wanted to see if he had an enhanced capacity for thought, and he was determined not to be accused of slipshod evidence.

We were in a restaurant around the corner from the LaFarge town house a week before Thanksgiving, and I had just asked Terrace when he expected to shout "Eureka."

"I hope there'll be at least five 'Eurekas,' " he said. "First, I am going to shout 'Eureka' when Nim shows solid evidence of an ability to construct gestural sentences according to grammatical rules. Second, when he starts to use a gestural language to talk about his imagination. Third, when he begins to generate hypotheses about people not present. Fourth, when he begins to discuss the past or future. Fifth, when Nim begins to talk about an inner world—his emotions and dreams."

"When can we expect the first 'Eureka'?"

FIRST MESSAGE FROM THE PLANET OF THE APES

"Summer of '75," said Terrace. "Now, you have to meet Stephanie. None of this would have been possible without her."

Ten minutes later, Terrace and Stephanie and I were sitting around the thick-carpeted conversation pit on the first floor of the LaFarge town house. They were both smiling, because only a few minutes before, as Stephanie was introducing me to her family in the dining area, Nim, from his high-chair, had spontaneously signed *eat.* Jennie Lee, Stephanie's twelve-year-old daughter from her first marriage, had then spooned some baby food into Nim's mouth, and he had swallowed it, smacked his lips, oblivious to all the eyes on him, and signed *eat* again. On the wall behind Nim was a blackboard with the chalked words: FINISH, EAT, DRINK, SIT, HUG, KISS, STAY, DON'T, STOP, GAME—words already part of his receptive repertory, plus some others, not yet capitalized: *stroller, diaper, napkin, trudge,* that Nim, who was just a year old, was working on. Terrace's technique of intense stimulation at an early age and Stephanie's happy home environment were obviously paying off: Nim was acquiring language *as fast as* a human hcild of the same age.

Stephanie LaFarge is tall, willowy, and extraordinary looking, far more so than her photographs suggest, since the camera seems to emphasize a raw-boned angularity in her features and filters out her most striking characteristic, which is a shrewd but good-natured watchfulness. Although she was friendly she was clearly not the sort of woman who enjoyed talking about herself to a stranger.

Only gradually, therefore, did she let it be known that her father was a CBS executive; that she had worked as the director of a primary unit at the West Side Montessori School; and that shortly she planned to begin work on her doctorate in psychology at Teachers College.

I asked her what kinds of reactions she got from people on the street when she had Nim with her.

"Most people, once they get over the initial surprise, are intrigued," she said. "But some are really offended by the sight of a woman with an infant ape in her arms."

Terrace mentioned that he expected a lot of people on and off the streets to be offended. Language-acquisition experiments with subhuman primates not only challenge a lot of age-old assumptions about animal and human behavior, but pose ticklish questions that spill out of the behavioral sciences into philosophy, theology, the law, and civil rights.

These assumptions can be traced back through humanism, empiricism, Christian theology, Judaism—all the way back to Aristotle, who, in *De Anima,* developed a treatise on the soul. In it, Aristotle distinguished between man, who was supposed to have a rational soul, and beasts, who were supposed to have only an animal spirit. Man with his rational soul was supposed to be thoughtful; but beasts were mere automatons thoughtlessly going through the motions assigned to them by Nature. This Aristotelian distinction between man and beasts was popularized by Plato in the

STUART BAUR

Phaedrus, and ever since then it has been part of the cultural baggage of the West. Man with his rational soul, so the argument goes, is capable of conceptual thought, which is dependent on language. Animals, who are not blessed with language, are therefore not capable of thought.

Terrace's gamble, if it succeeds, will, among other things, throw some light on these areas. Have some animals always possessed the mental hardware for language, but merely lacked the vocal apparatus? Have they been capable all along of a nonvocal language? And once they acquire it will they prove to be as capable of conceptual thought as man is?

This last question upsets many people, and it is not just the man in the street who is vaguely discomfited by the idea. And when it comes to *their own language* (there are some 4,000 known languages), people tend to be even smugger, each nationality convinced that its language is the best.

Goethe, Montaigne, and Ortega y Gasset said very similar things about their respective favorite. Each maintained that language is man's fundamental treasure, his prize, his trump, his ace in the hole, his final pleasure and consolation when everything else has soured; and he bristles at the idea of sharing it with a lower form of life.

And yet, as jealous as he is of language, man knows so little about its origins. How did language begin? What conditions had to prevail before the great multibranched language trees—Semitic, Egyptian, Berber, Cushitic, Germanic, Celtic, Italic, Slavic, Iranic, and Indic—developed? There are plenty of language-origin theories.

One is that language developed *onomatopoetically*—imitative of natural sounds; another, that it started with *work chants;* another, that it began as *babbleluck*—associations between spontaneous infant babbling sounds and features in the environment; still another, that it was *instinctivist*—that it suddenly appeared at a certain level of human cognitive evolution and was inborn thereafter; that it was *conventionalist*—that individuals deliberately agreed to create language in order to improve their lives; that it was *divine*—the gift of a creator; that it was *chance mutation*—the outcome of a random biological accident; and finally, that it was *gestural* in origin—that it began with hand and arm movements, like Nim was being taught, that later turned vocal. . . .

"May we join the party?"

It was Jennie Lee with Nim in her arms. When Stephanie gave her permission she climbed up into the waterbed near the conversation pit and burped Nim gently. Jennie is a pretty, bright-eyed twelve-year-old, and to Nim what Joshua was to Bruno—a sibling companion, with the difference that she is also a very competent surrogate mother.

Nim disengaged himself from Jennie's arms and climbed down from the waterbed. Once you get a look at Nim, Terrace had warned me, it is difficult to take your eyes off him. It was true. Nim has star quality. He is built like Antonio Rocca, the wrestler, with all his authority in his chest and arms. In profile, he looks like a weak-chinned old monarch; full face, remarkably like Carl Albert, the speaker of the House.

Terrace signed *come-gimmee-hug,* but Nim did not want to go-give-a-hug; he wanted to whirl like a hairy top, which he did for a while. Then he came scampering purposefully toward me; and for a wild moment I thought he was going to look me in the eye and shout: "Get me a lawyer!"

But he said no such thing, of course; he said nothing, nor did he look me in the eye; chimps, especially young ones, try to avoid eye contact. He tucked his nose into my armpit to smell me. So I smelled him back, curious to know if an infant chimp in a diaper had the cidery sour-milk aroma of an infant human in a diaper. Nim smelled, not unpleasantly, like a rotting dock.

"Bite him !" called Jennie from the waterbed. "Chimps love to be bitten. It's a sign of affection with them."

So that I might be able to boast when I am old that once-upon-a-time I sank my teeth into the vanguard of a scientific revolution, I bit Nim; and he let out a piercing hoot of pure pleasure and backed off; and we made eye contact for a few seconds and I got that strange reverberating jolt I always get when I look into the eyes of gorillas, orang-utans, gibbons, sportive lemurs—any primate. It is a jolt that comes from a certainty that something complicated and rich is going on inside their heads that they lack the words to express. Nim then touched base, hugging Terrace and then Stephanie, and climbed back up to Jennie on the waterbed.

It was time to leave, and I was about to say good night when I realized that I had not asked Stephanie the obvious question: surely, there was no other woman in all of America quite like her. She was running a very large family, bringing up a subhuman primate as part of that family, and participating in a revolutionary language-acquisition experiment that would not have been possible without her; but I did not yet know *why* she was doing it.

"Because," she said, "I plan to work as a clininal therapist with emotionally disturbed children. Which is another way of saying that I am interested in the rehabilitation of the mind; and, to me, that does not preclude the rehabilitation of the animal mind. . . ."

As I was leaving, Terrace invited me to attend Nim's first birthday party. "You'll get to meet the volunteers that way," he said. "Each one came into the experiment from a different angle and for a different reason. They're a remarkable group. You'll see, when you meet them. . . ."

Nim's first year on earth was celebrated four days late, on November 24, 1974, so that all the volunteers could get together on a Sunday at the LaFarge town house.

The first volunteer I met was Maggie Jakobson, a fifteen-year-old beauty who heard about the experiment with Nim and had attended the special Ameslan classes at N.Y.U. in the summer. Maggie had a WIN—Whip Inflation Now—button pinned upside down on her sweater so that it read NIM. When I mentioned that some realists in Washington were also wearing the button upside down too, but that "in D.C., NIM stands for No Immediate Miracles," she said: "Same with NIM in N.Y.C. What we're doing with Nim is a miracle, but it does require patience."

Maggie gives her spare time to Nim after classes at Calhoun High School. Lisa Paddon is doing it for college credit. Lisa has come from Hood College, in Maryland, just to work with Nim full time for six months.

Mrs. Penny Franklin and Mrs. Connie Garlock both knew about Terrace's plans for Nim before any of the other volunteers. Mrs. Franklin, a professional book editor, is an old friend of Stephanie's and the only volunteer with some experience with the first chimp, Bruno. Connie, who is now completing work on a degree in psychology at Columbia, was once Terrace's secretary. When she heard he had finally acquired Nim, she volunteered.

Mrs. Rena Cascone, a petite curly-haired brunette with a rich contralto voice, volunteered after reading a magazine article about the work Roger Fouts, one of the Gardners' former assistants, was doing in Oklahoma. She wrote to Fouts and he referred her to Terrace. Somehow, Mrs. Cascone, who has two careers going at once—professional singer and free-lance writer—manages to find more than five hours a week for Nim. "I make the time," she said. "It's important."

Laura Petitto, a senior at Ramapo College in New Jersey, got interested in ethology when she was a teen-ager and has worked since then in various zoos and at Jungle Habitat. Of all the volunteers, she is the one who will probably devote herself to a life spent with animals. After graduation from Ramapo she hopes to go to Africa to a field study project, similar to the one run by Jane Goodall in the Gombe Preserve.

Bill Tynan, after a hiatus, is completing his education at Columbia. Mr. Tynan, who has experience in cable television and was once an editor of *High Fidelity,* will be in charge of videotaping sessions with Nim once he starts signing regularly.

Kela Stevens, of all the volunteers, is the most proficient in Ameslan, for a good reason: she is putting herself through college as a professional translator for the deaf. This entails standing up in front of a class for 50 exhausting minutes and translating what she hears an instructor say into a gestural language that deaf students in the class can comprehend. She learned Ameslan on her own so that she might communicate with a deaf boy she had become fond of; and when she completes her undergraduate work she plans to go to law school and specialize in legal guidance for the deaf. "The deaf, in effect," she said, "have no legal rights at all. Whom can they communicate with? Deaf lawyers, who know Ameslan? There are none."

Carol Stewart brings more experience in gestural language rehabilitation to the project than all the other volunteers put together. Carol is present at all the sessions with Nim; so, strictly speaking, she is not a volunteer, but

FIRST MESSAGE FROM THE PLANET OF THE APES

a supervisor of volunteers. She has never worked with primates before, but has wide experience working with the profoundly mentally retarded—the mentally retarded who are deaf and suffer from cerebral palsy—the triply benighted. "The perpetual rockers, the ones who knock their heads against the wall, the eaters of their own excrement," she said bluntly. After exhausting years of work with a group of the profoundly mentally retarded at the Southbury Training School in Connecticut, Carol Stewart and Paula Wilson and Linda Goodman and Robin Wood taught them enough of the gestural language of the deaf so that they could communicate with their parents for the first time; in effect, they broke through the wall of silence the patients had been imprisoned behind since birth, and gave them at least the rudiments of human dignity. Since September, 1974, when Terrace enlisted her in his project, Carol has made enormous contributions to Nim's socialization and language acquisition. Because of her experience at Southbury she was remarkably successful in getting Nim to sit quietly, to attend to a volunteer teacher's face and hands, and to make the appropriate response when signed to by a teacher.

After a coffee and cake and beer and pizza birthday celebration for Nim on the first floor, Terrace and Stephanie led all the volunteers upstairs to the second floor to make plans for the next week. Certain adjustments had to be made if Nim were not to fall behind schedule.

Stephanie's father had suddenly died and she had to make the long drive to Chicago to attend the funeral. Carol Stewart, after working with Nim virtually every day, all day, for three months, was fatigued and had been ordered by her doctor to take a few days' rest. Rena Cascone had a cold. Penny Franklin, Laura Petitto, and Connie Garlock were simply tired. And yet, despite their fatigue, all the volunteers indomitably rearranged their lives so that Nim would not fall behind schedule.

An hour later, walking down the stairs of the town house that led to West 78th Street, I tried to calculate what it had cost Terrace and Stephanie and the volunteers to accomplish what they had achieved with Nim so far.

Terrace's experiment appears to be the most subtle and ambitious of all the experiments ever conducted with chimps. It is an attempt to breach the wall of silence that has separated man from the animal world ever since man fled the jungle canopy. It is also an investigation into how we acquire language, and what the distinguishing features of language are. If it succeeds it may even throw some light on the origins of language and the ultimate wilderness—the processes of the mind. All the other attempts—the Gardners, Premack, Rumbaugh—had generous grant support. Terrace is operating on a shoestring budget with a group of devoted volunteers.

I tried to calculate the cost to them, some of whom had come in from Connecticut and New Jersey twice a week. Altogether, something like 10,000 man-hours had already been expended on Nim: the cost in human terms was incalculable; but the results were impressive. Nim was acquiring language as fast as a human infant of the same age.

STUART BAUR

Turning for a last look at the town house, I saw that I had not closed the door properly. I hustled up the steps to do it right, and heard two young volunteers in the vestibule.

"Do you think he realizes the importance of what we're doing?"

"He asked enough questions."

"Anyone who doesn't realize needs a new central nervous system."

For Discussion and Further Application

1. What does it mean to say that "although all speech is language, not all language is speech"?
2. Why is Ameslan considered a language? Try to construct a definition of language by your answer.
3. According to the article's author, what was the "real importance" of Project Washoe?
4. Why did many critics of Project Washoe insist that the chimp's use of multi-sign sequences was not really the same as a child's first sentences?
5. According to the article, is there any evidence that chimps develop a gestural language of their own in the wild?
6. What five accomplishments does Terrace hope Nim will achieve using signs? Why do you think he orders them as he does?
7. Aristotle was a fourth-century B.C. Greek philosopher. What distinction did he make between humans and animals? Do you agree with Baur that Aristotle's distinction is still a part of our thinking?
8. Discuss several language-origin theories mentioned in the article.
9. What are the implications of a chimp constructing sentences "according to grammatical rules"? Talk about the concept of "grammar" as it is used here.
10. The "I" concept, or self-identity, is central to human language. Do any of the chimps described in the article show a sense of "I"?

FIRST MESSAGE FROM THE PLANET OF THE APES

MARTIN JOOS

too many clocks

In this essay, excerpted from the first two chapters of his book *The Five Clocks,* Martin Joos builds a case for accepting the variety of languages—or styles of language—we all use. (He labels the five styles *intimate, casual, consultative, formal,* and *frozen*.) Joos sets up a grid to analyze these various styles in terms of the speaker's age and willingness to accept responsibility as well as the speaker's experience and exposure to a variety of usages. Joos' own writing style is very terse. He packs a lot of complex psychological and social analysis, and he often uses tongue-in-cheek "asides" and what might seem to us "old-fashioned" slang. You may have to reread the article several times, but the insights Joos has to offer are worth the effort, even if you disagree with some of his judgments. Can you find any examples from your own experience to prove or refute his arguments?

> *Ballyhough railway station has two clocks which disagree by some six minutes. When one helpful Englishman pointed the fact out to a porter, his reply was 'Faith, sir, if they was to tell the same time, why would we be having two of them?'*

That more than one kind of English is likely to be in use at the same time and place is a notorious fact. So is sex, for that matter, or the weather. But our accommodations to those facts are not equally realistic. We have easily understood that evolution has so shaped our planet's flora and fauna that agriculture is best served by fluctuating weather and cyclical seasons. With a great deal more effort, we are coming to understand that sex is here to stay and may even have a sort of survival-value—that its seasons and its vagaries may conceivably be essential to the business of being human.

Long ago taught to give weather its highest praise by calling it 'seasonable,' we have been learning recently to treat sex with the same respect for facts. The intellectual gain is great, however few may value it. Much greater, some say, is the profit that comes from not sending children into adulthood with useless burdens of guilt.

English-usage guilt-feelings have not yet been noticeably eased by the work of linguistic scientists, parallel to the work done by the psychiatrists. It is still our custom unhesitatingly and unthinkingly to demand that the clocks of language all be set to Central Standard Time. And each normal American is taught thoroughly, if not to keep accurate time, at least to feel ashamed whenever he notices that a clock of his is out of step with the English Department's tower-clock. Naturally he avoids looking aloft when he can. Then his linguistic guilt hides deep in his subconscious mind and there secretly gnaws at the underpinnings of his public personality. Freud or Kinsey [well-known psychologists] may have strengthened his private self-respect, but in his social life he is still in uneasy bondage to the gospel according to Webster as expounded by Miss Fidditch.*

Shall the porter speak up? Well, it isn't likely to do much good this year. But the porter is a sort of Court Fool and won't lose his job for speaking up once. And if enough of us speak up, travelers may learn to read clocks with more sympathy and self-respect.

The Ballyhough situation was simple. But English, like national languages in general, has five clocks. And the times that they tell are not simply earlier and later; they differ sidewise too, and in several directions. Naturally. A community has a complex structure, with variously differing needs and occasions. How could it scrape along with only one pattern of English usage? (Webster, of course!—Well, . . .)

It would be very little better served with a single range of usages, differing along the length of a single scale. And yet our public theory of English is all laid out along just such a single yardstick. (Webster is one Webster, and Miss Fidditch is his prophet.)

We have not yet learned to speak of English as we speak of the weather and agriculture, and as we are slowly learning to speak of sex and survival. In the school folklore called 'grammar' for lack of effective challenge—a sort of numerology taught in high-schools instead of algebra, an astrology masquerading as astronomy in our colleges—we are bound to speak of English usage only in a simplistic way, like a proper Victorian maiden lady speaking of Men.

Ask a normal citizen to compare 'if they was to tell the same time' with 'if they were to tell the same time' and he will check by Miss Fidditch's tape: 'Bad, fair, good, better, best = correct.' And that's about all. Oh yes; he will deplore the conditions which prevail, he will mutter that he too has sinned and fallen short of Webster, and he will be worried about his son's English. Then he will wander off into spelling-reform and Communism.

But now if you press him for a program, he will suggest installing a master-clock system. He will promise to speak up in the next P.T.A. meeting for more and better grammar teaching, like they had in Webster's day. What he doesn't know is that he himself has two English-usage clocks as adequately adjusted as any railroad-man's watch, for use on different occasions, plus three others that are more or less reliable depending on his experiences and the distances to his horizons. And he will be baffled by your lunacy if you casually say what linguists know: That he built

*Joos' parody of an old maid schoolteacher who lives and dies by the rules of traditional grammar.

and adjusted those clocks himself, with less help than hindrance from schooling.

What he does know is that his usage varies, as he thinks. The fact is that his several usages do not vary enough to matter, any one of them. They alternate with each other, like his pajamas and overalls and committee-meeting suit, each tailored so as not to bind and so that he finds the pockets without looking. And he has one master-clock to tell him when to change. (Tsk, tsk! Mixed metaphor!—Pray for me, Miss F.)

Then when he happens to notice that the garments differ, he parrots her appraisals of better and worse. Finally he pleads 'No contest,' on the theory that he was surely wrong every time—that correctness is for teachers, who have the word from Webster. (Where did Webster get it from?—Excuse me, I'm busy.)

Bad, fair, good, better, best. Only the best is Correct. No busy man can be Correct. But his wife can. That's what women are for. That's why we have women to teach English and type our letters and go to church for us and discover for us that the English say 'Aren't I?' while we sinfully hunt golf balls in the rough on Sunday, and, when our partner finds two of them, ask 'which is me?' (Webster: colloq.—Professor K of Harvard: I speak colloq myself, and sometimes I write it.)

Only the porter . . . Only a few of us today are aware of the other scales of English usage. It is our business to consciously know about their social utility. We have to say 'consciously,' for, beneath their cant, the members of the community are unconsciously familiar with those other values: that is, in fact, what it means to 'be a member of' the community. The unaware familiarity is what makes the values effective and gives the individual his profit from them. The kids know that; that's why they don't listen to Miss Fidditch—they have their eye on the main chance. (Where does it say how to sweet-talk in French?—Who cares! She's [He's] American.)

Must usages differ? We might as well ask whether quadrupeds must have four legs and snakes have none. Each question is meaningful—to a believer in Original Sin. A scout from Mars would ask no such questions. He would take each usage as belonging to a current stage in a continuing evolution. And he would not confuse his research with a Golden-Age myth or a Progress theory—nor with a World-is-going-to-the-dogs fallacy either.

His basic research assumption would be: Since usage differences call for efforts to keep them under control, there must be rewards for the efforts. They must have survival-values. Then he would set about tabulating differences, efforts, and values. Rather soon, he would examine how the young advance toward better control and improved chances of survival. Example: 'Hi, Toots!'—'Don't be such a goof!' (Quiet there, Miss F. These are people preparing for examinations.)

Efforts and values are never perfectly in equilibrium. That is why usages change: they are constantly being readjusted to make up for the constant erosion that washes out the profits. . . . When you assume a fixed position, you're dead. Dead as Caesar or a Siberian mammoth. Or Webster.

When too many people had abandoned 'Ain't I?' we promptly used the tar-brush on 'Pleased to meet you.' To a social animal, the question of first importance always is 'What group am I in?' The second question is 'How do I stand within the group?'' Only third are the message transactions, namely 'How are things changing within my group?' A poor fourth is 'How's the weather?'—matters of information. Fifth (earlier only for pedants) is 'How does my group rank among other groups?'—with respect to language usage, this is 'correctness.'

Among other things—among a great many others!—the scout from Mars must examine the match-up between the bad-to-best scale of English usage and the parallel scales of occasions, of moods, and of men. It would be foolish to assume in advance that they are just bad-to-best men. (You mean that the Good Guys don't always flaunt Webster and the Bad Guys don't always flout Webster?—Precisely.)

* * *

Here are, in order of importance, four of the usage-scales of native central English:

AGE	STYLE	BREADTH	RESPONSIBILITY
senile	frozen	genteel	best
mature	formal	puristic	better
teenage	consultative	standard	good
child	casual	provincial	fair
baby	intimate	popular	bad

These four scales are essentially independent; relations among them are not identities. (But isn't the best English genteel?—That must be Miss Fidditch talking.)

AGE: The frame within which all other scales develop. Though this is the most important of them all, we shall have very little to say about the age-scale of usage because nothing can be done about it directly. . . .

STYLE: Here are the five clocks to which we shall principally devote our attention. They may be called 'higher' and 'lower' for convenience in referring to the tabulation; but that doesn't mean anything like relative superiority. . . .

BREADTH: This scale measures breadth of experience and of self-limitation. From popular English up to standard English, your experiences broaden your usages; and from there up to genteel you narrow them again to suit your personality. . . .

RESPONSIBILITY: Here at last is the actual usage-scale nearest to Miss Fidditch's mythical scale of excellence, and we borrow her scale-labels but not her meanings for them, eliminating her favorite synonym 'correct' for the top. . . .

Much as linguists hate to admit it, the responsibility scale does exist. . . .

• • •

. . . There is something about social living that creates a responsibility scale of usage; and when we have examined the natural basis of that scale, we shall see why the folklore calls it a quality scale.

The community's survival depends on cooperation; and adequate cooperation depends on recognizing the more and the less responsible types of persons around us. We need to identify the natural burden-bearers of the community so that we can give them the responsibility which is heaviest of all: we make them responsible for cooperation itself. Then the majority of us can function carefree in our square and round niches, free of the burden of maintaining the cooperation-net which joins us all. Some few of us have a strong interest in cooperation-nets without much competence in them; we are placed as letter-carriers and writers and legislators and teachers and so on; and for those jobs we are selected by tests which discriminate between interest and talent in the maintenance of cooperation.

In any case, the community places us principally by language-use tests which measure us on the various usage scales. Conversely, each of us selects others. For the present, we are interested in just one scale, namely responsibility—a personality scale and a usage scale running quite accurately parallel to each other.

We start very early learning to use this scale. It would be an exceptionally foolish ten-year-old who trusted a well-groomed sharper in preference to a judge in a bathing-suit. And he selects the more responsible person principally by listening, for the same reason that an employer wants an interview with each job-seeker—an interview for which no handbook is needed, for the oral code is public property.

The oral code for responsible personalities is indeed in part arbitrary, conventional: 'himself,' not 'hisself.' But the convention has a natural base, and in a very simple way. Responsible language . . . is explicit. It commits the speaker. The responsible speaker is under a sort of almost morbid compulsion to leave himself no way out of his commitment. The responsibility-dialect does not mumble; its grammar does not contradict itself; its semantics doesn't weasel. That is its basis; 'himself' and the rest are conventional, but they borrow their strength from the natural basis; they are overlays, but the basis is strong enough to overpower the illogicality of 'himself.'

. . . Through some historical accident—some random fluctuation in the distribution of 'himself' and 'hisself' among members of the community—it happened that 'himself' came to be regarded as relatively

MARTIN JOOS

more common in the responsibility-dialect. It may not have been actually more common there, but the community at large at least thought it was, and that was enough. Flocking did the rest. Those young people who aspired to responsibilities (perhaps only subconsciously aspired) selected 'himself' (normally without awareness of what they were doing or why), while those who aspired to irresponsible lives selected 'hisself' if it was conventionally available to them.

If it was not, they instead selected effete usages. Vulgarity and effeteness use equivalent signals in our culture. Each supplies its fellowship with passwords. For the community at large, the passwords are signals saying 'No responsibilities wanted!' And we take them at their word—for this part of our communication-system— the more certainly because the whole code works subconsciously.

Miss Fidditch's mistake is in trying to work out the code consciously and logically, instead of simply listening to what clearly responsible people actually say. Sometimes, however, she does listen; and then if she tries to teach what she has learned, and if her more responsible pupils learn to speak that way, Miss Fidditch is apt to imagine that her teaching is what taught them. That is an illusion. Responsibility earns respect; therefore most people (not all!) try for a step higher on the responsibility scale of English usage: simply to earn the respect of others, even irresponsible persons will try this if they don't feel the danger in it. In any case, that is why usages once labeled 'bad' always dwindle and ultimately vanish. Not because Miss Fidditch banned them! The kids aren't listening to her; they listen to Uncle David who is an aviator and to Dr. Henderson, perhaps also to historical and fictional characters if the school is doing its proper job. Miss Fidditch is convinced that bad English is gaining ground; she is only looking for burglars under the bed; statistics says the opposite, item by item. . . .

Finally, the community prefers the center of the scale: 'good' usage, not 'best.' It routinely rejects morbidly honest candidates for office, and the best English counts as the disqualification that makes a teacher.

For Discussion and Further Application

1. Do you agree or disagree with Joos' contention that many English speakers have "guilt-feelings" about their use of language? What does Joos mean by the statement, ". . . if enough of us speak up, travelers may learn to read clocks with more sympathy and self-respect"?
2. What opinion does Joos have of traditional methods of teaching English usage in high schools and colleges? Do you agree or disagree?
3. According to Joos, how do we develop our various styles? Who "adjusted" our clocks?

4. At one point in the article, Joos begins a paragraph with "Bad, fair, good, better, best. Only the best is correct. No busy man can be Correct. But his wife can. That's what women are for." How do you react to that statement? Is Joos seriously supporting "correctness" and sex roles, or is he speaking "tongue-in-cheek"?
5. What does being "a member of a community" have to do with levels of English usage?
6. What would be the basic research assumption of Joos' scout from Mars? Why do you think an individual's many styles of language survive? What functions do they serve?
7. Discuss how age affects language style.
8. According to Joos, is our formal style superior to our casual style? Why or why not?
9. What does Joos mean by the statement, "Your experiences broaden your usages"?
10. Joos claims that using language "low" on the responsibility scale (presumably, dialect forms like *hisself* or "in" slang) is a way of saying "No responsibilities wanted!" Do you agree with this analysis?

BENJAMIN LEE WHORF

languages and logic

By studying various American Indian languages, Benjamin Lee Whorf and his teacher Edward Sapir documented what linguists now label "the Whorf-Sapir hypothesis," a controversial theory that has had a major impact on twentieth-century studies of language and culture. Simply stated, the Whorf-Sapir hypothesis argues that language slices up the world for us, and different languages slice up the world differently. English, for example, seems to rely heavily on labeling reality in terms of separate objects and actions—subjects and verbs. An Indian language like Nootka, however, seems to view reality more as a flow or synthesis of motions or actions *without actors*. This article is excerpted from the longer article entitled "Language and Logic," first published in 1940 and reprinted in *Language, Thought, and Reality,* a collection of Whorf's major writings.

. . . Segmentation of nature is an aspect of grammar—one as yet little studied by grammarians. We cut up and organize the spread and flow of events as we do, largely because, through our mother tongue, we are parties to an agreement to do so, not because nature itself is segmented in exactly that way for all to see. Languages differ not only in how they build their sentences but also in how they break down nature to secure the elements to put in those sentences. This breakdown gives units of the lexicon [the collection of a language's meaningful units, a dictionary]. "Word" is not a very good "word" for them; "lexeme" has been suggested, and "term" will do for the present. By these more or less distinct terms we ascribe a semifictitious isolation to parts of experience. English terms, like "sky, hill, swamp," persuade us to regard some elusive aspect of nature's endless variety as a distinct THING, almost like a table or chair. Thus English and similar tongues lead us to think of the universe as a collection of rather distinct objects and events corresponding to words. Indeed this is the implicit picture of classical physics and astronomy—that the universe is essentially a collection of detached objects of different sizes.

The examples used by older logicians in dealing with this point are usually unfortunately chosen. They tend to pick out tables and chairs and apples on tables as test objects to demonstrate the object-like nature of reality and its one-to-one correspondence with logic. Man's artifacts and the agricultural products he severs from living plants have a unique degree of isolation; we may expect that languages will have fairly isolated terms for them. The real question is: What do different languages do, not with these artificially isolated objects but with the flowing face of nature in its motion, color, and changing form; with clouds, beaches, and yonder flight of birds? For, as goes our segmentation of the face of nature, so goes our physics of the Cosmos.

Here we find differences in segmentation and selection of basic terms. We might isolate something in nature by saying "It is a dripping spring." Apache erects the statement on a verb *ga*: "be white (including clear, uncolored, and so on)." With a prefix *nō-* the meaning of downward motion enters: "whiteness moves downward." Then *tó*, meaning both "water" and "spring" is prefixed. The result corresponds to our "dripping spring," but synthetically it is "as water, or springs, whiteness moves downward." How utterly unlike our way of thinking! The same verb, *ga*, with a prefix that means "a place manifests the condition" becomes *gohlga*: "the place is white, clear; a clearing, a plain." These examples show that some languages have means of expression—chemical combination, as I called it—in which the separate terms are not so separate as in English but flow together into plastic synthetic creations. Hence such languages, which do not paint the separate-object picture of the universe to the same degree as English and its sister tongues, point toward possible new types of logic and possible new cosmical pictures.

The Indo-European languages and many others give great prominence to a type of sentence having two parts, each part built around a class of word—substantives [nouns or words functioning as nouns] and verbs—which those languages treat differently in grammar. . . . This distinction is not drawn from nature; it is just a result of the fact that every tongue must have some kind of structure, and those tongues have made a go of exploiting this kind. The Greeks, especially Aristotle, built up this contrast and made it a law of reason. Since then, the contrast has been stated in logic in many different ways: subject and predicate, actor and action, things and relations between things, objects and their attributes, quantities and operations. And, pursuant again to grammar, the notion became ingrained that one of these classes of entities can exist in its own right but that the verb class cannot exist without an entity of the other class, the "thing" class, as a peg to hang on. . . .

Our Indian languages show that with a suitable grammar we may have intelligent sentences that cannot be broken into subjects and predicates. Any attempted breakup is a breakup of some English translation or paraphrase of the sentence, not of the Indian sentence itself. . . .

When we come to Nootka, [the language spoken by Indians living on Vancouver Island in British Columbia], the sentence without subject or predicate is the only type. The term "predication" is used, but it means "sentence." Nootka has no parts of speech; the simplest utterance is a sentence, treating of some event or event-complex. Long sentences are sentences of sentences (complex sentences), not just sentences of words. In Fig. 1 we have a simple, not a complex, Nootka sentence. The translation,

BENJAMIN LEE WHORF

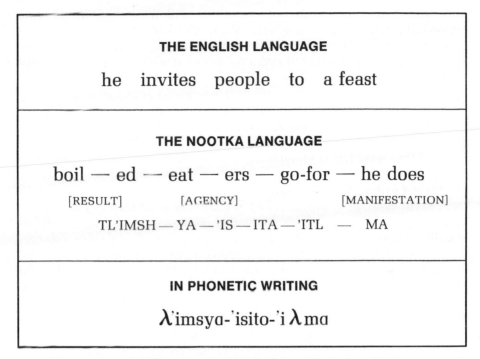

THE ENGLISH LANGUAGE

he   invites   people   to   a feast

THE NOOTKA LANGUAGE

boil — ed — eat — ers — go-for — he does

[RESULT]   [AGENCY]   [MANIFESTATION]

TL'IMSH — YA — 'IS — ITA — 'ITL   —   MA

IN PHONETIC WRITING

ƛimsya-ˑisito-ˑi ƛ ma

Here are shown the different ways in which English and Nootka formulate the same event. The English sentence is divisible into subject and predicate; the Nootka sentence is not, yet it is complete and logical. Furthermore, the Nootka sentence is just one word, consisting of the root *tl'imsh* with five suffixes.

"he invites people to a feast," splits into subject and predicate. Not so the native sentence. It begins with the event of "boiling or cooking," *tl'imsh;* then comes -*ya* ("result") = "cooked"; then -*'is* "eating" = "eating cooked food"; then -*ita* ("those who do") = "eaters of cooked food"; then -*'itl* ("going for"); then -*ma*, sign of third-person indicative, giving *tl'imshya'- isita'itlma*, which answers to the crude paraphrase, "he, or somebody, goes for (invites) eaters of cooked food."

The English technique of talking depends on the contrast of two artificial classes, substantives and verbs, and on the bipartitioned ideology of nature, already discussed. Our normal sentence, unless imperative, must have some substantive before its verb, a requirement that corresponds to the philosophical and also naïve notion of an actor who produces an action This last might not have been so if English had had thousands of verbs like "hold," denoting positions. But most of our verbs follow a type of segmentation that isolates from nature what we call "actions," that is, moving outlines.

Following majority rule, we therefore read action into every sentence, even into "I hold it." A moment's reflection will show that "hold" is no action but a state of relative positions. Yet we think of it and even see it as an action because language formulates it in the same way as it formulates more numerous expressions, like "I strike it," which deals with movements and changes.

We are constantly reading into nature fictional acting entities, simply because our verbs must have substantives in front of them. We have to say "It flashed" or "A light flashed," setting up an actor, "it" or "light," to perform what we call an action, "to flash." Yet the flashing and the light are one and the same! The Hopi language reports the flash with a simple verb, *rehpi*: "flash (occurred)." There is no division into subject and predicate, not even a suffix like -*t* of Latin *tona-t* "it thunders." Hopi can and does have verbs without subjects, a fact which may give that tongue potentialities, probably never to be developed, as a logical system for understanding some aspects of the universe. Undoubtedly modern science, strongly reflecting western Indo-European tongues, often does as we all do, sees actions and forces where it sometimes might be better to see states. On the other hand, "state" is a noun, and as such it enjoys the superior prestige traditionally attaching to the subject or thing class; therefore science is exceedingly ready to speak of states if permitted to manipulate the concept like a noun. Perhaps, in place of the "states" of an atom or a dividing cell, it would be better if we could manipulate as readily a more verblike concept but without the concealed premises of actor and action.

I can sympathize with those who say, "Put it into plain, simple English," especially when they protest against the empty formalism of loading discourse with pseudolearned words. But to restrict thinking to the patterns merely of English, and especially to those patterns which represent the acme of plainness in English, is to lose a power of thought which, once lost, can never be regained. . . . For this reason I believe that those who envision a future world speaking only one tongue, whether English, German, Russian, or any other, hold a misguided ideal and would do the evolution of the human mind the greatest disservice. Western culture has made, through language, a provisional analysis of reality and, without correctives, holds resolutely to that analysis as final. The only correctives lie in all those other tongues which by aeons of independent evolution have arrived at different, but equally logical, provisional analyses.

For Discussion and Further Application

1. How did older logicians try to prove reality had an "object-like" nature? How does Whorf refute their arguments?
2. Underlying Whorf's analysis is the controversial assumption that "reality" depends on our perception of it. Whorf claims further that our perception is shaped

by the language we use. This inevitably raises another debate: whether we can perceive or think without language. Can we?

3. Discuss how the statements "It is a dripping spring" and "As water, or springs, whiteness moves downward" imply different perceptions of reality.

4. According to Whorf, what quality do most English verbs share?

5. "We are constantly reading into nature fictional acting entities, simply because our verbs must have substantives (or nouns) in front of them." The structure of the language we speak forces us to attribute every action to an actor. Can you think of any specific examples of actions that might not require "actors" if it weren't for the structure of our language?

6. Discuss how such an actor/action, subject/verb structure to our language might have left its mark on aspects of our culture like religion, law, or philosophy.

7. Can different uses of language —poetry, for example—create perceptions of reality that go beyond the normal structure our language imposes? Why or why not?

language
and equal treatment
of the sexes

The following article was excerpted from the McGraw-Hill Book Company's "Guidelines for Equal Treatment of the Sexes" which was issued to all McGraw-Hill staff members and authors in 1974. The "Guidelines" are an attempt, as the Introduction asserts, "to eliminate sexist assumptions from McGraw-Hill Book Company publications and to encourage a greater freedom for all individuals to pursue their interests and realize their potentials." The excerpts reprinted here deal specifically with language and the role language has played in reinforcing inequality. What are the implications of a major publishing house setting up explicit suggestions for altering language use?

The word *sexism* was coined, by analogy to *racism*, to denote discrimination based on gender. In its original sense, *sexism* referred to prejudice against the female sex. In a broader sense, the term now indicates any arbitrary stereotyping of males and females on the basis of their gender.

• • •

Women and men should be treated with the same respect, dignity, and seriousness. Neither should be trivialized or stereotyped. . . . Women should not be described by physical attributes when men are being described by mental attributes or professional position. Instead, both sexes should be dealt with in the same terms. References to a man's or a woman's appearance, charm, or intuition should be avoided when irrelevant.

NO	YES
Henry Harris is a shrewd lawyer and his wife Ann is a striking brunette.	The Harrises are an attractive couple. Henry is a handsome blond and Ann is a striking brunette.
	OR
	The Harrises are highly respected in their fields. Ann is an accomplished musician and Henry is a shrewd lawyer.
	OR
	The Harrises are an interesting couple. Henry is a shrewd lawyer and Ann is very active in community (or church or civic) affairs.

A. In descriptions of women, a patronizing or girl-watching tone should be avoided, as should sexual innuendoes, jokes, and puns. Examples of practices to be avoided: focusing on physical appearance (a buxom blonde); using special female-gender word forms (poetess, aviatrix, usherette); treating women as sex objects or portraying the typical woman as weak, helpless, or hysterical; making women figures of fun or objects of scorn and treating their issues as humorous or unimportant.

Examples of stereotypes to be avoided: scatterbrained female, fragile flower, goddess on a pedestal, catty gossip, henpecking shrew, apron-wearing mother, frustrated spinster, ladylike little girl. Jokes at women's expense—such as the woman driver or nagging mother-in-law clichés—are to be avoided.

NO	YES
the fair sex; the weaker sex	women
the distaff side	the female side or line
the girls or the ladies (when adult females are meant)	the women
girl, as in: I'll have my girl check that.	I'll have my secretary (or my assistant) check that. (Or use the person's name.)
lady used as a modifier, as in lady lawyer	lawyer (A woman may be identified simply through the choice of pronouns, as in: The lawyer made her summation to the jury. Try to avoid gender modifiers altogether. When you *must* modify, use woman or female, as in: a course on women writers, or the airline's first female pilot.)
the little woman; the better half; the ball and chain	wife
female-gender word forms, such as authoress, poetess, Jewess	author, poet, Jew
female-gender or diminutive word forms, such as suffragette, usherette, aviatrix	suffragist, usher, aviator (or pilot)
libber (a put-down)	feminist; liberationist
sweet young thing	young woman; girl
co-ed (as a noun) (*Note:* Logically, co-ed should refer to any student at a co-educational college or university. Since it does not, it is a sexist term.)	student
housewife	homemaker for a person who works at home, or rephrase with a more precise or more inclusive term

NO	YES
career girl or career woman	name the woman's profession: attorney Ellen Smith; Marie Sanchez, a journalist or editor or business executive or doctor or lawyer or agent
cleaning woman, cleaning lady, or maid	housekeeper; house or office cleaner
The sound of the drilling disturbed the housewives in the neighborhood.	The sound of the drilling disturbed everyone within earshot (or everyone in the neighborhood).
Housewives are feeling the pinch of higher prices.	Consumers (customers or shoppers) are feeling the pinch of higher prices.

B. In descriptions of men, especially men in the home, references to general ineptness should be avoided. Men should not be characterized as dependent on women for meals, or clumsy in household maintenance, or as foolish in self-care.

To be avoided: characterizations that stress men's dependence on women for advice on what to wear and what to eat, inability of men to care for themselves in times of illness, and men as objects of fun (the henpecked husband).

C. Women should be treated as part of the rule, not as the exception.

Generic terms, such as doctor and nurse, should be assumed to include both men and women, and modified titles such as "woman doctor" or "male nurse" should be avoided. Work should never be stereotyped as "woman's work" or as "a man-sized job." Writers should avoid showing a "gee-whiz" attitude toward women who perform competently. ("Though a woman, she ran the business as well as any man" or "Though a woman, she ran the business efficiently.")

D. Women should be spoken of as participants in the action, not as possessions of the men. Terms such as pioneer, farmer, and settler should not be used as though they applied only to adult males.

NO	YES
Pioneers moved West, taking their wives and children with them.	Pioneer families moved West. OR Pioneer men and women (or pioneer couples) moved West, taking their children with them.

E. Women should not be portrayed as needing male permission in order to act or to exercise rights (except, of course, for historical or factual accuracy).

NO	YES
Jim Weiss allows his wife to work part-time.	Judy Weiss works part-time.

• • •

McGRAW-HILL BOOK COMPANY

In references to humanity at large, language should operate to include women and girls. Terms that tend to exclude females should be avoided whenever possible.

A. The word *man* has long been used not only to denote a person of male gender, but also generically to denote humanity at large. To many people today, however, the word *man* has become so closely associated with the first meaning (a male human being) that they consider it no longer broad enough to be applied to any person or to human beings as a whole. In deference to this position, alternative expressions should be used in place of *man* (or derivative constructions used generically to signify humanity at large) whenever such substitutions can be made without producing an awkward or artificial construction. In cases where *man*-words must be used, special efforts should be made to ensure that pictures and other devices make explicit that such references include women.

Here are some possible substitutions for *man*-words:

NO	YES
mankind	humanity, human beings, human race, people
primitive man	primitive people or peoples; primitive human beings; primitive men and women
man's achievements	human achievements
If a man drove 50 miles at 60 mph . . .	If a person (or driver) drove 50 miles at 60 mph . . .
the best man for the job	the best person (or candidate) for the job
manmade	artificial; synthetic; manufactured; constructed; of human origin
manpower	human power; human energy; workers; workforce
grow to manhood	grow to adulthood; grow to manhood or womanhood

B. The English language lacks a generic singular pronoun signifying *he* or *she*, and therefore it has been customary and grammatically sanctioned to use masculine pronouns in expressions such as "one . . . *he*," "anyone . . . *he*," and "each child opens *his* book." Nevertheless, avoid when possible the pronouns *he*, *him*, and *his* in reference to the hypothetical person or humanity in general.

Various alternatives may be considered:

(1) Reword to eliminate unnecessary gender pronouns.

NO	YES
The average American drinks his coffee black.	The average American drinks black coffee.

LANGUAGE AND EQUAL TREATMENT OF THE SEXES

NO	YES
(2) Recast into the plural.	Most Americans drink their coffee black.

(3) Replace the masculine pronoun with *one, you, he* or *she, her* or *his*, as appropriate. (Use *he* or *she* and its variations sparingly to avoid clumsy prose.)

(4) Alternate male and female expressions and examples.

NO	YES
I've often heard supervisors say, "He's not the right man for the job," or "He lacks the qualifications for success."	I've often heard supervisors say, "She's not the right person for the job," or "He lacks the qualifications for success."

(5) To avoid severe problems of repetition or inept wording, it may sometimes be best to use the generic *he* freely, but to add, in the preface and as often as necessary in the text, emphatic statements to the effect that the masculine pronouns are being used for succinctness and are intended to refer to both females and males. . . .

C. Occupational terms ending in *man* should be replaced whenever possible by terms that can include members of either sex unless they refer to a particular person.

NO	YES
congressman	member of Congress; representative (but *Congressman* Koch and Congress-*woman* Holzman)
businessman	business executive; business manager
fireman	fire fighter
mailman	mail carrier; letter carrier
salesman	sales representative; salesperson; sales clerk
insurance man	insurance agent
statesman	leader; public servant
chairman	the person presiding at (or chairing) a meeting; the presiding officer; the chair; head; leader; coordinator; moderator
cameraman	camera operator
foreman	supervisor

D. Language that assumes all readers are male should be avoided.

NO	YES
you and your wife	you and your spouse
when you shave in the morning	when you brush your teeth (or wash up) in the morning

• • •

McGRAW-HILL BOOK COMPANY

The language used to designate and describe females and males should treat the sexes equally.

A. Parallel language should be used for women and men.

NO	YES
the men and the ladies	the men and the women; the ladies and the gentlemen; the girls and the boys
man and wife	husband and wife

Note that *lady* and *gentleman*, *wife* and *husband*, and *mother* and *father* are role words. *Ladies* should be used for women only when men are being referred to as *gentlemen*. Similarly, women should be called *wives* and *mothers* only when men are referred to as *husbands* and *fathers*. Like a male shopper, a woman in a grocery store should be called a *customer*, not a *housewife*.

B. Women should be identified by their own names (e.g., Indira Gandhi). They should not be referred to in terms of their roles as wife, mother, sister, or daughter unless it is in these roles that they are significant in context. Nor should they be identified in terms of their marital relationships (Mrs. Gandhi) unless this brief form is stylistically more convenient (than, say Prime Minister Gandhi) or is paired up with similar references to men.

(1) A woman should be referred to by name in the same way that a man is. Both should be called by their full names, by first or last name only, or by title.

NO	YES
Bobby Riggs and Billie Jean	Bobby Riggs and Billie Jean King
Billie Jean and Riggs	Billie Jean and Bobby; King and Riggs;
Mrs. King and Riggs	Ms. King (because she prefers Ms.) and Mr. Riggs
Mrs. Meir and Moshe Dayan	Golda Meir and Moshe Dayan or Mrs. Meir and Dr. Dayan

(2) Unnecessary reference to or emphasis on a woman's marital status should be avoided. Whether married or not, a woman may be referred to by the name by which she chooses to be known, whether her name is her original name or her married name.

C. Whenever possible, a term should be used that includes both sexes. Unnecessary references to gender should be avoided.

NO	YES
college boys and co-eds	students

D. Insofar as possible, job titles should be nonsexist. Different

185

nomenclature should not be used for the same job depending on whether it is held by a male or by a female. . . .

NO	YES
steward or purser or stewardess	flight attendant
policeman and policewoman	police officer
maid and houseboy	house or office cleaner; servant

E. Different pronouns should not be linked with certain work or occupations on the assumption that the worker is always (or usually) female or male. Instead either pluralize or use *he or she* and *she or he.*

NO	YES
the consumer or shopper . . . she	consumers or shoppers . . . they
the secretary . . . she	secretaries . . . they
the breadwinner . . . his earnings	the breadwinner . . . his or her earnings *or* breadwinners . . . their earnings.

F. Males should not always be first in order of mention. Instead, alternate the order, sometimes using: *women and men, gentlemen and ladies, she or he, her or his.*

For Discussion and Further Application

1. The examples cited in these guidelines describe both conscious and unconscious sexism in language. Which, in your opinion, are most destructive to an individual's self-image and why?
2. Can you give comparable examples of conscious and unconscious racism embedded in language?
3. What are stereotypes? Can you think of any other common sexist stereotypes—masculine or feminine—besides those mentioned? What about racial stereotypes? Class stereotypes? Regional stereotypes? Suggest some alternate, neutral descriptions to replace the stereotypes you identify.
4. Discuss how the civil rights movement has already forced certain changes in language use over the last twenty years.
5. These guidelines raise the complicated issue of "legislating" speech patterns. Do minority groups have a right to dictate changes? Is it really possible to alter the speech patterns of the community at large?
6. Analyze a recent piece of your own writing and, using the guidelines as a reference, point out any examples of "sexism" embedded in your language.
7. Find examples in current newspaper articles or magazine advertisements of sexist images and words.

McGRAW-HILL BOOK COMPANY

NORMAN D. HINTON

the language of
jazz musicians

The piece that follows is an interesting example of a glossary—a collection of specialized terms—which attempts to provide definitions and derivations of jazz slang. It was compiled in 1959. How many of the words defined are familiar to you? As you read, keep a count of how many have been assimilated into current dialects and note any changes that occur as the slang becomes more commonly used.

This glossary makes no pretensions to completeness. It is simply a list of words used by jazz musicians in their everyday speech with equals. Some of the etymologies may seem fanciful; these men do not worry themselves about the origins of their words. I believe, however, that the etymologies are correct, and I can vouch for the use of the words.

Apple, the, *n*. New York City. Derivation obscure, but dates from the late '30's, when New York was the center of jazz in America. Occ. [occasional]. o.f. [old-fashioned].

ax, *n*. Any of the solo reed or (less commonly) brass instruments. Orig. a saxophone. Fr. fancied resemblance in shape plus the abbr. *sax*. Occ.

bad, *adj*. & *adv*. Good. However, at times, it may mean "bad," and the listener must determine meaning fr. context, tone of voice, facial expression, etc. Occ., older.

beat, *n*. & *v*. *(p.p.)* (1) As *n*., musical rhythm, "the beat" (fr. *beat* time). (2) As *v*., tired, exhausted (preservation of old p.p.; comm. [common] usage particularly adopted by jazzmen. *OED* citations from 1830 on). Both comm. (Actually 1 & 2 *altogether* separate terms.)

blow, *v*. Orig. to play a wind instrument. Generalized to performing upon any instrument (thus, one can "blow guitar"). Probably fr. fact that all solo instruments in traditional jazz are wind instr. Comm.

box, *n*. A piano (undoubtedly fr. shape of upright piano and spinet, usually found in jazz night clubs). Comm., rec. [recent].

bread, *n*. Money. A double pun—(1) "dough," (2) bread, the necessity. Occ., rec. (Invented by Dizzy Gillespie.)

bring down, *v*. To make one feel low. See *put down*. Occ., rec. in this sense. (Obs.—to make one feel good—out of use since the '30's.)

bug, *v*. To bother, especially to get one in such a state that he cannot play well. Extended to mean getting annoyed at anything.

cat, n. Orig., one who was "hep." Obs. in this sense; now, any person. (Thus, a musician can now speak of a "square cat"—a contradiction in terms in the '30's.) Comm.

changes, n. The chords for whatever melody is being used as a basis for improvisation. Comm., older.

chase, n. A 32-bar chorus divided so that two men (usually) take alternate four- or eight-bar sections. Occ.

chick, n. A girl. Not specifically a jazzman's term, but very common.

clinker, n. A missed note, or other error in playing. Largely replaced by *goof* (q.v.). Occ., o.f.

combo, n. A small band, a "combination" of from three to ten pieces. Basic, comm.

come on, v. Strictly, to begin a chorus, but almost always used with an approving or disparaging phrase—"Man, you came on like the end." Older (one of the oldest words still in use), comm.

cool, n. & *adj.* Agreeing with the generally received aesthetic standards of the modern jazzman. Basic, comm.

corny, *adj.* Non-jazz, extremely commercial music. Origin doubtful, but since it is often expanded to "corn-fed" and "corn-ball" (or may actually have been a clipped form of one of these words), I think it once meant "country" music: polkas, square dance music, etc. Comm., basic, older.

crazy, *adj.* Like *cool* and almost interchangeable with it. Fr. description of bop as "crazy music." Has to do most basically with harmonies used in playing, but generalized like *cool.* Comm., basic.

cut, *v.i.* & *t.* (1) (intr.) To leave. Usually to "cut out" (cut = leave out, leave). "Man, nothin's happening, let's cut out!" Occ., rec. (2) (tr.) To play an instrument better than another musician, or to produce better jazz than another. Also said of whole orchestras. The winner in a musical contest is said to have "cut" the other. Comm., older (even pre-'30's).

cute, *adv.* (Playing) in an ingenious, intriguing manner. Occ., in an amusing manner. Occ., rec.

dig, v. To understand and agree with: not limited to music alone. (Perhaps fr. a sense of "getting to the bottom" of things.) Comm., older, basic.

end, the, n. The best, the most pleasing. Like *most* (q.v.), but better. *Absolute end,* n., intensified form. Comm., basic.

eyes, n. An expression denoting approval. "I've got eyes for that" means "I like it." Extreme approval is expressed by the qualifying words "big" or "bulging." Invented by Lester Young. Comm.

fake, v. To improvise. Sometimes also means to pretend to know a tune, but usually has meaning above. Comm., older.

flip, v. To approve wildly. Orig. to "flip one's wig" (akin to "blow one's top," but never denotes anger for jazzmen). Usually indicates response to another's solo. Comm.

funky, n. An old word, orig. meaning earthy or odorous. Now, a piece or player imbued with the basic spirit of the blues, although in a modern idiom. Occ. (The *original* meaning is obs.; the newer meaning is rec.)

gas, *v. & n.* To please, or, as noun, spoken of a situation which pleases— "It's a gas!" *gasser, n.* Something which pleases extremely. Origin unknown, at least to me. Occ.

go, *expl.* Really a fan's word, to express excitement at a particularly "swingin' " solo. Often used derisively, sometimes approvingly, by musicians. (The fan's full phrase is "Go, man, go!") Occ.

gone, *adj.* In the ultimate state of happiness, usually inspired by music. *Real gone, adj.,* intensified form. (Perhaps from dope addiction, but it is equally possible that the borrowing went the other way.) Occ., older, the gonest, *n. The most, etc.*

goof, *n. & v.* A mistake in playing, and to make that mistake. Extended to all errors. Comm., basic.

greatest, *n.* See *most, end.* Comm.

head arrangement. A musical arrangement which is not written down and never has been, but is known by all the members of the ensemble. Usually the product of group effort. Comm.

hep, *v.* See *hip.* O.f.

hip, *v.* "In the know," or one of the elite. Occ. means simply to understand. Comm., basic.

horn, *n.* Any musical instrument, but especially (and originally *only*) the wind instruments. (See *blow* for a similar extension.) Comm.

jazz, *n.* Nonsense, completely worthless information or attitude. "Don't hand me that jazz" = "quit kidding." Comm., rec.

jive, *n.* Same as *jazz.* Occ., o.f.

lead, *n.* The top, or melody part in an arrangement: therefore, the melodic line. Lead man, *n.* One who playes the "lead" in his section of the ensemble. Comm., basic.

least, the *n.* Opposite of *the most.* Occ.

like, *interj.* Means little or nothing. Used to fill up gaps in the sentence. Comm., rec.

Man, *interj.* Used in direct address. Comm., basic.

Mickey, *adj.* "Corny," old-fashioned, "ricky-tick" music. Short for "Mickey Mouse music," but usually abbreviated. Originally referred to the sort of pseudo-jazz that accompanied animated cartoons. Sometimes referred to as "businessman's bounce." Occ., o.f.

moldy fig. One who likes or plays "traditional" jazz exclusively. Comm. (Refers mostly to fans, not musicians.) Often abbr. *fig.*

most, *n.* The best, the most in line with jazzmen's aesthetic standards; see *cool, crazy.* Comm.

number, *n.* A tune. Perhaps from the fact that bands give their arrangements numbers rather than names, to make filing easier. Comm., basic.

pad, *n.* A bed. Extended to mean bedroom, or even apartment. Occ.

put down, *v.* To belittle, criticize adversely, another man's playing. Perhaps related to *bring down* (q.v.). Occ., rec.

ride-out, n. The final chorus of an arrangement. (In dixieland, the clarinet "rides" above the ensemble.) Occ., o.f.

riff, n. & v. A short musical phrase (usually 4 or 8 bars), whose chords, repeated the length of a chorus, become the basis for improvisation. To play a riff. Origin doubtful. Comm., older, basic.

see, v. To read music. Occ., rec.

session, n. Shortened form of obs. *jam session;* an informal gathering of musicians playing for their own amusement. Occ., older.

square, n. Not in accordance with the jazzman's aesthetic standards. Probably comes from steady 1-2-3-4 rhythm without variation. Many musicians, while saying the word, will make a motion similar to band director's indication for 4/4 time—the hand moves in a square for the four beats. Comm., older, basic.

swing, v. To play well in all senses, technically and otherwise, but especially to have the basic feel for jazz rhythms. A man can play well harmonically and rhythmically, but he will not swing without a feel for "the beat." Comm., older, basic.

swingin', adj. Actually, the participle of swing, but used for many non-musical things. The highest term of approval. May be applied to anything a jazzman likes, or any person. (Although the verb is of long standing, the use of the participle is relatively recent.) Comm., basic.

too much, adj. Same as *the most, the greatest.* Comm.

way out, adj. Departing greatly from the norm; especially said of unusual (or unusually good) treatment of melody or harmony; now of anything that seems especially good—though still used in the original sense too. Occ., older (found on records in the '30's).

wig, v. To think; to play extremely intellectual music. Occ., rec.

wild, adj. Same as *crazy, cool.* Occ.

worst, the, n. Opposite of *most, end,* etc. See *least.* Occ.

write, v. To make an arrangement. writer, n. Arranger. Comm.

you know, inter. phr. Means nothing (see *like*), but used as a question at the end of a statement.

For Discussion and Further Application

1. Why do you think jazz has had such an important influence on American language?
2. Are there any words in the glossary that rock or country and western music has borrowed from jazz?
3. What additional words have rock and country and western music added to the language?
4. Write your own glossary for the specialized language of another group: sports reporters, politicians, the military, computer technologists, the police, or wine tasters are just a few possibilities.
5. What does this glossary prove about the susceptibility of majority dialects to minority group influence?

NORMAN D. HINTON

H. JACK GEIGER

all god's dangers

The following article is a book review of *The Life of Nate Shaw*, a biography (really an autobiography) of an "illiterate" black sharecropper born in 1885 whose life spanned eighty-eight years of Southern history. The review is interesting for several reasons. First, it briefly chronicles Nate Shaw's history, which parallels the difficult, torn history of the South moving into the twentieth century—the futile poverty of tenant farming, the radical Alabama Sharecropper Union of the 1930s, and the recent civil rights movement. The review also gives a sample of oral history at its best. Theodore Rosengarten, author of the biography, used a tape recorder to capture Nate Shaw's own words. The quotes from Shaw in the review reflect the strength and vitality of the man's dialect: he is illiterate—he can neither read nor write—yet he recreates from memory the complexity of the history he has lived through. Finally, this selection is a good example of book review technique. The reviewer offers us a taste of the book being reviewed, he gives us a sense of what the book tries to do, and he judges its success.

On a cold January morning in 1969, a young white graduate student from Massachusetts, stumbling along the dim trail of a long-defunct radical organization of the 1930's, the Alabama Sharecropper Union, heard that there was a survivor and went looking for him. In a rural settlement 20 miles or so from Tuskegee in east-central Alabama he found him—the man he calls Nate Shaw—a black man, 84 years old, in full possession of every moment of his life and every facet of its meaning.

Right off, the student asked a first question: "Why did you join the union?" It was as if he had touched a switch that had been waiting, for decades, to be thrown. Nate Shaw answered, uninterrupted, for eight hours. He talked of white landlords, bankers, fertilizer agents, mule traders, gin operators, sheriffs, judges; of black tenant farmers, wives, children, communities; of cotton and corn and boll weevils; of the black South, the cotton economy, the "Southern way of life" and of the day, at last, when he found its injustice unendurable and confronted it with a gun. "Oh," said Nate Shaw, "there's so much I remember till I just can't breathe it!"

Theodore Rosengarten, the student, had found a black Homer, bursting with his black Odyssey and able to tell it with awesome intellectual power, with passion, with the almost frightening power of memory in a man who could neither read nor write but who sensed that the substance of his own life, and a million other black lives like his, were the very fiber of the nation's history.

Knowing this, Rosengarten came back again and again for four years with a tape recorder, and Nate Shaw, remembering it all from the ruins of slavery to the present, talked.

And so we have Nate Shaw's life in a big book, every word of it his own. And we have a major figure that has been missing (by no accident) from the mainstream of American literature and white American consciousness for more than a century: the strong, tough, autonomous, powerful rural Southern black man, self-possessed, ego intact, a whole man, unbroken by a system whose every purpose was to exploit, shatter and destroy him.

We have more. We have a black Faulkner (and what an appropriate irony it is that Faulkner's black counterpart should prove, if only in the merest technical sense of the word, to be illiterate—about as illiterate as Homer!) describing that black tenant farmer's world, which was the bedrock on which the Snopeses* and the landed gentry played out their struggles. It is all there: the dizzying genealogies, the careful inventories, the richness and variety of characters and the complexities of purpose, white and black.

We have the social, economic, political and racial relations of the cotton system and a piece of the radical Southern history of the thirties. More important, this book demonstrates that The Movement—the freedom movement, the civil rights movement, the black power movement—did not suddenly begin in the 1960's. It was not the primary creation of Northern blacks and Northern white liberals, but was there in the South all along, in men and women like Nate Shaw who were prepared to go along and get along only until they found that moment, that issue and time and circumstance, when it was important to put their lives on the line for something more than survival: freedom. And, if they had to die, they would take some whites with them.

Now let me get out of Nate Shaw's way, for one does not read this book—one listens to it, and gasps, and nods in agreement, or laughs, or frowns, as one does in conversation. This is no mere oral history. Nate Shaw strides directly off the page and into our consciousness, a living presence, talking, shouting, sorrowing, laughing, exulting, speaking poetry, speaking history, thinking and feeling—and he makes us hear him.

There is Shaw, for example, on life in the South:

"I never tried to beat nobody out of nothin since I been in this world, never has, but I understands that there's a whole class of people tries to beat the other class of people out of what they has. I've had it put on me; I've seen it put on others, with these eyes. O, it's plain: if every man thoroughly got his rights, there wouldn't be so many rich people in the world—I spied that a long time ago ... O, it's desperately wrong. ... I found out all of that because they tried to take I don't know what all away from me."

*William Faulkner was a major twentieth-century American novelist. In a series of novels, he created the Snopeses, a "poor white" family whose history he traces through several generations.

H. JACK GEIGER

This is how Nate Shaw found out. He was the son of a tenant farmer, a tough and sometimes cruel man. He grew up behind plow handles, working the earth, with no time for what passed for black schooling in the Alabama of the 1890's. He learned the backbreaking, bodywrenching futility of endless days in the field in the tenant-farming system: "ain't nothin but go day, come night, God send Sunday."

From his childhood experience, he learned the racial economics of tenant farming. The white man rents his land to the black farmer, supplies "furnish"—seed money, fertilizer money, food money—and takes a "mortgage" on the crop, the black man's house, furniture, tools, mules, cattle, horses and anything else he can get away with. The black man plows the land, plants the cotton, fights the boll weevil, chops away the weeds, picks the cotton and brings it in. The white man sets the price on the cotton, does his own arithmetic on the "furnish" money—and takes everything. Until next year, when, still in debt, the black tenant farmer starts all over.

"They took what cotton he made but there weren't no corn to take," Shaw says of his father. "Took his horse and wagon, went in the pen and took his fattening hog, what meat my daddy was raising for his family. I was big enough and old enough to stretch my eyes at conditions and abominate what I seed. So I seed that twice: My daddy stripped of everthing he had . . . Of course, years ago I heard that President Lincoln freed the colored people; but it didn't amount to a hill of beans . . . when they got freedom, really. Had to do whatever the white man directed em to do, couldn't voice their heart's desire. That was the way of life I was born and raised into."

Nate Shaw meant to change that. He grew, married, started his own family, tenant-farmed for years and then saw his chance to get out from under, by working a double day, hauling lumber for money while he and his sons raised cotton and corn. He paid off his debts, bought his own land and sweated his way up: his own house, and barn—both of which he built himself—two mules, two horses, two automobiles, a blacksmith's shop, some hogs and cattle, some money in the bank. He was his own man.

These were, perhaps, the happiest years of his life, and the daily rhythms and smells and *feel* of that life on the Southern earth comes through with incredible clarity. Shaw remembers how many acres he farmed in 1906, and what he planted, and how many bales he made, and what cotton brought that year, and what white man tried to rip him off, and for how much, and how he neatly sidestepped it. And he remembers it again for 1907, and the year after that, and every year since.

He remembers work, which he loved. We come to know Nate Shaw the farmer, hunter, log cutter, lumber hauler, swamp drainer, house-builder, mule trainer, beekeeper, hog raiser, blacksmith, maker of ax handles, basket weaver. There are long and loving descriptions of the crafts of rural survival, and the knowledge of the earth ("this here land would have to grunt just to sprout peas"). He remembers mules, which he loved with a passion. What is one to say of a man who remembers the names, weights, colors, gaits and dispositions of mules he owned 60 years ago, of mules his neighbors owned 60 years ago, of mules he merely saw on the road 60 years ago?

The more Shaw prospered, the more the whites hungered to take what he had, and he knew it. When the Alabama Sharecroppers Union came, early in the Depression, it was as if all his life had prepared him for it: "And durin of the pressure year, a union began to operate in this country, called it the Sharecroppers Union . . . and I knowed what was goin on was a turn-about on the southern man, white and colored . . . And I heard about it bein a organization for the poor class of people—that's what I wanted to get into, too . . . From my boy days comin along, ever since I been in God's world, I've never had no rights, no choice in nothin that the white man didn't want me to have—even been cut out of education, book learnin, been deprived of that."

Then this "illiterate" man asked: "How could I favor such ruins as have been the past?"

The climactic moment approached. Whites, enraged by the union, increased their pressure. In December, 1932, bearing a fraudulent mortgage note from a white man, four armed sheriff's deputies came to seize a neighbor and fellow union member's livestock, and Shaw knew that his would be next because "my name was just ringin in it."

"Somebody got to stand up," Shaw said—it is the definitive phrase, the determining decision of his life. "If I'm sworn to stand up for all the poor colored farmers—and poor white farmers if they'd taken a notion to join—I've got to do it. . . . So I stood up against this Southern way of life . . . If a man comes to take away what I have and he don't have a fair claim against me, I'll die before I stand quiet as a fence post and let him do it. If I die trying to defend myself, why, let me go. I'm going to try, definitely."

Shaw tried. He told the sheriffs they'd have to kill him. They shot him three times in the back. Alone, he shot back and ran them off. He fled to Tuskegee, was hunted down, jailed, given a sham trial and sentenced to 12 years in prison.

Here, once again, he bent but did not break. "I went through prison quiet as a plank of wood," he told Rosengarten, because he understood the wastefulness of confrontation when he had no power at all. All he did was refuse parole three times rather than tell the whites what they wanted to learn about the union (40 years later, he was still careful to "disremember" the union organizer's name), serve every day of his time and come out intact.

But the world had changed, he was 59, a mule-driving man in a tractor-farming country. He worked prodigiously, as was his need, but more of his life now was in his 10 children, their land and their futures. His wife died. "I'd stayed with her 40-odd years, and that was short, short" he says tenderly. Later, he remarried. Surrounded by his family and community, he retired. Then, in his 85th year, Rosengarten found him.

H. JACK GEIGER

Why is all this so important, so powerful beyond its own literary merit? Because everyone needs to learn what Southern whites and blacks know: that there have always been, and are now, Nate Shaws: black men intact at the core, skilled workmen, powerful thinkers, loving husbands and fathers, who were the pillars of the black community's strength. They were ready to come out shooting if they had to, but they were also wise. In a world where the threat of violence to them was daily and almost casual, they could at least determine for themselves the moment and the issue over which they would take their stand. They may be a minority among the oppressed, but they are the source of all movements for freedom. We need to know more about the ways in which such men and women are formed, in the face of crushing adversity. There are clues in Nate Shaw's life, and this is one of the values of this book.

Another is that it puts the Southern movements of the 1960's in a new perspective. Historians are only now beginning to give full attention to the radical Southern efforts of the Depression years—the Southern Tenant Farmers Union, which successfully organized sharecropper strikes in Mississippi, the Alabama Sharecroppers Union and others. Through them, impoverished black (and some white) tenant farmers organized and fought, 40 years before either S.N.C.C. or Martin Luther King, and long before the Moynihans of the world started trying to convince us that there were, and are, few such men among the blacks. Instead, it tells us more vividly than anything before it what it was like, then, and in some ways now, to be poor and black and Southern.

It is equally important that it is told by a black man, by one whose whole life was in and of that black experience, one who had never left it, gone north, gone to college, returned to describe it with behavioral science's tools or the novelist's typewriter. Nate Shaw is a primary source. These are not the confessions of Nat Turner. They are the assertions of Nate Shaw.

And how he asserts them! "If you don't like what I have done, then you are against the man I am today. I ain't going to take no backwater about it. If you don't like me for the way I have lived, get on off in the woods and bushes and shut your mouth and let me go for what I'm worth. And if I come out of my scrapes, all right; if I don't come out, don't let it worry you; this is me. . . . And for God's sake don't come up messin with me. . . . I'd fight this morning for my rights, I'd do it—and for other folks' rights if they'll push along."

Musing, near the end, he issues what could be a manifesto for all the movements for black power, Chicano power, poor people's power and social change. "How many people is it today that it needs and requires to carry out this movement? How many is it knows just what it's going to take? It's taken time, untold time, and more time it'll take before it's finished. Who's to do it? It's the best people of the United States . . . the uneducated, unknowledged ones that's living here in this country. They goin to win!

195

They goin to win!"

He died on November 5, 1973. If there is a heaven, and if the angels have any sense at all, they are sitting attentively in great semicircular ranks, and there at the center, I would like to believe, is Nate Shaw—telling his story, rolling out his history, making real what it means to be rural, and Southern, and black, and a whole man. The rest of us don't have to wait. We can read it now.

For Discussion and Further Application

1. What are the differences between biography and autobiography?
2. Discuss Nate Shaw's dialect as it is recorded in the review. What are some of its distinctive features?
3. Was Nate Shaw "illiterate"? Discuss the usual definitions of illiteracy. What other linguistic skills did Nate Shaw develop that more "literate" users of language have lost?
4. The review claims *The Life of Nate Shaw* has "literary merit." What does the reviewer mean? On the basis of what you've read in the review, do you agree or disagree?
5. Why does the reviewer claim Nate Shaw's biography is so important?
6. According to the reviewer, what perspective does Nate Shaw's biography give the civil rights movement of the 1960s?
7. Should book (or movie) reviewers concentrate on describing their material and leave evaluation to the reader? Why or why not?

H. JACK GEIGER

ALDOUS HUXLEY

the arts of selling

The piece reprinted below, a chapter from Aldous Huxley's *Brave New World Revisited* (1958), is a detailed
analysis of advertising psychology and its close ties to political propaganda. The rules
of the advertising game are more stringent than those for political propaganda because,
as Huxley explains, advertising is subject to a gentlemen's agreement of sorts. But, as
he goes on to describe, all propaganda—whether it "sells" a tyrant's power, a candidate
running for office, or toothpaste—plays on the hidden fears, desires, and ignorance of
the public. Huxley investigates several "arts" involved in selling and analyzes the
apparent contradiction of allowing advertising in a "democratic" culture: propaganda
violates the very nature of a democracy.

The survival of democracy depends on the ability of large numbers of people to make realistic
choices in the light of adequate information. A dictatorship, on the other
hand, maintains itself by censoring or distorting the facts, and by appealing, not to reason, not to enlightened self-interest, but to passion and
prejudice, to the powerful "hidden forces," as Hitler called them, present
in the unconscious depths of every human mind.

In the West, democratic principles are proclaimed and many able and
conscientious publicists do their best to supply electors with adequate
information and to persuade them, by rational argument, to make realistic
choices in the light of that information. All this is greatly to the good. But
unfortunately propaganda in the Western democracies, above all in
America, has two faces and a divided personality. In charge of the editorial
department there is often a democractic Dr. Jekyll—a propagandist who
would be very happy to prove that John Dewey [an American philosopher]
had been right about the ability of human nature to respond to truth and
reason. But this worthy man controls only a part of the machinery of mass
communication. In charge of advertising we find an anti-democratic, because anti-rational, Mr. Hyde—or rather a Dr. Hyde, for Hyde is now a Ph.D.
in psychology and has a master's degree as well in the social sciences. This
Dr. Hyde would be very unhappy indeed if everybody always lived up to
John Dewey's faith in human nature. Truth and reason are Jekyll's affair,
not his. Hyde is a motivation analyst, and his business is to study human
weaknesses and failings, to investigate those unconscious desires and fears
by which so much of men's conscious thinking and overt doing is determined. And he does this, not in the spirit of the moralist who would like to
make people better, or of the physician who would like to improve their
health, but simply in order to find out the best way to take advantage of

their ignorance and to exploit their irrationality for the precuniary benefit of his employers. But after all, it may be argued, "capitalism is dead, consumerism is king"—and consumerism requires the services of expert salesmen versed in all the arts (including the more insidious arts) of persuasion. Under a free enterprise system commercial propaganda by any and every means is absolutely indispensable. But the indispensable is not necessarily the desirable. What is demonstrably good in the sphere of economics may be far from good for men and women as voters or even as human beings. An earlier, more moralistic generation would have been profoundly shocked by the bland cynicism of the motivation analysts. Today we read a book like Mr. Vance Packard's *The Hidden Persuaders,* and are more amused than horrified, more resigned than indignant. Given Freud, given Behaviorism, given the mass producer's chronically desperate need for mass consumption, this is the sort of thing that is only to be expected. But what, we may ask, is the sort of thing that is to be expected in the future? Can a campaign in favor of rationality be successful in the teeth of another and even more vigorous campaign in favor of irrationality? These are questions which, for the moment, I shall not attempt to answer, but shall leave hanging, so to speak, as a backdrop to our discussion of the methods of mass persuasion in a technologically advanced democratic society.

The task of the commercial propagandist in a democracy is in some ways easier and in some ways more difficult than that of a political propagandist employed by an established dictator or a dictator in the making. It is easier inasmuch as almost everyone starts out with a prejudice in favor of beer, cigarettes and iceboxes, whereas almost nobody starts out with a prejudice in favor of tyrants. It is more difficult inasmuch as the commercial propagandist is not permitted, by the rules of his particular game, to appeal to the more savage instincts of his public. The advertiser of dairy products would dearly love to tell his readers and listeners that all their troubles are caused by the machinations of a gang of godless international margarine manufacturers, and that it is their patriotic duty to march out and burn the oppressors' factories. This sort of thing, however, is ruled out, and he must be content with a milder approach. But the mild approach is less exciting than the approach through verbal or physical violence. In the long run, anger and hatred are self-defeating emotions. But in the short run they pay high dividends in the form of psychological and even (since they release large quantities of adrenalin and noradrenalin) psychological satisfaction. People may start out with an initial prejudice against tyrants; but when tyrants or would-be tyrants treat them to adrenalin-releasing propaganda about the wickedness of their enemies—particularly of enemies weak enough to be persecuted—they are ready to follow him with enthusiasm. In his speeches Hitler kept repeating such words as "hatred," "force," "ruthless," "crush," "smash"; and he would accompany these violent words with even more violent gestures. He would yell, he would

ALDOUS HUXLEY

scream, his veins would swell, his face would turn purple. Strong emotion (as every actor and dramatist knows) is in the highest degree contagious. Infected by the malignant frenzy of the orator, the audience would groan, and sob and scream in an orgy of uninhibited passion. And these orgies were so enjoyable that most of those who had experienced them eagerly came back for more. Almost all of us long for peace and freedom; but very few of us have much enthusiasm for the thoughts, feelings and actions that make for peace and freedom. Conversely almost nobody wants war or tyranny; but a great many people find an intense pleasure in the thoughts, feelings and actions that make for war and tyranny. These thoughts, feelings and actions are too dangerous to be exploited for commercial purposes. Accepting this handicap, the advertising man must do the best he can with the less intoxicating emotions, the quieter forms of irrationality.

Effective rational propaganda becomes possible only when there is a clear understanding, on the part of all concerned, of the nature of symbols and of their relations to the things and events symbolized. Irrational propaganda depends for its effectiveness on a general failure to understand the nature of symbols. Simple-minded people tend to equate the symbol with what it stands for, to attribute to things and events some of the qualities expressed by the words in terms of which the propagandist has chosen, for his own purposes, to talk about them. Consider a simple example. Most cosmetics are made of lanolin, which is a mixture of purified wool fat and water beaten up into an emulsion. This emulsion has many valuable properties: it penetrates the skin, it does not become rancid, it is mildly antiseptic and so forth. But the commercial propagandists do not speak about the genuine virtues of the emulsion. They give it some picturesquely voluptuous name, talk ecstatically and misleadingly about feminine beauty and show pictures of gorgeous blondes nourishing their tissues with skin food. "The cosmetic manufacturers," one of their numbers has written, "are not selling lanolin, they are selling hope." For this hope, this fraudulent implication of a promise that they will be transfigured, women will pay ten or twenty times the value of the emulsion which the propagandists have so skillfully related, by means of misleading symbols, to a deep-seated and almost universal feminine wish—the wish to be more attractive to members of the opposite sex. The principles underlying this kind of propaganda are extremely simple. Find some common desire, some widespread unconscious fear or anxiety; think out some way to relate this wish or fear to the product you have to sell; then build a bridge of verbal or pictorial symbols over which your customer can pass from fact to compensatory dream, and from the dream to the illusion that your product, when purchased, will make the dream come true. "We no longer buy oranges, we buy vitality. We do not buy just an auto, we buy prestige." And so with all the rest. In toothpaste, for example, we buy, not a mere cleanser and antiseptic, but release from the fear of being sexually repulsive. In vodka and whiskey we are not buying a protoplasmic poison which, in small doses, may depress

THE ARTS OF SELLING

the nervous system in a psychologically valuable way; we are buying friendliness and good fellowship, the warmth of Dingley Dell and the brilliance of the Mermaid Tavern. With our laxatives we buy the health of a Greek god, the radiance of one of Diana's nymphs. With the monthly best seller we acquire culture, the envy of our less literate neighbors and the respect of the sophisticated. In every case the motivation analyst has found some deep-seated wish or fear, whose energy can be used to move the consumer to part with cash and so, indirectly, to turn the wheels of industry. Stored in the minds and bodies of countless individuals, this potential energy is released by, and transmitted along, a line of symbols carefully laid out so as to bypass rationality and obscure the real issue.

Sometimes the symbols take effect by being disproportionately impressive, haunting and fascinating in their own right. Of this kind are the rites and pomps of religion. These "beauties of holiness" strengthen faith where it already exists and, where there is no faith, contribute to conversion. Appealing, as they do, only to the aesthetic sense, they guarantee neither the truth nor the ethical value of the doctrines with which they have been, quite arbitrarily, associated. As a matter of plain historical fact, the beauties of holiness have often been matched and indeed surpassed by the beauties of unholiness. Under Hitler, for example, the yearly Nuremberg rallies were masterpieces of ritual and theatrical art. "I had spent six years in St. Petersburg before the war in the best days of the old Russian ballet," writes Sir Nevile Henderson, the British ambassador to Hitler's Germany, "but for grandiose beauty I have never seen any ballet to compare with the Nuremberg rally." One thinks of Keats—"beauty is truth, truth beauty." Alas, the identity exists only on some ultimate, supramundane level. On the levels of politics and theology, beauty is perfectly compatible with nonsense and tyranny. Which is very fortunate; for if beauty were incompatible with nonsense and tyranny, there would be precious little art in the world. The masterpieces of painting, sculpture and architecture were produced as religious or political propaganda, for the greater glory of a god, a government or a priesthood. But most kings and priests have been despotic and all religions have been riddled with superstition. Genius has been the servant of tyranny and art has advertised the merits of the local cult. Time, as it passes, separates the good art from the bad metaphysics. Can we learn to make this separation, not after the event, but while it is actually taking place? That is the question.

In commercial propaganda the principle of the disproportionately fascinating symbol is clearly understood. Every propagandist has his Art Department, and attempts are constantly being made to beautify the billboards with striking posters, the advertising pages of magazines with lively drawings and photographs. There are no masterpieces; for masterpieces appeal only to a limited audience, and the commercial propagandist is out to captivate the majority. For him, the ideal is a moderate excellence. Those who like this not too good, but sufficiently striking, art may be

ALDOUS HUXLEY

expected to like the products with which it has been associated and for which it symbolically stands.

Another disproportionately fascinating symbol is the Singing Commercial. Singing Commercials are a recent invention; but the Singing Theological and the Singing Devotional—the hymn and the psalm—are as old as religion itself. Singing Militaries, or marching songs, are coeval with war, and Singing Patriotics, the precursors of our national anthems, were doubtless used to promote group solidarity, to emphasize the distinction between "us" and "them," by the wandering bands of paleolithic hunters and food gatherers. To most people music is intrinsically attractive. Moreover, melodies tend to ingrain themselves in the listener's mind. A tune will haunt the memory during the whole of a lifetime. Here, for example, is a quite uninteresting statement or value judgment. As it stands nobody will pay attention to it. But now set the words to a catchy and easily remembered tune. Immediately they become words of power. Moreover, the words will tend automatically to repeat themselves every time the melody is heard or spontaneously remembered. Orpheus has entered into an alliance with Pavlov—the power of sound with the conditioned reflex. For the commercial propagandist, as for his colleagues in the fields of politics and religion, music possesses yet another advantage. Nonsense which it would be shameful for a reasonable being to write, speak or hear spoken can be sung or listened to by that same rational being with pleasure and even with a kind of intellectual conviction. Can we learn to separate the pleasure of singing or of listening to song from the all too human tendency to believe in the propaganda which the song is putting over? That again is the question.

Thanks to compulsory education and the rotary press, the propagandist has been able, for many years past, to convey his messages to virtually every adult in every civilized country. Today, thanks to radio and television, he is in the happy position of being able to communicate even with unschooled adults and not yet literate children.

Children, as might be expected, are highly susceptible to propaganda. They are ignorant of the world and its ways, and therefore completely unsuspecting. Their critical faculties are undeveloped. The youngest of them have not yet reached the age of reason and the older ones lack the experience on which their new-found rationality can effectively work. In Europe, conscripts used to be playfully referred to as "cannon fodder." Their little brothers and sisters have now become radio fodder and television fodder. In my childhood we were taught to sing nursery rhymes and, in pious households, hymns. Today the little ones warble the Singing Commercials. Which is better—"Rheingold is my beer, the dry beer," or "Hey diddle-diddle, the cat and the fiddle"? "Abide with me" or "You'll wonder where the yellow went, when you brush your teeth with Pepsodent"? Who knows?

"I don't say that children should be forced to harass their parents into buying products they've seen advertised on television, but at the same time I cannot close my eyes to the fact that it's being done every day." So writes the star of one of the many programs beamed to a juvenile audience. "Children," he adds, "are living, talking records of what we tell them every day." And in due course these living, talking records of television commercials will grow up, earn money and buy the products of industry. "Think," writes Mr. Clyde Miller ecstatically, "think of what it can mean to your firm in profits if you can condition a million or ten million children, who will grow up into adults trained to buy your product, as soldiers are trained in advance when they hear the trigger words, Forward March!" Yes, just think of it! And at the same time remember that the dictators and the would-be dictators have been thinking about this sort of thing for years, and that millions, tens of millions, hundreds of millions of children are in process of growing up to buy the local despot's ideological product and, like well-trained soldiers, to respond with appropriate behavior to the trigger words implanted in those young minds by the despot's propagandists.

Self-government is in inverse ratio to numbers. The larger the constituency, the less the value of any particular vote. When he is merely one of millions, the individual elector feels himself to be impotent, a negligible quantity. The candidates he has voted into office are far away, at the top of the pyramid of power. Theoretically they are the servants of the people; but in fact it is the servants who give orders and the people, far off at the base of the great pyramid, who must obey. Increasing population and advancing technology have resulted in an increase in the number and complexity of organizations, an increase in the amount of power concentrated in the hands of officials and a corresponding decrease in the amount of control exercised by electors, coupled with a decrease in the public's regard for democratic procedures. Already weakened by the vast impersonal forces at work in the modern world, democratic institutions are now being undermined from within by the politicians and their propagandists.

Human beings act in a great variety of irrational ways, but all of them seem to be capable, if given a fair chance, of making a reasonable choice in the light of available evidence. Democratic institutions can be made to work only if all concerned do their best to impart knowledge and to encourage rationality. But today, in the world's most powerful democracy, the politicians and their propagandists prefer to make nonsense of democratic procedures by appealing almost exclusively to the ignorance and irrationality of the electors. "Both parties," we were told in 1956 by the editor of a leading business journal, "will merchandize their candidates and issues by the same methods that business has developed to sell goods. These include scientific selection of appeals and planned repetition. . . . Radio spot announcements and ads will repeat phrases with a planned intensity. Billboards will push slogans of proven power. . . . Candidates need, in addition to rich voices and good diction, to be able to look 'sincerely' at the TV camera."

ALDOUS HUXLEY

The political merchandisers appeal only to the weaknesses of voters, never to their potential strength. They make no attempt to educate the masses into becoming fit for self-government; they are content merely to manipulate and exploit them. For this purpose all the resources of psychology and the social sciences are mobilized and set to work. Carefully selected samples of the electorate are given "interviews in depth." These interviews in depth reveal the unconscious fears and wishes most prevalent in a given society at the time of an election. Phrases and images aimed at allaying or, if necessary, enhancing these fears, at satisfying these wishes, at least symbolically, are then chosen by the experts, tried out on readers and audiences, changed or improved in the light of the information thus obtained. After which the political campaign is ready for the mass communicators. All that is now needed is money and a candidate who can be coached to look "sincere." Under the new dispensation, political principles and plans for specific action have come to lose most of their importance. The personality of the candidate and the way he is projected by the advertising experts are things that really matter.

In one way or another, as vigorous he-man or kindly father, the candidate must be glamorous. He must also be an entertainer who never bores his audience. Inured to television and radio, that audience is accustomed to being distracted and does not like to be asked to concentrate or make a prolonged intellectual effort. All speeches by the entertainer-candidate must therefore be short and snappy. The great issues of the day must be dealt with in five minutes at the most—and preferably (since the audience will be eager to pass on to something a little livelier than inflation or the H-bomb) in sixty seconds flat. The nature of oratory is such that there has always been a tendency among politicians and clergymen to over-simplify complex issues. From a pulpit or a platform even the most conscientious of speakers finds it very difficult to tell the whole truth. The methods now being used to merchandise the political candidate as though he were a deodorant positively guarantee the electorate against ever hearing the truth about anything.

For Discussion and Further Application

1. What does Huxley mean when he says, "Irrational propaganda depends for its effectiveness on a general failure to understand the nature of symbols"?
2. How can an understanding of the nature of symbols aid an aware consumer?
3. Huxley claims that where an advertisement has been successful, "the motivational analyst has found some deep-seated wish or fear, whose energy can be used to move the consumer to part with cash." Can you find current examples of this?
4. According to Huxley, how does advertising undermine democratic institutions?
5. Can you find any example of current political candidates who fit Huxley's description of media politicans, selected by merchandisers for their ability to "sell"? Describe what they are "selling" and how they "sell" it.
6. Is Huxley a pessimist or an optimist about the ability of people to govern themselves? Do you agree with his opinion?

THE ARTS OF SELLING

JACK SHAKELY

sweet charity

Charitable fund raising has become a big business, inheriting many of the techniques and sometimes shady practices developed for more commercial enterprises. One dominant style of advertising that flourished in the 1950s was the "hard sell." Charitable solicitation inevitably tried out the style. The following essay, excerpted from a longer article entitled "The Ethics of Charitable Solicitation," describes the production and costs behind the scenes of one such notorious fund-raising operation. Besides its inherent interest as an exposé of the hard-sell methods of business, "Sweet Charity" is an excellent example of expository writing techniques. The writer is well organized; he uses transitions effectively; and most obviously, he makes his points with a barrage of specific facts.

As late as the 1930's most charity appeals were ill-conceived and naive, based more on the Christian doctrine of tithing than attacking human ills or injustices. A 1933 issue of *Fortune* magazine quoted then Father Fulton Sheen as saying, "Philanthropy is not absolute in its end but sacramental—a means of spiritual sanctification." The Christian Church went this one better, stating that the need wasn't as important as the charity. The need was important "merely as an occasion for the exercise of the soul." This set the *Fortune* reporter to musing, "It is doubtless a noble thing for the poor to assist the rich in the salvation of their souls. But it is a mean role to play."

It isn't any wonder that most solicitations of that era were of the "give, it's good for you" genre. And it isn't any wonder that when some of the hard-sell methods of business were moved into the charity arena, the resulting flood of donations caused dancing in the streets.

Remember the famous dollar bill letter? A hospital on the East coast sent out the first one in the 1950's, a fund raising letter with a real one dollar bill attached that asked the donor to return the dollar plus a contribution. The letter was two things: a whopping success and a lie.

The hospital knew it would be successful. An earlier letter from the *Wall Street Journal,* with a German Reichsbank note for 100,000 marks attached, pointed out the horrors of inflation and the need to stay on top of the financial news. It was the most successful subscriber solicitation letter in the newspaper's history.

While the Reichsmark was worthless and was nothing more than a clever device for attracting attention to the letter's content, the dollar bill did have a value (this was the 1950's, remember) and imparted a gratuitous obligation on the prospective donor. Most important, the letter that accompanied the dollar was a lie from top to bottom.

The letter opened with a statement that the dollar bill was in fact the real McCoy and that you could "keep it if you want to, after you've read this letter—but I don't believe you will, then."

Then the lie took over. "I've made an investment—of a thousand dollars—in human nature—in human kindness. I've mailed a thousand dollars—in a thousand letters to a thousand people picked at random." Actually, the investment was considerably more than that. The hospital (not the letter-writer as suggested) sent out 175,000 letters, not 1,000 as stated, and the recipients of those letters were certainly not picked at random "because I believe that everyone is really kind, way down inside," as the letter stated, but were selected from proven lists of past donors to similar causes or related organizations.

The letter continued to develop the untruthful theme that only a thousand letters are being sent. "This thousand dollars is my subscription to the ABC Hospital—and I'm investing in the belief that every one will bring back several more—at least another—with it. So our subscription which I'm starting in this way will be at least two thousand—maybe five—for there's going to be a lot of you sending a five or a ten—or more—when you mail my dollar back."

In the sixth paragraph, after the "little old me and little old you" idea has been firmly established, we read this: "Remember—both my dollar and your dollars go to help crippled children." Incredibly, this is the ONLY reference to the works of the charity in the entire letter. And regretably this is the biggest lie of all.

Most of the money didn't go to the children at all. It went to pay for the mailing.

There was no theft, no mis-management of the funds. It is just a fact of life that this type of letter is enormously expensive to produce and control. At current prices, here's why:

Of the 175,000 dollar bills sent out, 25,000 never came back. The cost so far, then, is $25,000. Next, the process of attaching the bill to the letter with a spot of glue, called "tipping," is a costly operation, driving the cost for the total package (outside envelope, letter, tipping, reply envelope) to about twenty cents per unit, or $36,000. Total so far, $61,000. Because there was money in the envelope, sending the letter at the nonprofit bulk rate was too risky. First class postage adds another $17,500, making the total now $78,500. In order to increase the potential return rate, the business reply envelope was necessary. This means that postage on all returned envelopes will be paid by the hospital. There were 150,000 replies (we told you it was a successful letter) at twelve cents each, or another $18,000.

The mailing lists which are "picked at random" cost between $25 and $40 per thousand names. Using an average of $30 per thousand, that's

$5,250 more. $101,750. Add $25 per thousand for addressing and processing, for a total of $106,000.

The hospital is a legitimate nonprofit organization that hopes for continued giving from these 150,000 donors. Therefore, each gift must be acknowledged and thanked. Although the acknowledgments are mass produced, they must be sent first class. The total cost for the postage and printing of the thank you letter is about $28,000. Total—$131,000.

The 150,000 contributions must be processed. The envelopes must be opened, the checks and cash processed and recorded, the thank-you envelope addressed and the name and address of the donor entered into the (probably computerized) permanent file. Assuming that the entire process takes a little over five minutes for each donor, and using a rock-bottom figure of three dollars per hour, you can easily add another $45,000 to the total, or $176,000. Although the person who wrote the letter obviously got some pay and there are other administrative overhead, let's leave it at that.

This letter is a classic in every respect. First, it has been called "the most successful fund raising letter" ever mailed. It received a phenomenal 80 percent response, a response rate ten to 40 times what can normally be expected.

But more than that, it is a classic example of a lack of ethics in both cost and content. The letter said almost nothing about charity, its works or why the money was needed. It led you to believe that one man had put up the money, it led you to believe that only a relatively small number of people would receive the letter and that the amount to be raised was to be a very small sum. The letter contained the ultimate in unsolicited "merchandise," a dollar bill.

"Remember, both my dollar and your dollars go to help crippled children," the letter said. Well, the 150,000 "my" dollars that were returned didn't go to help the crippled children; they went back to the bank. Then there are "your" dollars. How much was raised? $270,000—another reason why the letter is considered so successful. Subtract the cost figure so laboriously arrived at earlier and you get $94,000 net. That's a lot of money and the children could use it, but more than half—68 percent—of the donated money was spent to pay for the raising of that money. If the letter had been less successful, pulling, say, 20 percent (still a very good percentage) the crippled children could have *lost* as much as $120,000.

For Discussion and Further Application

1. In evaluating the "dollar bill letter," the author reaches two seemingly contradictory conclusions. What are they?
2. Discuss the psychology underlying the apparent effectiveness and success of such a fund-raising campaign.

JACK SHAKELY

3. Using the examples quoted from the "dollar bill letter," analyze the language used. How does the letter writer get across his sales pitch?
4. Can you give any examples from TV or radio advertising of the hard-sell technique still in operation?
5. Many sales pitches and ads today use "soft-sell" techniques instead. What do you think the term means? Cite examples from current advertising.
6. Do you think the hospital fund-raising drive would have been successful if it made a straightforward appeal for funds without the gimmick of enclosing the dollar bill? Why or why not?
7. The author claims the dollar bill letter is a "classic example of a lack of ethics in both cost and content." Why? Do you agree or disagree?
8. Analyze the organization and transitions Shakely uses in writing the article.

NORMAN MAILER

ego

The article reprinted below was written in 1971, just after
Muhammad Ali lost the first important fight of his come-
back to Joe Frazier. In the process of narrating that fight, Norman Mailer catches up with
Ali and gives us a powerful description of his growth and unique development as a
fighter. Mailer's controversial analysis delves into Ali's defeat, adding almost mythical
dimensions to Ali's complexity. Both Mailer's interpretation and his writing style go
beyond the usual techniques of traditional sports reporting. Rather than simply describe
an event, he builds Ali into a symbol of evolving black consciousness, a strategist, the
"first psychologist of the body." In doing this, Mailer's own use of language and
technique—his uniquely personal style as a writer—"out-Ali" Ali. The fighter who
emerges at the end of Mailer's description is not a defeated ex-champion, but a fallen
angel, only temporarily prone to mortal risks.

It is the great word of the 20th Century. If there is
a single word our century has added to the po-
tentiality of language, it is ego. Everything we have done in this century,
from monumental feats to nightmares of human destruction, has been a
function of that extraordinary state of the psyche which gives us authority
to declare we are sure of ourselves when we are not.

Muhammad Ali begins with the most unsettling ego of all. Having
commanded the stage, he never pretends to step back and relinquish his
place to other actors—like a six-foot parrot, he keeps screaming at you that
he is the center of the stage. "Come here and get me, fool," he says. "You
can't, 'cause you don't know who I am. You don't know *where* I am. I'm
human intelligence and you don't even know if I'm good or evil." This has
been his essential message to America all these years. It is intolerable to our
American mentality that the figure who is probably most prominent to us
after the President is simply not comprehensible, for he could be a demon
or a saint. Or both! Richard Nixon, at least, appears comprehensible. We
can hate him or we can vote for him, but at least we disagree with each other
about him. What kills us about a.k.a. [also known as] Cassius Clay is that the
disagreement is inside us. He is *fascinating*—attraction and repulsion must
be in the same package. So, he is obsessive. The more we don't want to
think about him, the more we are obliged to. There is a reason for it. He is
America's Greatest Ego. . . .

•   •   •

Ego is driving a point through to a conclusion you are obliged to reach
without knowing too much about the ground you cross between. You suffer
for a larger point. Every good prizefighter must have a large ego, then,
because he is trying to demolish a man he doesn't know too much about, he
is unfeeling—which is the ground floor of ego, and he is full of techniques

—which are the wings of ego. What separates the noble ego of the prize-fighters from the lesser ego of authors is that the fighter goes through experiences in the ring which are occasionally immense, incommunicable except to fighters who have been as good, or to women who have gone through every minute of an anguish-filled birth, experiences which are finally mysterious. Like men who climb mountains, it is an exercise of ego which becomes something like soul—just as technology may have begun to have transcended itself when we reached the moon. So, two great fighters in a great fight travel down subterranean rivers of exhaustion and cross mountain peaks of agony, stare at the light of their own death in the eye of the man they are fighting, travel into the crossroads of the most excruciating choice of karma as they get up from the floor against all the appeal of the sweet swooning catacombs of oblivion—it is just that we do not see them this way, because they are not primarily men of words, and this is the century of words, numbers, and symbols. Enough.

We have come to the point. There are languages other than words, languages of symbol and languages of nature. There are languages of the body. And prizefighting is one of them. . . . Boxing is a rapid debate between two sets of intelligence. It takes place rapidly because it is conducted with the body rather than the mind. If this seems extreme, let us look for a connection. Picasso could never do arithmetic when he was young because the number seven looked to him like a nose upside down. So to learn arithmetic would slow him up. He was a future painter—his intelligence resided somewhere in the coordination of the body and the mind. He was not going to cut off his body from his mind by learning numbers. But most of us do. We have minds which work fairly well and bodies which sometimes don't. But if we are white and want to be comfortable we put our emphasis on learning to talk with the mind. Ghetto cultures, black, Puerto Rican and Chicano cultures having less expectation of comfort tend to stick with the wit their bodies provide. They speak to each other with their bodies, they signal with their clothes. They talk with many a silent telepathic intelligence. And doubtless feel the frustration of being unable to express the subtleties of their states in words, just as the average middle-class white will feel unable to carry out his dreams of glory by the uses of his body. If black people are also beginning to speak our mixture of formal English and jargon-polluted American with real force, so white corporate America is getting more sexual and more athletic. Yet to begin to talk about Ali and Frazier, their psyches, their styles, their honor, their character, their greatness and their flaws, we have to recognize that there is no way to comprehend them as men like ourselves—we can only guess at their insides by a real jump of our imagination into the science Ali invented—he was the first psychologist of the body.

• • •

A kid as wild and dapper and jaybird as the president of a down-home college fraternity, bow-tie, brown-and-white shoes, sweet, happy-go-lucky, *raucous*, he [Clay/Ali] descended on Vegas for the second Patterson-Liston fight. He was like a beautiful boy surrounded by doting aunts. The classiest-looking middle-aged Negro ladies were always flanking him in Vegas as if to set up a female field of repulsion against any evil black magnetic forces in the offing. And from the sanctuary of his ability to move around crap tables like a kitten on the frisk, he taunted black majestic king-size Liston before the fight and after the fight. "You're so ugly," he would jeer, crap table safely between them, "that I don't know how you can get any uglier."

"Why don't you sit on my knee and I'll feed you your orange juice," Liston would rumble back.

"Don't insult me, or you'll be sorry 'cause you're just an ugly slow bear." They would pretend to rush at one another. Smaller men would hold them back without effort. They were building the gate for the next fight. And Liston was secretly fond of Clay. He would chuckle when he talked about him. It was years since Liston had failed to knock out his opponent in the first round. His charisma was majestic with menace. One held one's breath when near him. He looked forward with obvious amusement to the happy seconds when he would take Clay apart and see the expression on that silly face. In Miami he trained for a three-round fight. In the famous fifth round when Clay came out with caustic in his eyes and could not see, he waved his gloves at Liston, a look of abject horror on his face, as if to say, "Your younger brother is now an old blind beggar. Do not strike him." And did it with a peculiar authority. For Clay looked like a ghost with his eyes closed, tears streaming, his extended gloves waving in front of him like a widow's entreaties. Liston drew back in doubt, in bewilderment, conceivably in concern for his new great reputation as an exbully; yes, Liston reacted like a gentleman, and Clay was home free. His eyes watered out the caustic, his sight came back. He cut Liston up in the sixth. He left him beaten and exhausted. Liston did not stand up for the bell to the seventh. Maybe Clay had even defeated him earlier that day at the weigh-in when he had harangued and screamed and shouted and whistled and stuck his tongue out at Liston. The Champ had been bewildered. No one had been able ever to stare him in the eyes these last four years. Now a boy was screaming at him, a boy reported to belong to Black Muslims, no, stronger than that, a boy favored by Malcolm X who was braver by reputation than the brave, for he could stop a bullet any day. Liston, afraid only, as he put it, of crazy men, was afraid of the Muslims for he could not contend with their allegiance to one another in prison, their puritanism, their discipline, their martial ranks. The combination was too complex, too unfamiliar. Now, their boy, in a pain of terror or in a mania of courage, was screaming at him at the weigh-in. Liston sat down and shook his head, and looked at the Press, now become his friend, and wound his fingers in circles around his ear, as if saying, Whitey to Whitey, "That black boy is nuts." So Clay made Liston Tom it, and when Liston missed the first jab he threw in the fight by a foot and a half, one knew the night would not be ordinary in the offing.

For their return bout in Boston, Liston trained as he had never before, Clay got a hernia. Liston trained again. Hard training as a fighter grows older seems to speak of the dull deaths of the brightest cells in all the favorite organs; old fighters react to training like beautiful women to washing floors. But Liston did it twice, once for Clay's hernia, and again for their actual fight in Maine, and the second time he trained, he aged as a fighter, for he had a sparring partner, Amos Lincoln, who was one of the better heavy-weights in the country. They had wars with one another every afternoon in the gym. By the day before the fight, Liston was as relaxed and sleepy and dopey as a man in a steambath. He had fought his heart out in training, and done it under constant pressure from Clay who kept telling the world that Liston was old and slow and could not possibly win. And their fight created a scandal, for Liston ran into a short punch in the first round and was counted out, unable to hear the count. The referee and timekeeper missed signals with one another while Clay stood over fallen Liston screaming. "Get up and fight!" It was no night for the fight game, and a tragedy for Clay since he had trained for a long and arduous fight. He had developed his technique for a major encounter with Liston and was left with a horde of unanswered questions including the one he could never admit—which was whether there had been the magic of a real knockout in his punch or if Liston had made—for what variety of reasons!—a conscious decision to stay on the floor. It did him no good.

He had taken all the lessons of his curious life and the outrageously deep comprehension he had of the motivations of his own people—indeed, one could even approach the beginnings of a Psychology of the Blacks by studying his encounters with fighters who were black—and had elaborated that into a technique for boxing which was almost without compare. A most cultivated technique. For he was no child of the slums. His mother was a gracious pale-skinned lady, his father a bitter wit pride-oriented on the family name of Clay—they were descendants of Henry Clay, the orator, on the white side of the family, nothing less, and Cassius began boxing at 12 in a police gym, and from the beginning was a phenomenon of style and the absence of pain, for he knew how to use his physical endowment. Tall, relatively light, with an exceptionally long reach even for his size, he developed defensive skills which made the best use of his body. Working apparently on the premise that there was something obscene about being hit, he boxed with his head back and drew it further back when attacked, like a kid who is shy of punches in a street fight, but because he had a waist which was more supple than the average fighter's neck, he was able to box with his arms low, surveying the fighter in front of him, avoiding punches by the speed of his feet, the reflexes of his waist, the long spoiling deployment of his arms which were always tipping over fighters off-balance. Added to this was his psychological comprehension of the vanity and confusion of other fighters. A man in the ring is a performer as well as a gladiator. Elaborating his technique from the age of 12, Clay knew how to work on the vanity of other performers, knew how to make them feel ridiculous and so force them into crucial mistakes, knew how to set such a tone from the first round—later he was to know how to begin it a year before he would even meet the man. Clay knew that a fighter who had been put in psychological knots before he got near the ring had already lost half, three quarters, no, all of the fight could be lost before the first punch. That was the psychology of the body.

Now, add his curious ability as a puncher. He knew that the heaviest punches, systematically delivered, meant little. There are club fighters who look like armadillos and alligators—you can bounce punches off them forever and they never go down. You can break them down only if they are in a profound state of confusion, and the bombardment of another fighter's fists is never their confusion but their expectation. So Clay punched with a greater variety of mixed intensities than anyone around, he played with punches, was tender with them, laid them on as delicately as you put a postage stamp on an envelope, then cracked them in like a riding crop across your face, stuck a cruel jab like a baseball bat held head on into your mouth, next waltzed you in a clinch with a tender arm around your neck, winged away out of reach on flying legs, dug a hook with the full swing of a baseball bat hard into your ribs, hard pokes of a jab into the face, a mocking soft flurry of pillows and gloves, a mean forearm cutting you off from coming up on him, a cruel wrestling of your neck in a clinch, then elusive again, gloves snake-licking your face like a whip. By the time Clay had defeated Liston once and was training for the second fight, by the time Clay, now champion and renamed Muhammad Ali, and bigger, grown up quickly and not so mysteriously (after the potent ego-soups and marrows of his trip through Muslim Africa) into a Black Prince, Potentate of his people, new Poombah of Polemic, yes, by this time, Clay—we will find it more natural to call him Ali from here on out (for the Prince will behave much like a young god)—yes, Muhammad Ali, Heavyweight Champion of the World, having come back with an amazing commitment to be leader of his people, proceeded to go into training for the second Liston fight with a commitment and then a genius of comprehension for the true intricacies of the Science of Sock. He alternated the best of sparring partners and the most ordinary, worked rounds of dazzling speed with Jimmy Ellis—later, of course, to be champion himself before Frazier knocked him out—rounds which displayed the high esthetic of boxing at its best, then lay against the ropes with other sparring partners, hands at his sides as if it were the 11th or 13th round of an excruciating and exhausting fight with Liston where Ali was now so tired he could not hold his hands up, could just manage to take punches to the stomach, rolling with them, smothering them with his stomach, absorbing them with backward moves, sliding along the ropes, steering his sparring partner with passive but off-setting moves of his limp

NORMAN MAILER

arms. For a minute, for two minutes, the sparring partner—Shotgun Sheldon was his name—would bomb away on Ali's stomach much as if Liston
were tearing him apart in later rounds, and Ali weaving languidly, sliding
his neck for the occasional overhead punch to his face, bouncing from the
rope into the punches, bouncing back away from punches, as if his torso
had become one huge boxing glove to absorb punishment, had penetrated
through into some further conception of pain, as if pain were not pain if you
accepted it with a relaxed heart, yes, Ali let himself be bombarded on the
ropes by the powerful bull-like swings of Shotgun Sheldon, the expression
on his face as remote, and as searching for the last routes into the nerves of
each punch going in as a man hanging on a subway strap will search into
the meaning of the market quotations he has just read on the activities of a
curious stock. So Ali relaxed on the ropes and took punches to the belly
with a faint disdain, as if, curious punches, they did not go deep enough
and after a minute of this, or two minutes, having offered his body like the
hide of a drum for a mad drummer's solo, he would snap out of his
communion with himself and flash a tattoo of light and slashing punches,
mocking as the lights on water, he would dazzle his sparring partner, who,
arm-weary and punched out, would look at him with eyes of love, complete
was his admiration. And if people were ever going to cry watching a boxer
in training, those were the moments, for Ali had the far-off concentration
and disdain of an artist who simply cannot find anyone near enough or
good enough to keep him and his art engaged, and all the while was
perfecting the essence of his art which was to make the other fighter fall
secretly, helpless, in love with him. Bundini, a special trainer, an alter ego
with the same harsh, demoniac, witty, nonstop powers of oration as Ali
himself—he even looked a little like Ali—used to weep openly as he
watched the workouts.

Training session over, Ali would lecture the Press, instruct them—
looking beyond his Liston defense to what he would do to Patterson,
mocking Patterson, calling him a rabbit, a white man's rabbit, knowing he
was putting a new beam on Patterson's shoulders, an outrageously helpless
and heavy beam of rage, fear, hopeless anger and secret black admiration
for the all-out force of Ali's effrontery. And in the next instant Ali would be
charming as a movie star on the make speaking tenderly to a child. If he was
Narcissus, so he was as well the play of mood in the water which served as
mirror to Narcissus. It was as if he knew he had disposed of Patterson
already, that the precise attack of calling him a rabbit would work on the
weakest link—wherever it was—in Patterson's tense and tortured psyche
and Patterson would crack, as indeed, unendurably for himself, he did,
when their fight took place. Patterson's back gave way in the early rounds,
and he fought twisted and in pain, half crippled like a man with a sac-
roiliac, for 11 brave and most miserable rounds before the referee would
call it and Ali, breaking up with his first wife then, was unpleasant in the
ring that night, his face ugly and contemptuous, himself well on the way to

becoming America's most unpopular major American. That, too, was part of the art—to get a public to the point of hating him so much the burden on the other fighter approached the metaphysical—which is where Ali wanted it. White fighters with faces like rock embedded in cement would trade punch for punch, Ali liked to get the boxing where it belonged—he would trade metaphysic for metaphysic with anyone.

So he went on winning his fights and growing forever more unpopular. How he inflamed the temper of boxing's white establishment, for they were for most part a gaggle of avuncular drunks and hard-bitten hacks who were ready to fight over every slime-slicked penny, and squared a few of their slippery crimes by getting fighters to show up semblance-of-sober at any available parish men's rally and charity church breakfast—"Everything I am I owe to boxing," the fighter would mumble through his dentures while elements of gin, garlic, and goddess-of-a-girlie from the night before came off in the bright morning fumes.

Ali had them psyched. He cut through moribund coruscated dirty business corridors, cut through cigar smoke and bushwah, hypocrisy and well-aimed kicks to the back of the neck, cut through crooked politicians, and patriotic pus, cut like a laser, point of the point, light and impersonal, cut to the heart of the rottenest meat in boxing, and boxing was always the buried South Vietnam of America, buried for 50 years in our hide before we went there, yes, Ali cut through the flag-dragooned salutes of drunken dawns and said, "I got no fight with those Vietcongs," and they cut him down, thrust him into the three and a half years of his martyrdom. Where he grew. Grew to have a little fat around his middle and a little of the complacent muscle of the clam to his world-ego. And grew sharper in the mind as well, and deepened and broadened physically. Looked no longer like a boy, but a sullen man, almost heavy, with the beginnings of a huge expanse across his shoulders. And developed the patience to survive, the wisdom to contemplate future nights in jail, grew to cultivate the suspension of belief and the avoidance of disbelief—what a rack for a young man! As the years of hope for reinstatement, or avoidance of prison, came up and waned in him, Ali walked the tightrope between bitterness and apathy, and had enough left to beat Quarry and beat Bonavena, beat Quarry in the flurry of a missed hundred punches, ho! how his timing was off! beat him with a calculated whip, snake-lick whip, to the corrugated sponge of a dead flesh over Quarry's Irish eyes—they stopped it after the third on cuts—then knocked out Bonavena, the indestructible, never stopped before, by working the art of crazy mixing in the punches he threw at the rugged—some of the punches Ali threw that night would not have hurt a little boy—the punch he let go in the 15th came in like a wrecking ball from outer space. Bonavena went sprawling across the ring. He was a house coming down.

Yet it may have been the blow which would defeat him later. For Ali had been tired with Bonavena, lackluster, winded, sluggish, far ahead on points but in need of the most serious work if he were to beat Frazier. The punch in the last round was obliged, therefore, to inflame his belief that the forces of magic were his, there to be called upon when most in need, that the silent leagues of black support for his cause—since their cause was as his own—were like some cloak of midnight velvet, there to protect him by black blood, by black sense of tragedy, by the black consciousness that the guilt of the world had become the hinge of a door that they would open. So they would open the way to Frazier's chin, the blacks would open the aisle for his trip to the gods.

Therefore he did not train for Frazier as perhaps he had to. He worked, he ran three miles a day when he could have run five, he boxed some days and let a day and perhaps another day go, he was relaxed, he was confident, he basked in the undemanding winter sun of Miami, and skipped his rope in a gym crowded with fighters, stuffed now with working fighters looking to be seen, Ali comfortable and relaxed like the greatest of movie stars, he played a young fighter working out in a corner on the heavy bag—for of course every eye was on him—and afterward doing sit-ups in the back room and having his stomach rubbed with liniment, he would talk to reporters. He was filled with confidence there was no black fighter he did not comprehend to the root of the valve in the hard-pumping heart, and yes, Frazier, he assured everybody, would be easier than they realized. Like a little boy who had grown up to take on a mountain of responsibility he spoke in the deep relaxation of the wise, and teased two of the reporters who were present and fat. "You want to drink a lot of water," he said, "good cold water instead of all that liquor rot-your-gut," and gave the smile of a man who had been able to intoxicate himself on water (although he was, by repute, a fiend for soft sweet drinks), "and fruit and good clean vegetables you want to eat and chicken and steak. You lose weight then," he advised out of kind secret smiling thoughts, and went on to talk of the impact of the fight upon the world. "Yes," he said, "you just think of a stadium with a million people, 10 million people, you could get them all in to watch they would all pay to see it live, but then you think of the hundreds of millions and the billions who are going to see this fight, and if you could sit them all down in one place, and fly a jet plane over them, why that plane would have to fly for an hour before it would reach the end of all the people who will see this fight. It's the greatest event in the history of the world, and you take a man like Frazier, a good fighter, but a simple hard-working fellow, he's not built for this kind of pressure, the eyes," Ali said softly, "of that many people upon him. There's an experience to pressure which I have had, fighting a man like Liston in Miami the first time, which he has not. He will cave in under the pressure. No, I do not see any way a man like Frazier can whup me, he can't reach me, my arms are too long, and if he does get in and knock me down I'll never make the mistake of Quarry and Foster or Ellis of rushing back at him, I'll stay away until my head clears, then I begin to pop him again, pop! pop!" a few jabs, "no there is no way this man can beat me,

215

EGO

this fight will be easier than you think."

There was one way in which boxing was still like a street fight and that was in the need to be confident you would win. A man walking out of a bar to fight with another man is seeking to compose his head into the confidence that he will certainly triumph—it is the most mysterious faculty of the ego. For that confidence is a sedative against the pain of punches and yet is the sanction to punch your own best. The logic of the spirit would suggest that you win only if you deserve to win; the logic of the ego lays down the axiom that if you don't think you will win, you don't deserve to. And, in fact, usually don't; it is as if not believing you will win opens you to the guilt that perhaps you have not the right, you are too guilty.

So training camps are small factories for the production of one rare psychological item—an ego able to bear huge pain and administer drastic punishment. The flow of Ali's ego poured over the rock of every distraction, it was an ego like the flow of a river of constant energy fed by a hundred tributaries of black love and the love of the white left. The construction of the ego of Joe Frazier was of another variety. His manager, Yancey "Yank" Durham, a canny foxy light-skinned Negro with a dignified mien, a gray head of hair, gray mustache and a small but conservative worthy's paunch, plus the quick-witted look of eyes which could spot from a half-mile away any man coming toward him with a criminal thought, was indeed the face of a consummate jeweler who had worked for years upon a diamond in the rough until he was now and at last a diamond, hard as the transmutation of black carbon from the black earth into the brilliant sky-blue shadow of the rarest shining rock. What a fighter was Frazier, what a diamond of an ego had he, and what a manager was Durham. Let us look.

Sooner or later, fight metaphors, like fight managers, go sentimental. They go military. But there is no choice here. Frazier was the human equivalent of a war machine. He had tremendous firepower. He had a great left hook, a left hook frightening even to watch when it missed, for it seemed to whistle; he had a powerful right. He could knock a man out with either hand—not all fighters can, not even very good fighters. Usually, however, he clubbed opponents to death, took a punch, gave a punch, took three punches, gave two, took a punch, gave a punch, high speed all the way, always working, pushing his body and arms, short for a heavyweight, up through the middle, bombing through on force, reminiscent of Jimmy Brown knocking down tacklers. Frazier kept on coming, hard and fast, a hang-in, hang-on, go-and-get-him, got-him, got-him, slip and punch, take a punch, wing a punch, whap a punch, never was Frazier happier than with his heart up on the line against some other man's heart, let the bullets fly—his heart was there to stand up at the last. Sooner or later, the others almost all fell down. Undefeated like Ali, winner of 23 out of 26 fights by knockout, he was a human force, certainly the greatest heavyweight force to come along since Rocky Marciano. (If those two men had ever met, it would have been like two Mack trucks hitting each other head-on, then backing up to hit each other again—they would have kept it up until the wheels were off the axles and the engines off the chassis.) But this would be a different kind of fight. Ali would run. Ali would keep hitting Frazier with long jabs, quick hooks and rights while backing up, backing up, staying out of reach unless Frazier could take the punishment and get in. That was where the military problem began. For getting in against the punishment he would take was a question of morale, and there was a unique situation in this fight—Frazier had become the white man's fighter, Mr. Charley was rooting for Frazier, and that meant blacks were boycotting him in their heart. That could be poison to Frazier's morale, for he was twice as black as Clay and half as handsome, he had the rugged decent life-worked face of a man who had labored in the pits all his life, he looked like the deserving modest son of one of those Negro cleaning women of a bygone age who worked from 6 in the morning to midnight every day, raised a family, endured and occasionally elicited the exasperated admiration of white ladies who would kindly remark, "That woman deserves something better in her life." Frazier had the mien of the son, one of many, of such a woman, and he was the hardest-working fighter in training many a man had ever seen, he was conceivably the hardest-working man alive in the world, and as he went through his regimen, first boxing four rounds with a sparring partner, Kenny Norton, a talented heavyweight from the coast with an almost unbeaten record, then working on the heavy bag, then the light bag, then skipping rope, 10 to 12 rounds of sparring and exercise on a light day. Frazier went on with the doggedness, the concentration, and the pumped-up fury of a man who has had so little in his life that he can endure torments to get everything, he pushed the total of his energy and force into an absolute abstract exercise of will so it did not matter if he fought a sparring partner or the heavy bag, he lunged at each equally as if the exhaustions of his own heart and the clangor of his lungs were his only enemies, and the head of a fighter or the leather of the bag as it rolled against his own head was nothing but some abstract thunk of material, not a thing, not a man, but thunk! thunk! something of an obstacle, thunk! thunk! thunk! to beat into thunk! oblivion. And his breath came in rips and sobs as he smashed into the bag as if it were real, just that heavy big torso-sized bag hanging from its chain but he attacked it as if it were a bear, as if it were a great fighter and they were in the mortal embrace of a killing set of exchanges of punches in the middle of the eighth round, and rounds of exercise later, skipping rope to an inhumanly fast beat for this late round in the training day, sweat pouring like jets of blood from an artery, he kept swinging his rope, muttering. "Two-million-dollars-and-change, two-million-dollars-and-change," railroad train chugging into the terminals of exhaustion. And it was obvious that Durham, jeweler to his diamond, was working to make the fight as abstract as he could for Frazier, to keep Clay out of it—for they would not call him Ali in their camp—yes. Frazier was fortifying his ego by depersonalizing his opponent, Clay was thunk! the heavy bag, thunk! and thunk!—Frazier was looking to get no messages from that cavern on velvet when black people sent their good wishes to Ali at midnight, no, Frazier would insulate himself with prodigies of work, hardest-working man in the hell-hole of the world, and on and on he drove himself into the depressions each day of killing daily exhaustion.

That was one half of the strategy to isolate Frazier from Ali, hard work and thinking of thunking on inanimate Clay; the other half was up to Durham who was running front relations with the blacks of North Philly who wandered into the gym, paid their dollar, and were ready to heckle on Frazier. In the four rounds he boxed with Norton, Frazier did not look too good for a while. It was 10 days before the fight and he was in a bad mood when he came in, for the word was through the gym that they had discovered one of his favorite sparring partners, just fired that morning, was a Black Muslim and had been calling Ali every night with reports, that was the rumor, and Frazier, sullen and cold at the start, was bopped and tapped, then walloped by Norton moving fast with the big training gloves in imitation of Ali, and Frazier looked very easy to hit until the middle of the third round when Norton, proud of his something like 20 wins and one loss, beginning to get some ideas himself about how to fight champions, came driving in to mix it with Frazier, have it out man to man and caught a right which dropped him, left him looking limp with that half-silly smile sparring partners get when they have been hit too hard to justify any experience or any money they are going to take away. Up till then the crowd had been with Norton. There at one end of the Cloverlay gym, a street-level storefront room which could have been used originally by an automobile dealer, there on that empty, immaculate Lysol-soaked floor, designed when Frazier was there for only Frazier and his partners to train (as opposed to Miami where Ali would rub elbows with the people) here the people were at one end, the end off the street, and they jeered whenever Norton hit Frazier, they laughed when Norton made him look silly, they called out, "Drop the mother," until Durham held up a gentlemanly but admonishing finger in request for silence. Afterward, however, training completed, Durham approached them to answer questions, rolled with their sallies, jived the people back, subtly enlisted their sympathy for Frazier by saying, "When I fight Clay, I'm going to get him somewhere in the middle rounds," until the blacks quipping back said angrily, "You ain't fighting him, Frazier is."
    "Why you call him Clay?" another asked. "He Ali."
    "His name is Cassius Clay to me," said Durham.
    "What you say against his religion?"
    "I don't say nothing about his religion and he doesn't say anything about mine. I'm a Baptist."
    "You going to make money on this?"

"Of course," said Durham, "I got to make money. You don't think I work up this sweat for nothing."

They loved him. He was happy with them. A short fat man in a purple suit wearing his revival of the wide-brim bebop hat said to Durham, "Why don't you get Norton to manage? He was beating up on your fighter," and the fat man cackled for he had scored and could elaborate the tale for his ladies later how he had put down Yank who was working the daily rite on the edge of the black street for his fighter, while upstairs, dressed, and sucking an orange, sweat still pouring, gloom of excessive fatigue upon him, Frazier was sitting through his two-hundredth or two-thousandth interview for this fight, reluctant indeed to give it at all. "Some get it, some don't," he had said for refusal, but relented when a white friend who had done road work with him interceded, so he sat there now against a leather sofa, dark blue suit, dark T-shirt, mopping his brow with a pink-red towel, and spoke dispiritedly of being ready too early for the fight. He was waking up an hour too early for roadwork each morning now. "I'd go back to sleep but it doesn't feel good when I do run."

"I guess the air is better that hour of the morning."

He nodded sadly. "There's a limit to how good the air in Philly can get."

"Where'd you begin to sing?" was a question asked.

"I sang in church first," he replied, but it was not the day to talk about singing. The loneliness of hitting the bag still seemed upon him as if in his exhaustion now, and in the thoughts of that small insomnia which woke him an hour too early every day, was something of the loneliness of all blacks who work very hard and are isolated from fun and must wonder in the just-awakened night how large and pervasive was the curse of a people. "The countdown's begun," said Frazier, "I get impatient about now."

For the fight, Ali was wearing red velvet trunks, Frazier had green. Before they began, even before they were called together by the referee for instructions, Ali went dancing around the ring and glided past Frazier with a sweet little-boy smile, as if to say, "You're my new playmate. We're going to have fun." Ali was laughing. Frazier was having nothing of this and turned his neck to embargo him away. Ali, having alerted the crowd by this big first move, came prancing in again. When Frazier looked ready to block him, Ali went around, evading a contact, gave another sweet smile, shook his head at the lack of high spirit. "Poor Frazier," he seemed to say.

At the weigh-in early that afternoon Ali looked physically resplendent; the night before in Harlem, crowds had cheered him; he was coming to claim his victory on the confluence of two mighty tides—he was the mightiest victim of injustice in America and he was also—the 20th Century was nothing if not a tangle of opposition—he was also the mightiest narcissist in the land. Every beard, dropout, homosexual, junkie, freak, swinger, and plain simple individualist adored him. Every pedantic liberal soul who had once loved Patterson now paid homage to Ali. The mightiest of the black psyches and the most filigreed of the white psyches were ready to roar him home, as well as every family-loving hard-working square American who genuinely hated the war in Vietnam. What a tangle of ribbons he carried on his lance, enough cross purposes to be the knight-resplendent of television, the fell hero of the medium, and he had a look of unique happiness on television when presenting his program for the course of the fight, and his inevitable victory. He would be as content then as an infant splashing the waters of the bathinette. If he was at once a saint and a monster to any mind which looked for category, any mind unwilling to encounter the thoroughly dread-filled fact that the 20th Century breed of man now in birth might be no longer half good and half evil—generous and greedy by turns—but a mutation with Cassius Muhammed for the first son—then that mind was not ready to think about 20th Century Man. (And indeed Muhammad Ali had twin poodles he called Angel and Demon.) So now the ambiguity of his presence filled the Garden before the fight was fairly begun, it was as if he had announced to that plural billion-footed crowd assembled under the shadow of the jet which would fly over them that the first enigma of the fight would be the way he would win it, that he would initiate his triumph by getting the crowd to laugh at Frazier, yes, first premise tonight was that the poor black man in Frazier's soul would go berserk if made a figure of roll-off-your-seat amusement.

The referee gave his instructions. The bell rang. The first 15 seconds of a fight can be the fight. It is equivalent to the first kiss in a love affair. The fighters each missed the other. Ali blocked Frazier's first punches easily, but Ali then missed Frazier's head. That head was bobbing as fast as a third fist. Frazier would come rushing in, head moving like a fist, fists bobbing too, his head working above and below his forearm, he was trying to get through Ali's jab, get through fast and sear Ali early with the terror of a long fight and punches harder than he had ever taken to the stomach, and Ali in turn, backing up, and throwing fast punches, aimed just a trifle, and was therefore a trifle too slow, but it was obvious Ali was trying to shiver Frazier's synapses from the start, set waves of depression stirring which would reach his heart in later rounds and make him slow, deaden nerve, deaden nerve went Ali's jab flicking a snake tongue, whoo-eet! whoo-eet! but Frazier's head was bobbing too fast, he was moving faster than he had ever moved before in the bobbing nonstop never-a-backward step of his, slogging and bouncing forward, that huge left hook flaunting the air with the confidence it was enough of a club to split a tree, and Ali, having missed his jabs, stepped nimbly inside the hook and wrestled Frazier in the clinch. Ali looked stronger here. So by the first 45 seconds of the fight, they had each surprised the other profoundly. Frazier was fast enough to slip through Ali's punches, and Ali was strong enough to handle him in the clinches. A pattern had begun. Because Ali was missing often, Frazier was in under his shots like a police dog's muzzle on your arm, Ali could not

NORMAN MAILER

slide from side to side, he was boxed in, then obliged to go backward, and would end on the ropes again and again with Frazier belaboring him. Yet Frazier could not reach him. Like a prestidigitator Ali would tie the other's punches into odd knots, not even blocking them yet on his elbows or his arms, rather throwing his own punches as defensive moves, for even as they missed, he would brush Frazier to the side with his forearm, or hold him off, or clinch and wrestle a little of the will out of Frazier's neck. Once or twice in the round a long left hook by Frazier just touched the surface of Ali's chin, and Ali waved his head in placid contempt to the billions watching as if to say, "This man has not been able to hurt me at all."

The first round set a pattern for the fight. Ali won it and would win the next. His jab was landing from time to time and rights and lefts of no great consequence. Frazier was hardly reaching him at all. Yet it looked like Frazier had established that he was fast enough to get in on Ali and so drive him to the ropes and to the corners, and that spoke of a fight which would be determined by the man in better condition, in better physical condition rather than in better psychic condition, the kind of fight Ali could hardly want for his strength was in his pauses, his nature passed along the curve of every dialectic, he liked, in short, to fight in flurries, and then move out, move away, assess, take his time, fight again. Frazier would not let him. Frazier moved in with the snarl of a wolf, his teeth seemed to show through his mouthpiece, he made Ali work. Ali won the first two rounds but it was obvious he could not continue to win if he had to work all the way. And in the third round Frazier began to get to him, caught Ali with a powerful blow to the face at the bell. That was the first moment where it was clear to all that Frazier had won a round. Then he won the next. Ali looked tired and a little depressed. He was moving less and less and calling upon a skill not seen since the fight with Chuvalo when he had showed his old ability, worked on all those years ago with Shotgun Sheldon, to lie on the ropes and take a beating to the stomach. He had exhausted Chuvalo by welcoming attacks on the stomach but Frazier was too incommensurable a force to allow such total attack. So Ali lay on the ropes and wrestled him off, and moved his arms and waist, blocking punches, slipping punches, counter-ing with punches—it began to look as if the fight would be written on the ropes, but Ali was getting very tired. At the beginning of the fifth round, he got up slowly from his stool, very slowly. Frazier was beginning to feel that the fight was his. He moved in on Ali jeering, his hands at his side in mimicry of Ali, a street fighter mocking his opponent, and Ali tapped him with long light jabs to which Frazier stuck out his mouthpiece, a jeer of derision as if to suggest that the mouthpiece was all Ali would reach all night.

There is an extortion of the will beyond any of our measure in the exhaus-tion which comes upon a fighter in early rounds when he is already too tired to lift his arms or take advantage of openings there before him, yet the fight is not a third over, there are all those rounds to go, contractions of torture, the lungs screaming into the dungeons of the soul, washing the throat with a hot bile that once belonged to the liver, the legs are going dead, the arms move but their motion is limp, one is straining into another will, breathing into the breath of another will as agonized as one's own. As the fight moved through the fifth, the sixth and the seventh, then into the eighth, it was obvious that Ali was into the longest night of his career, and yet with that skill, that research into the pits of every miserable contingency in boxing, he came up with odd somnambulistic variations, holding Frazier off, riding around Frazier with his arm about his neck, almost entreating Frazier with his arms extended, and Frazier leaning on him, each of them slowed to a pit-a-pat of light punches back and forth until one of them was goaded up from exhaustion to whip and stick, then hook and hammer and into the belly and out, and out of the clinch and both looking exhausted, and then Frazier, mouth bared again like a wolf, going in and Ali waltzing him, tying him, tapping him lightly as if he were a speed bag, just little flicks, until Frazier, like an exhausted horse finally feeling the crop, would push up into a trot and try to run up the hill. It was indeed as if they were both running up a hill. As if Frazier's offensive was so great and so great was Ali's defense that the fight could only be decided by who could take the steepest pitch of the hill. So Frazier, driving, driving, trying to drive the heart out of Ali, put the pitch of that hill up and up until they were ascending an unendurable slope. And moved like somnambulists slowly working and rubbing one another, almost embracing, next to locked in the slow moves of lovers after the act until, reaching into the stores of energy reaching them from cells never before so used, one man or the other would work up a contractive spasm of skills and throw punches at the other in the straining slow-motion hypnosis of a deepening act. And so the first eight rounds went by. The two judges scored six for Frazier, two for Ali. The referee had it even. Some of the Press had Ali ahead—it was not easy to score. For if it were an alley fight, Frazier would win. Clay was by now hardly more than the heavy bag to Frazier. Frazier was dealing with a man not a demon. He was not respectful of that man. But still! It was Ali who was landing the majority of punches. They were light, they were usually weary, but some had snap, some were quick, he was landing two punches to Frazier's one. Yet Frazier's were hardest. And Ali often looked as tender as if he were making love. It was as if he could now feel the whole absence of that real second fight with Liston, that fight for which he had trained so long and so hard, the fight which might have rolled over his laurels from the greatest artist of pugilism to the greatest brawler of them all—maybe he had been prepared on the night to beat Liston at his own, be more of a slugger, more of a man crude to crude than Liston. Yes, Ali had never been a street fighter and never a whorehouse knock-it-down stud, no, it was more as if a man with the exquisite reflexes of Nureyev had learned to throw a knockout punch with either hand and so had become champion of

222

NORMAN MAILER

the world without knowing if he was the man of all men or the most delicate of the delicate with special privilege endowed by God. Now with Frazier, he was in a sweat bath (a mudpile, a knee, elbow, and death-thumping chute of a pit) having in this late year the fight he had sorely needed for his true greatness as a fighter six and seven years ago, and so whether ahead, behind or even, terror sat in the rooting instinct of all those who were for Ali for it was obviously Frazier's fight to win, and what if Ali, weaknesses of character now flickering to the surface in a hundred little moves, should enter the vale of prizefighting's deepest humiliation, should fall out half conscious on the floor and not want to get up. What a death to his followers.

The ninth began. Frazier mounted his largest body attack of the night. It was preparations-for-Liston-with-Shotgun-Sheldon, it was the virtuosity of the gym all over again, and Ali, like a catcher handling a fast-ball pitcher, took Frazier's punches, one steamer, another steamer, wing! went a screamer, a steamer, warded them, blocked them, slithered them, winced from them, absorbed them, took them in and blew them out and came off the ropes and was Ali the Magnificent for the next minute and thirty seconds. The fight turned. The troops of Ali's second corps of energy had arrived, the energy for which he had been waiting long agonizing heart-sore vomit-mean rounds. Now he jabbed Frazier, he snake-licked his face with jabs faster than he had thrown before, he anticipated each attempt of Frazier at counterattack and threw it back, he danced on his toes for the first time in rounds, he popped in rights, he hurt him with hooks, it was his biggest round of the night, it was the best round yet of the fight, and Frazier full of energy and hordes of sudden punishment was beginning to move into that odd petulant concentration on other rituals besides the punches, tappings of the gloves, stares of the eye, that species of mouthpiece-chewing which is the prelude to fun-strut in the knees, then Queer Street, then waggle on out, drop like a steer.

It looked like Ali had turned the fight, looked more like the same in the 10th, now reporters were writing another story in their mind where Ali was not the magical untried Prince who had come apart under the first real pressure of his life but was rather the greatest Heavyweight Champion of all time for he had weathered the purgatory of Joe Frazier.

But in the 11th, that story also broke. Frazier caught him, caught him again and again, and Ali was near to knocked out and swayed and slid on Queer Street himself, then spent the rest of the 11th and the longest round of the 12th working another bottom of Hell, holding off Frazier who came on and on, sobbing, wild, a wild honor of a beast, man of will reduced to the common denominator of the will of all of us back in that land of the animal where the idea of man as a tool-wielding beast was first conceived. Frazier looked to get Ali forever in the 11th and the 12th, and Ali, his legs slapped and slashed on the thighs between each round by Angelo Dundee, came out for the 13th and incredibly was dancing. Everybody's story switched again. For if Ali won this round, the 14th and 15th, who could know if he could

223

not win the fight? . . . He won the first half of the 13th, then spent the second half on the ropes with Frazier. They were now like crazy death-march-maddened mateys coming up the hill and on to home, and yet Ali won the 14th, Ali looked good, he came out dancing for the 15th, while Frazier, his own armies of energy finally caught up, his courage ready to spit into the eye of any devil black or white who would steal the work of his life, had equal madness to steal the bolt from Ali. So Frazier reached out to snatch the magic punch from the air, the punch with which Ali topped Bonavena, and found it and thunked Ali a hell and hit Ali a heaven of a shot which dumped Muhammed into 50,000 newspaper photographs—Ali on the floor! Great Ali on the floor was out there flat singing to the sirens in the mistiest fogs of Queer Street (same look of death and widowhood on his far-gone face as one had seen in the fifth blind round with Liston) yet Ali got up. Ali came sliding through the last two minutes and thirty-five seconds of this heathen holocaust in some last exercise of the will, some iron fundament of the ego not to be knocked out; and it was then as if the spirit of Harlem finally spoke and came to rescue and the ghosts of the dead in Vietnam, something held him up before arm-weary triumphant near-crazy Frazier who had just hit him the hardest punch ever thrown in his life and they went down to the last few seconds of a great fight, Ali still standing and Frazier had won.

The world was talking instantly of a rematch. For Ali had shown America what we all had hoped was secretly true. He was a man. He could bear moral and physical torture and he could stand. And if he could beat Frazier in the rematch we would have at last a national hero who was hero of the world as well, and who could bear to wait for the next fight? Joe Frazier, still the champion, and a great champion, said to the press, "Fellows, have a heart—I got to live a little. I've been working for 10 long years." And Ali, through the agency of alter-ego Bundini, said—for Ali was now in the hospital to check on the possible fracture of a jaw—Ali was reported to have said, "Get the gun ready—we're going to set traps." Oh, wow. Could America wait for something so great as the Second Ali-Frazier?

For Discussion and Further Application

1. Why does Mailer claim we find Ali so fascinating?
2. Mailer insists that every good fighter must have a large ego. Why?
3. How can prizefighting be described as "a language of the body"?
4. Do you agree with Mailer's contention that the white middle class emphasizes "learning to talk with the mind" but ghetto cultures "speak to each other with their bodies, they signal with their clothes"?
5. Mailer claims Ali was the "first psychologist of the body." What does he mean?

6. Part of Mailer's style is his use of vivid metaphors and similes. For example, Ali's punches vary from postage stamps on an envelope to a baseball bat in the mouth. Find some other examples and explain why they either work or do not work well.
7. Mailer frequently uses lengthy series of run-on sentences. Find some examples and describe whether or not they serve a purpose. Do you think they help or hinder Mailer's style?
8. Can you account for any differences between Mailer's style at the beginning of the article and his style toward the end?
9. Select several sentences at random from the article and analyze as best you can how they are put together.
10. Write a short passage imitating Mailer's style. Try, for example, to describe one of Ali's more recent fights the way Mailer would; then write a short passage describing the fight in a traditional sports reporter's prose.

JOHN McPHEE

the capital of the pines

The following article is excerpted from a chapter of John McPhee's book, *The Pine Barrens*. A little known section in southern New Jersey, the Pine Barrens has a unique culture and history. McPhee thoroughly researched the book, which first appeared as a series of articles in *The New Yorker* magazine, through trips to the region. There he got to know the inhabitants and their history firsthand. As you read, notice the techniques he uses to describe the town of Chatsworth and its people. What makes his writing so effective?

Chatsworth, in Woodland Township, is the principal community in the Pine Barrens. It is six miles north of the approximate center of the pines at Hog Wallow, and is surrounded on all sides by deep forest. From the air, two miles away, Chatsworth is not visible under the high cover of oaks and pines. The town consists of three hundred and six people, seventy-four houses, ten trailers, a firehouse, a church, a liquor store, a post office, a school, two sawmills, and one general store. Somehow, Chatsworth is a half-tone more attractive than any other town in the pines. The people are apparently just a little competitive about the appearance of their houses, most of which are painted, and this gives Chatsworth a measure of distinction from its "suburbs"—the word used in Chatsworth for small settlements nearby in the woods, such as Leektown, Butler Place, Speedwell, and Jones Mill. People in Chatsworth pay twenty-four dollars a truckload to bring in topsoil so that they can grow lawns. That sort of thing notwithstanding, individualism and personal independence are as important there as they are in the rest of the pines. Two-thirds of Chatsworth's people make their living in Woodland Township—mainly from cranberries and blueberries and from "working for the state highway" and patrolling the woods as fire wardens or foresters. Half the people classify themselves as self-employed. Most of them are descended from English, Irish, and German ancestors who settled in the Pine Barrens in the eighteenth century, and the headstones in the Chatsworth cemetery bear names such as Brower, Bozarth, Dunfee, Leek, Applegate, Ritzendollar, and Buzby.

On the southwest corner of the town's principal intersection is the Chatsworth General Store, the entrance to which was cut into a corner of the building on an angle, so that the door itself, aproned with concrete steps, is the most prominent exterior feature of the building. The door was apparently designed to attract people from both intersecting streets, although the store has no competition for a ten-mile sweep in all directions. When I first stopped in there, I noticed on its shelves the usual run of cold cuts, canned foods, soft drinks, crackers, cookies, cereals, and sardines, and also Remington twelve-gauge shotgun shells, Slipknot friction tape, Varsity gasket cement, Railroad Mills sweet snuff, and State-Wide well restorer. Wrapping string unwound from a spool on a wall shelf and ran through eyelets across the ceiling and down to a wooden counter. A glass counter top next to the wooden one had been rubbed cloudy by hundreds of thousands of coins and pop bottles, and in the case beneath it were twenty-two rectangular glass dishes, each holding a different kind of penny candy. Beside the candy case was a radiator covered with an oak plank. Chatsworth loafers sat there. There were no particular loafers. Almost everyone who came into the store spent a little time on the oak plank. There were three Esso pumps on the sidewalk outside. Esso had been sold there since 1921. Just inside the door, a red kerosene pump was set in the floor. I was told that as many as four hundred gallons of kerosene had been sold through it in a week. Kerosene is widely used in the pines, both for heat and for light.

The general store was built in 1865. It was owned and run from 1894 until 1939 by Willis Jefferson Buzby, who was known as the King of the Pineys. After Buzby's death, the place was taken over by his son Willis Jonathan Buzby, who assumed his father's title, and who is still called the King of the Pineys, although he and his wife, Kate, recently sold the business to another Chatsworth couple and retired to their house across the street. "We're the original pineys," Mrs. Buzby said to me in the store one day. "People come here and say, 'We're looking for the pineys,' and I say, 'They're right here,' and they say, 'No, we mean the people who live in caves and intermarry,' and I say, 'I don't know of any such people. We're pineys. We live right here.' " Mrs. Buzby is a small woman with gray hair and bright eyes. "We've had electric in here since 1932," she went on. "People come here now and see all the electric fixtures and say, 'My goodness, I didn't know the pineys lived like this.' Some of these homes don't look so good on the outside, but in the inside they have everything—refrigerators, radios, television."

Her husband, who has a forward bend in his walk and is a man of quick motions, said over his shoulder as he moved off to fill an order, "I'm a piney and I'm proud of it."

"Live in caves and intermarry, hah," Mrs. Buzby went on. "No one ever lived in caves that I heard of. I don't know of anyone around here except one family that's intermarried, and I've lived here all my life. Illegitimacy is low. In the city, you can do what you like. Here, you make a misstep and everyone knows it. There are some drifters, but not many. We have very few new people in town—perhaps half a dozen."

Mrs. Buzby's maiden name was Ritzendollar. When she went to high school, in Pemberton, on the periphery of the pinelands, she stayed there during the week, and when the roads were bad in winter she had to stay in Pemberton for as much as a month without going home. Her husband went to a one-room school in Chatsworth and did not go on to high school. They have one daughter, Theresa, who married a boy she met at Pemberton High School. Their son-in-law now does acoustical research at the University of Michigan. The Buzbys have two granddaughters. One went to Radcliffe and majored in art, married a graduate of the Harvard Medical School, and lives in Palo Alto, California. The other is now at Wellesley. A Wellesley banner was tacked to a canned-goods shelf in the Chatsworth General Store.

On the store bulletin board was a proclamation signed by Peter T. Brower, mayor of Woodland Township, forbidding all men to shave for six weeks. Violators would be fined two dollars, which would be used to help cover the costs of a coming celebration of the centennial of the township's incorporation. Almost every man in Chatsworth had grown a grisly stubble. Buzby had let his own beard go for the better part of a week. Now he got out an electric razor and plugged it into an outlet. "I better shave," he said, rubbing the machine against his face. "I look like a God-damned Rip Van Winkle. It costs you two bucks to shave now."

Out of a mud-colored 1948 De Soto came an old woman in a gray dress that reached her ankles. She bought two cans of beans and one slab of uncut bacon. She complained to Mrs. Buzby about a slab of bacon she had bought two weeks before, and she went out.

An old man in a straw hat, a faded blue shirt, and khaki trousers stopped in for his Philadelphia *Inquirer*. He reminisced with Mrs. Buzby. They talked of the school they went to, in Chatsworth, years ago. There was a big coal stove in the middle of the schoolroom. The oldest boys could throw erasers hard enough to knock the stovepipe out of the wall. When a doctor was scheduled to visit the school, the children ran into the woods to avoid vaccinations. The old man complained bitterly about a teacher who had whipped him for someone else's misdemeanor. As the old man was leaving, Mrs. Buzby drew him out on the origin of the word "pineys." He said, "Pineys is a freak name that was invented in New York City."

A Ford station wagon stopped at one of the Esso pumps, and Mrs. Peter Brower, the wife of the Mayor, pumped herself three dollars and seventy cents' worth of gas. She waved at Buzby and drove away. Buzby got out a book, read the pump from inside the store, and recorded what Brower owed.

An old blue-and-white Chevrolet succeeded Mrs. Brower at the pumps. In it was a tan and extremely tired-looking young woman with long tawny hair. She wore a green blouse. Two small children were crawling on her. Buzby went out. She undid two of her blouse buttons and reached inside. She removed a bill, unfolded it, and handed it to Buzby. He pumped a dollar's worth of gas.

A young man wearing a sleeveless shirt and dungarees asked Mrs. Buzby for a pack of cigarettes and a soft drink. "That will be fifty cents out of your jeans." she said.

Buzby, who frequently addressed remarks not to one person but to the loitering audience in general, announced that he had never had a drink or a smoke. "I got the thirty cents and I can do what I damned please with it," he said.

Charlie Applegate, custodian of the Chatsworth school and the husband of a teacher there, sat down on the oak plank for a while. In the course of a conversation, he told me that he once made seven hundred dollars in six weeks gathering wild blueberries. He is tanned, has gray hair, and speaks softly. He has a canoe, and loves to spend his free time on Pine Barrens rivers. "The woods are not built up, because they're so far from everything," he said. "In ten or fifteen years, they're going to build up. There's a proposal for a jetport. Most of the younger people are for it. The older people are not."

Buzby entered the conversation, saying, "As I look at it, damned if I'd want a jetport out there. It's going to be God-damned noisy."

"People from all over moving in would create problems," Applegate went on. "We have no crimes here. *That* would come to an end."

The statement—often heard in the Pine Barrens—that there is no crime in the pines is essentially true, with only a few exceptions, but among these exceptions some absorbing practices and events have been recorded. Fifty years ago, mounted state police patrolled the pines from barracks in Chatsworth. Now state police from barracks outside the woods patrol the pines, but only as a minor part of their work, which is almost wholly taken up with problems that arise elsewhere. A trooper at the Red Lion barracks, west of the woods, said to me one day, "There's no crime rate at all in the pines. They're loners in there. They take care of most of their troubles by themselves." Criminal events involving local people are infrequent. In 1912, a cranberry grower was returning to his bog with money to pay his scoopers when he came to a bridge that had been barricaded on the road from Atsion to Hampton Furnace. The men who had set up the barricade shot the grower and took the money. People still talk about it. Fred Brown once took me to the bridge and pantomimed the crime as he imagined it had happened. A man disappeared from Chatsworth in 1947, his bones were found in 1954, and the case has never been solved or explained. Two old men in Chatsworth fought over a woman in 1963, and one murdered the other. Stickups are all but unthinkable in the pines. Tavernkeepers and storekeepers say that the possibility almost never crosses their minds, and never did at all before the night in 1964 when a man with a silk stocking over his head and a gun in his hand walked into Hedger House, a bar isolated in the woods three miles north of Chatsworth. The man said that he wanted all the money in the cash register. By the accounts of those who were there, the men at the bar looked at the holdup man in surprise and disbelief. After a long moment in which nothing happened, except that one man is said to have continued his drinking, there was an explosion of gunfire from the back of the room and the holdup man fell to the floor and died.

Moonshining has been practiced in the pines for more years than there has been an Internal Revenue Service, but it is done only on a mild scale today. The trooper at Red Lion told me, "All they have to do is dig a hole in the ground four feet deep and set up a still in a swamp. I've only been on two still raids in my life, but that's how they set it up. We don't go looking for moonshiners, to tell you the truth." Any fruit or grain will make whiskey, and the pineys use blueberries, apples, corn, or peaches. Sometimes outsiders come in—from places like Perth Amboy, Jersey City, Newark, or New York—and set up big-syndicate stills at dead ends of the sand roads. Such stills are highly efficient alcohol plants, which cost about fifty thousand dollars. They last a short time, usually, while Cadillacs move in and out of the pines carrying hoods who think they are alone in the remotest place they have ever seen. But all the time they are being watched by the pineys, who tell the police. Syndicate moonshiners could spoil the woods for small-scale, native moonshiners, and the moonshiners of the Pine Barrens have always made extraordinary efforts to keep their forest, for their purposes, free and clear. The age of blimps is over now, but not long ago blimps in great numbers were based at Lakehurst Naval Air Station, on the northeastern border of the central pinelands, and it was common for the big airships to return to Lakehurst with holes in their envelopes. As the blimps hung over the woods, moonshiners frequently shot at them, in the mistaken belief that the sailors in them were sweeping the woods with binoculars in search of stills.

I once asked David Harrison, the chief fire warden of the Pine Barrens area, how many moonshiners are in the pines today.

"We don't know," he said. "We leave them alone. They leave us alone. Look at it this way: If we go in there and report them and they get arrested, they might spend six months in jail; then when they come out—if they wanted to get even—they could burn down half of New Jersey."

When crime occurs in the Pine Barrens, it is usually the work of outsiders, for whom the woods hold sinister attractions simply because they are so vast. From a gangland point of view, it makes better sense to put a body in the Pine Barrens than in the Hudson River. Another state trooper said to me, "Anybody who wanted to commit a murder—all he'd have to do is ride back there with a shovel. They'd never find that body. I always did figure there's a lot of bodies in there. You get in those woods and you can get lost. You could kill a person very easily and throw the body in there, and within three or four weeks the buzzards would have taken care of everything except the bones, and they would be scattered. The sand roads attract suicides. They use shotguns, or hoses from their exhaust pipes. In there, since 1900, there have been gangland killings, lovers'-lane killings, feud murders, and bootleggers' shoot-outs. Three years ago, a body in city clothes was found near Hampton Furnace. The case is still under investigation."

At about three o'clock, one July afternoon, in the height of the blueberry harvest, Charlie Leek, the foreman of a blueberry field, came into the Chatsworth General Store to drink a bottle of soda and to cool off. Many people in Chatsworth have small blueberry fields of their own—two to twenty-five acres. A reasonable crop picked from fifteen acres will gross ten thousand dollars. Charlie works for one of the larger growers, looking after about a hundred acres of blueberries and cranberries. I had met him at Buzby's a week or so earlier. He is a big, good-looking man with big gestures, dark hair, a weathered face, flashing blue eyes, frequent smiles, and a solid but capacious middle. He is about fifty, and he has a manner that suggests that he is not afraid to work and not afraid not to work. That day, he wore a blue suit, dark-blue trousers, and construction worker's shoes. Sitting on the oak plank, he got into a discussion with an old man about the bread their mothers used to make. Despite the considerable difference in the two men's ages, their mothers, Charlie told me, were sisters. "This is Horace Adams, my cousin," he said. "Everybody's a relation in this burg. Yes, Horace's mother and mine used to make their own yeast, too—out of potato water and hops. Modern women aren't up to that."

"They give you cold beans," Horace Adams said. "How is the picking going, Charlie?"

"I got so disgusted I just walked away for a while," Charlie said. "I don't know where they're getting the booze, but some of them got a bucket of water out there and I bet that water is ninety proof."

Blueberry pickers in the Pine Barrens are almost all brought in from outside, but they are not migrant workers. They come mainly from Philadelphia, in privately owned school buses that bear the words "Farm Labor Transport." For the most part, the buses are driven by the men who own them, and the drivers, like their passengers, come from the city. The drivers are mainly Negroes, and so are the passengers. The drivers read newspapers and magazines all day and get three cents a pint on the berries their passengers pick. It is up to the drivers to find the pickers, and they start cruising Philadelphia streets before dawn, offering a day's work to anyone they can find, sometimes picking up men who are so drunk that they have no idea what they are getting into and who sober up in the blazing sun of the Pine Barrens wondering how they got there. Busloads vary every day. About a third of the people are steady sober pickers who make daily trips in the same bus. There are always some who do almost no work and are simply taking advantage of a chance to have a day in the country. There is usually a high percentage of schoolchildren, some of whom appear to be too young to have working papers, but at least they seem to enjoy themselves and to be there by choice. Women in their eighties ride the farm-labor transports, too. So, occasionally, do prostitutes, who go with their customers out of the blueberry clearings into the woods. Some pickers spend more in this manner than they earn during the rest of the day. Some become so drunk in the fields that they fall down in the hot sand between the blueberry bushes and pass out. "We got everything from hoochy-coochy girls on up today," Charlie told me. Pickers are paid seven cents a pint. Picking begins when the dew dries on the bushes—and is not done on rainy days—because the blue of a blueberry is a protective wax, and it comes off on the hands if the berries are wet. Some of the wax comes off anyway, and pickers' hands are always blue. A real star can earn eighteen dollars in a day, but most pickers make about ten dollars, and those who do not pick steadily make less than that. Bus drivers clear from twenty-five to fifty dollars a day. Sometimes pickers of any sort are so scarce that growers have to compete for the favor of the drivers, and on days like that the drivers have been paid as much as ninety dollars. When the pickers get into the buses and start the ride back to Philadelphia, the drivers sell them wine. On arrival in the city, some people are drunk and have spent their day's pay in the buses. (This sorry scene is not repeated during the cranberry harvest in the fall, when the bogs are flooded an inch or so over the vines, and the cranberries, which float, are batted free by motorized water rakes until they form a great scarlet berry boom—hundreds of thousands of cranberries bobbing and drifting with the wind or on a slow drainage current to a corner of the bog, where they are hauled in.)

The cultivated blueberry was developed in the Pine Barrens. More cultivated blueberries are grown there than are grown in Michigan, the No. 2 blueberry state. In 1911, Miss Elizabeth White, one of four daughters of a cranberry grower who lived about ten miles north of Chatsworth, read a publication of the United States Department of Agriculture in which a Dr. Frederick Coville described the possibilities of crossing various wild blueberries and producing superior offspring. Miss White invited Dr. Coville to use Whitesbog, her family's property, for his experiments. She gave small boards with various-sized holes in them to all pineys who were interested, and said that she would pay for blueberry bushes at a rate scaled to the size of the largest hole that the berries would not go through. Of the first hundred and twenty bushes, she and Coville threw away a hundred and eighteen. From the remaining two, they eventually made thirty-five thousand hybrid cuttings. Of the resulting bushes, they threw away all but four, from which modern cultivated blueberries, in their numerous varieties, were developed. Some of the varieties were given the names of pineys who had collected for Miss White—Grover, Rubel, Sam, Stanley, Harding, Adams, Dunfee. Miss White was in her thirties when the experiments began, and the first commercial shipments were made in 1916. In 1952, she invited landscape architects from the state highway department to Whitesbog and showed them through her blueberry fields. Miss White was over six feet tall, she carried a cane and wore a Whistler's Mother dress that was as neat as a pin. Her ankles were black from the dirt of the fields, and her hands were midnight-blue from the wax of the berries. In her home, she served each of her visitors a blueberry that was the size of a baseball, as they recall it, heaped over with sugar and resting in a pool of cream. Then she asked them to consider planting blueberry bushes along the Garden

JOHN McPHEE

State Parkway. Miss White died a few months after that. Blueberry bushes were planted later in profusion on the margins of the parkway where it runs along the edge of the Pine Barrens.

The Rubel blueberry was named for Charlie Leek's uncle Rube Leek. The Stanley was named for Charlie's older brother. Both varieties are grown in the blueberry patch where Charlie is foreman. He told me this in his pick-up truck on the way out there from Buzby's store. He had asked me if I would like to have a look at a packing house. On the way, we went past Charlie's home, in Leektown—a settlement of six houses, five of which are occupied by people named Leek. Charlie's place is low, miscellaneously built, dark, and tarpapered. There are many fragments of machinery and several defunct vehicles in the yard. "My son Jim lives in that white house across the road from me, where I was born," he said. Looking closely, I saw traces of the white paint that had apparently covered it when Charlie was a boy.

"What did your father do?" I asked him.

"Worked in the wildwoods," he said. "Sphagnum. Wild huckleberries. Cranberries." He said that he himself had tried working outside the pines once but that he couldn't stand it and had finally come back. While he was employed at an aluminum plant on the Delaware River, he used to drink a fifth of whiskey a day, on the job. "Working with hot metal, you sweat it out," he said. "But if you drink, you abuse your family. You'll abuse your best friend, if you don't look out. I haven't had a drink since I quit that place, in 1941. It's not hard for a man to make his living here in the pines, if he ever lived here. You got wealthy men here. No one bothers you. If you don't feel good, you don't have to work. If you want to get some food, you just take your gun and go out and get it—in season. I don't outlaw. I used to. My son does a little outlawing. He has a car with a sun roof, and he and a friend hunt with it. They go through the woods and they see a deer and they stand up through the sun roof and shoot. You can do what you want to do down here. Most jobs, you have somebody breathing down your neck when you're working. Most of your natives around here aren't used to that, I can tell you that."

We had come to a clearing where thousands of blueberry bushes grow. In the center of it was the packing house—a small, low building with open and screenless windows on all sides. In front of it was a school bus marked "Farm Labor Transport." The driver stood beside his bus. He was a tall and amiable-looking man, with bare feet. He wore green trousers and a T-shirt. The end of the working day had come. Pickers were swarming around a pump—old women, middle-aged men, a young girl. A line was waiting to use an outhouse near the pump. Inside the packing house, berries half an inch thick were rolling up a portable conveyor belt and, eventually, into pint boxes. Charlie's sister was packing the boxes. Charlie's daughter-in-law was putting cellophane over them. And Charlie's son Jim was supervising the operation. Charlie picked up a pint box in which berries were mounded high, and he told me with disgust that some supermarket chains knock off these mounds of extra berries and put them in new boxes, getting three or four extra pints per twelve-box tray. At one window, pickers were turning in tickets of various colors, and they were given cash in return. One picker, who appeared to be at least in his sixties, tapped Charlie on the arm and showed him a thick packet of tickets held together with a rubber band. "I found these," the man said. "They must have fallen out of your son's pocket." He gave the packet to Charlie, who thanked him and counted the tickets.

Charlie said, "These tickets are worth seventy-five dollars."

After loading for the return trip to Philadelphia, many buses stop in Chatsworth, so that the pickers can buy food and soft drinks at the general store. At 6 P.M. that day, they stood four and five deep all along the Buzbys' counters. One after another, they bought Coca-Cola in cold quart bottles and cookies in family-size boxes. One woman, short and middle-aged, wore a gray flannel skirt over a pair of blue-gray cotton slacks. One old man, who had swollen ankles, wore no socks, and parts of his shoes had been cut away to relieve his toes. He bought a quart of orange soda and a bag of potato chips. Half of the crowd seemed to be teen-aged. Noise was high. When the pickers had gone to their buses, Mrs. Buzby said to me, "A couple of the drivers came in here earlier to buy soda water. They use it to cut the wine."

For Discussion and Further Application

1. What type of writing is McPhee engaging in here? Explain why you think it is or is not effective.
2. There are three major sections to this article. Summarize the main idea in each section.
3. Describe a grocery store where you shop. Imitate McPhee's description of the Chatsworth General Store.
4. From the examples of McPhee quotes, analyze the "pineys' " dialect. What are some of its distinctive characteristics?
5. Try writing a few lines of dialogue in the manner of people among whom you grew up.

JOHN McPHEE

GAY TALESE

new york

Gay Talese wrote "New York" for *Esquire* magazine in 1960. Some of his descriptions are obviously dated— this is New York City fifteen years ago. Even now, however, his descriptions capture a certain timeless sense of the city that still dominates our impressions, whether we've actually been there or not. As you read, try to determine what makes Talese's writing so effective.

New York is a city of things unnoticed. It is a city with cats sleeping under parked cars, two stone armadillos crawling up St. Patrick's Cathedral, and thousands of ants creeping on top of the Empire State Building. The ants probably were carried up there by wind or birds, but nobody is sure; nobody in New York knows any more about the ants than they do about the panhandler who takes taxis to the Bowery; or the dapper man who picks trash out of Sixth Avenue trash cans; or the medium in the West Seventies who claims, "I am clairvoyant, clairaudient and clairsensuous."

New York is a city for eccentrics and a center for odd bits of information. New Yorkers blink twenty-eight times a minute, but forty when tense. Most popcorn chewers at Yankee Stadium stop chewing momentarily just before the pitch. Gumchewers on Macy's escalators stop chewing momentarily just before they get off—to concentrate on the last step. Coins, paper clips, ball-point pens, and little girls' pocketbooks are found by workmen when they clean the sea lion's pool at the Bronx Zoo.

A Park Avenue doorman has parts of three bullets in his head—there since World War I. Several young gypsy daughters, influenced by television and literacy, are running away from home because they don't want to grow up and become fortune-tellers. Each month a hundred pounds of hair is delivered to Louis Feder on 545 Fifth Avenue, where blond hairpieces are made from German women's hair; brunette hairpieces from Italian women's hair; but no hairpieces from American women's hair which, says Mr. Feder, is weak from too frequent rinses and permanents.

Some of New York's best informed men are elevator operators, who rarely talk, but always listen—like doormen. Sardi's doormen listen to the comments made by Broadway's first-nighters walking by after the last act. They listen closely. They listen carefully. Within ten minutes they can tell you which shows will flop and which will be hits.

On Broadway each evening a big, dark, 1948 Rolls-Royce pulls into

Forty-sixth street—and out hop two little ladies armed with Bibles and signs reading, "The Damned Shall Perish." These ladies proceed to stand on the corner screaming at the multitudes of Broadway sinners, sometimes until three a.m., when their chauffeur in the Rolls picks them up and drives them back to Westchester.

By this time Fifth Avenue is deserted by all but a few strolling insomniacs, some cruising cabdrivers, and a group of sophisticated females who stand in store windows all night and day wearing cold, perfect smiles. Like sentries they line Fifth Avenue—these window mannequins who gaze onto the quiet street with tilted heads and pointed toes and long rubber fingers reaching for cigarettes that aren't there.

At five a.m. Manhattan is a town of tired trumpet players and homeward-bound bartenders. Pigeons control Park Avenue and strut unchallenged in the middle of the street. This is Manhattan's mellowest hour. Most *night* people are out of sight—but the *day* people have not yet appeared. Truck drivers and cabs are alert, yet they do not disturb the mood. They do not disturb the abandoned Rockefeller Center, or the motionless night watchmen in the Fulton Fish Market, or the gas-station attendant sleeping next to Sloppy Louie's with the radio on.

At five a.m. the Broadway regulars either have gone home or to all-night coffee shops where, under the glaring light, you see their whiskers and wear. And on Fifty-first Street a radio press car is parked at the curb with a photographer who has nothing to do. So he just sits there for a few nights, looks through the windshield, and soon becomes a keen observer of life after midnight.

"At one a.m.," he says, "Broadway is filled with wise guys and with kids coming out of the Astor Hotel in white dinner jackets—kids who drive to dances in their fathers' cars. You also see cleaning ladies going home, always wearing kerchiefs. By two a.m. some of the drinkers are getting out of hand, and this is the hour for bar fights. At three a.m. the last show is over in the nightclubs, and most of the tourists and out-of-town buyers are back in hotels. And small-time comedians are criticizing big-time comedians in Hanson's Drugstore. At four a.m., after the bars close, you see the drunks come out—and also the pimps and prostitutes who take advantage of drunks. At five a.m., though, it is mostly quiet. New York is an entirely different city at five a.m."

At six a.m. the early workers begin to push up from the subways. The traffic begins to move down Broadway like a river. And Mrs. Mary Woody jumps out of bed, dashes to her office and phones dozens of sleepy New Yorkers to say in a cheerful voice, rarely appreciated: "Good morning. Time to get up." For twenty years, as an operator of Western Union's Wake-Up Service, Mrs. Woody has gotten millions out of bed.

By seven a.m. a floridly robust little man, looking very Parisian in a blue beret and turtleneck sweater, moves in a hurried step along Park Avenue visiting his wealthy lady friends—making certain that each is given a brisk, before-breakfast rubdown. The uniformed doormen greet him warmly and call him either "Biz" or "Mac" because he is Biz Mackey, a ladies' masseur *extraordinaire*. He never reveals the names of his customers, but most of them are middle-aged and rich. He visits each of them in their apartments, and has special keys to their bedrooms; he is often the first man they see in the morning, and they lie in bed waiting for him.

The doormen that Biz passes each morning are generally an obliging, endlessly articulate group of sidewalk diplomats who list among their friends some of Manhattan's most powerful men, most beautiful women and snootiest poodles. More often than not, the doormen are big, slightly Gothic in design, and the possessors of eyes sharp enough to spot big tippers a block away in the year's thickest fog. Some East Side doormen are as proud as grandees, and the uniforms, heavily festooned, seem to come from the same tailor who outfitted Marshal Tito.

Shortly after seven-thirty each morning hundreds of people are lined along Forty-second Street waiting for the eight a.m. opening of the ten movie houses that stand almost shoulder-to-shoulder between Times Square and Eighth Avenue. Who are these people who go to the movies at eight a.m.? They are the city's insomniacs, night watchmen, and people who can't go home, do not want to go home, or have no home. They are derelicts, homosexuals, cops, hacks, truck drivers, cleaning ladies and restaurant men who have worked all night. They are also alcoholics who are waiting at eight a.m. to pay forty cents for a soft seat and to sleep in the dark, smoky theatre. And yet, aside from being smoky, each of Times Square's theatres has a special quality, or lack of quality, about it. At the Victory Theatre one finds horror films, while at the Times Square Theatre they feature only cowboy films. There are first-run films for forty cents at the Lyric, while at the Selwyn there are always second-run films for thirty cents. But if you go to the Apollo Theatre you will see, in addition to foreign films, people in the lobby talking with their hands. These are deaf-and-dumb movie fans who patronize the Apollo because they read the subtitles. The Apollo probably has the biggest deaf-and-dumb movie audience in the world.

New York is a city of 38,000 cabdrivers, 10,000 bus drivers, but only one chauffeur who has a chauffeur. The wealthy chauffeur can be seen driving up Fifth Avenue each morning, and his name is Roosevelt Zanders. He earns $100,000 a year, is a gentleman of impeccable taste and, although he owns a $23,000 Rolls-Royce, does not scorn his friends who own Bentleys. For $150 a day, Mr. Zanders will drive anyone anywhere in his big, silver Rolls. Diplomats patronize him, models pose next to him, and each day he receives cables from around the world urging that he be waiting at Idlewild, on the docks, or outside the Plaza Hotel. Sometimes at night, however, he is too tired to drive anymore. So Bob Clarke, his chauffeur, takes over and Mr. Zanders relaxes in the back.

New York is a town of 3000 bootblacks whose brushes and rhythmic rag-snaps can be heard up and down Manhattan from midmorning to midnight. They dodge cops, survive rainstorms, and thrive in the Empire State Building as well as on the Staten Island Ferry. They usually wear dirty shoes.

New York is a city of headless men who sit obscurely in subway booths all day and night selling tokens to people in a hurry. Each weekday more than 4,500,000 riders pass these money changers who seem to have neither heads, faces, nor personalities—only fingers. Except when giving directions, their vocabulary consists largely of three words: "How many, please?"

In New York there are 200 chestnut vendors, and they average $25 on a good day peddling soft, warm chestnuts. Like many vendors, the chestnut men do not own their own rigs—they borrow or rent them from pushcart makers such as David Amerman.

Mr. Amerman, with offices opposite a defunct public bathhouse on the Lower East Side, is New York's master builder of pushcarts. His father and grandfather before him were pushcart makers, and the family has long been a household word among the city's most discriminating junkmen, fruit vendors and hot-dog peddlers.

In New York there are 500 mediums, ranging from semi-trance to trance to deep-trance types. Most of them live in New York's West Seventies and Eighties, and on Sundays some of these blocks are communicating with the dead, vibrating to trumpets, and solving all problems.

The Manhattan Telephone Directory has 776,300 names, of which 3316 are Smith, 2835 are Brown, 2444 are Williams, 2070 are Cohen—and one is Mike Krasilovsky. Anyone who doubts this last fact has only to look at the top of page 876 where, in large black letters, is this sign: "There is only one Mike Krasilovsky. Sterling 3-1990."

In New York the Fifth Avenue Lingerie shop is on Madison Avenue; The Madison Pet Shop is on Lexington Avenue; the Park Avenue Florist is on Madison Avenue, and the Lexington Hand Laundry is on Third Avenue. New York is the home of 120 pawnbrokers and it is where Bishop Sheen's brother, Dr. Sheen, shares an office with one Dr. Bishop.

New York is a town of thirty tattooists where interest in mankind is skin-deep, but whose impressions usually last a lifetime. Each day the tattooists go pecking away over acres of anatomy. And in downtown Manhattan, Stanley Moskowitz, a scion of a distinguished family of Bowery skin-peckers, does a grand business.

When it rains in Manhattan, automobile traffic is slow, dates are broken and, in hotel lobbies, people slump behind newspapers or walk aimlessly about with no place to sit, nobody to talk to, nothing to do. Taxis are harder to get; department stores do between fifteen and twenty-five percent less business, and the monkeys in the Bronx Zoo, having no audience, slouch grumpily in their cages looking more bored than the lobby-loungers.

While some New Yorkers become morose with rain, others prefer it, like to walk in it, and say that on rainy days the city's buildings seem somehow cleaner—washed in an opalescence, like a Monet painting. There are fewer suicides in New York when it rains. But when the sun is shining, and New Yorkers seem happy, the depressed person sinks deeper into depression, and Bellevue Hospital gets more suicide calls.

New York is a town of 8485 telephone operators, 1364 Western Union messenger boys, and 112 newspaper copyboys. An average baseball crowd at Yankee Stadium uses over ten gallons of liquid soap per game—an unofficial high mark for cleanliness in the major leagues; the stadium also has the league's top number of ushers (360), sweepers (72), and men's rooms (34).

New York is a town in which the brotherhood of Russian Bath Rubbers, the only union advocating sweatshops, appears to be heading for its last rubdown. The union has been going in New York City for years, but now most of the rubbers are pushing seventy and are deaf—from all the water and the hot temperatures.

Each afternoon in New York a rather seedy saxophone player, his cheeks blown out like a spinnaker, stands on the sidewalk playing *Danny Boy* in such a sad, sensitive way that he soon has half the neighborhood peeking out of windows tossing nickels, dimes and quarters at his feet. Some of the coins roll under parked cars, but most of them are caught in his outstretched hand. The saxophone player is a street musician named Joe Gabler; for the past thirty years he has serenaded every block in New York and has sometimes been tossed as much as $10 a day in coins. He is also hit with buckets of water, empty beer cans and eggs, and chased by wild dogs. He is believed to be the last of New York's ancient street musicians.

New York is a town of nineteen midget wrestlers. They all can squeeze into the Hotel Holland's elevator, six can sleep in one bed, eight can be comfortably transported to Madison Square Garden in the chauffeur-driven Cadillac reserved for the midget wrestlers.

In New York from dawn to dusk to dawn, day after day, you can hear the steady rumble of tires against the concrete span of the George Washington Bridge. The bridge is never completely still. It trembles with traffic. It moves in the wind. Its great veins of steel swell when hot and contract when cold; its span often is ten feet closer to the Hudson River in summer than in winter. It is an almost restless structure of graceful beauty which, like an irresistible seductress, withholds secrets from the romantics who gaze upon it, the escapists who jump off it, the chubby girl who lumbers across its 3500-foot span trying to reduce, and the 100,000 motorists who each day cross it, smash into it, shortchange it, get jammed up on it.

When street traffic dwindles and most people are sleeping in New York, some neighborhoods begin to crawl with cats. They move quickly through the shadows of buildings; night watchmen, policemen, garbage collectors and other nocturnal wanderers see them—but never for long.

There are 200,000 stray cats in New York. A majority of them hang around the fish market, or in Greenwich Village, and in the East and West Side neighborhoods where garbage cans abound. No part of the city is without its strays, however, and all-night garage attendants in such busy neighborhoods as Fifty-fourth Street have counted as many as twenty of them around the Ziegfeld Theatre early in the morning. Troops of cats patrol the waterfront piers at night searching for rats. Subway trackwalkers have discovered cats living in the darkness. They seem never to get hit by trains, though some are occasionally liquidated by the third rail. About twenty-five cats live seventy-five feet below the west end of Grand Central Terminal, are fed by the underground workers, and never wander up into the daylight.

New York is a city in which large, cliff-dwelling hawks cling to skyscrapers and occasionally zoom to snatch a pigeon over Central Park, or Wall Street, or the Hudson River. Bird watchers have seen these peregrine falcons circling lazily over the city. They have seen them perched atop tall buildings, even around Times Square. About twelve of these hawks patrol the city, sometimes with a wingspan of thirty-five inches. They have buzzed women on the roof of the St. Regis Hotel, have attacked repairmen on smokestacks, and, in August, 1947, two hawks jumped women residents in the recreation yard of the Home of the New York Guild for the Jewish Blind. Maintenance men at the Riverside Church have seen hawks dining on pigeons in the bell tower. The hawks remain there for only a little while. And then they fly out to the river, leaving pigeons' heads for the Riverside maintenance men to clean up. When the hawks return, they fly in quietly—unnoticed, like the cats, the headless men, the ants, the ladies' masseur, the doorman with three bullets in his head, and most of the other offbeat wonders in this town without time.

For Discussion and Further Application

1. Talese tries to give an overall impression of the city by piling up many very specific details. What qualities do most of Talese's details have in common?
2. Describe Talese's organization. How does he hold all his specifics together?
3. What details date the essay? Which ones do you think are still true today?
4. Talese uses facts to create metaphors, then smashes the metaphors back to facts. Analyze his description of the George Washington Bridge.
5. Imitate Talese's style. Describe the life of a street you know well.

ANDREW MALCOLM

chemists in timber revolution on verge of test-tube trees

The following article, a feature article researching experiments and recent developments in the timber revolution, is an example of effective newspaper writing. Notice the difference in paragraphing. The article appears as it was originally written—in narrow, standard-sized newspaper columns. One or at most several sentences form a paragraph because longer units would be too massive, defeating one practical reason for paragraphing, ease of eye movement. As it is, the indenting breaks up the long columns, allowing the eye to catch the beginning of each new main idea or support. Notice that the same principles of effective organization still apply, however. The first five paragraphs could really be combined into one longer expository paragraph. The lead paragraph sets up the topic sentence: ". . . the nation's timberlands are today undergoing a major technological and scientific revolution. . . ." The following four paragraphs provide specific, supporting evidence. As you read, notice the way the rest of the article is organized.

FORT BRAGG, Calif.—Quietly like a tree growing, the nation's timberlands are today undergoing a major technological and scientific revolution that is radically changing the face of the country's vast woodlands.

Chemists in clean white coats are on the verge of creating test-tube trees, living growths with roots and needles created not naturally from seeds but chemically from the cells of another tree.

Other scientists in hard hats scour the woods for seeds and branch cuttings to crossbreed into "super trees," magnificent, fast-growing specimens bred especially for commercial attributes like the hybrid corns that revolutionized farming 20 years ago.

Sweating sawmill operators study computerized television monitors that automatically diagram the best cut for radically thinner sawblades to maximize the use of each log.

Elsewhere, helmeted helicopter pilots scatter tons of tree seeds artificially colored to fool hungry birds. Paul Bunyanesque machines roam the forests, snipping entire trees off at ground level and passing them through pulpers that consume 40-foot logs in nine seconds. Entire forests are fertilized and thinned like common carrot patches to produce harvestable growth decades sooner than nature can.

Significance for Consumers

These developments observed during several recent trips to timber camps, sawmills, plywood factories and forests in these heavily wooded areas of the Northwest, carry tremendous future significance for the nation's consumers, their woodlands, their housing, the economy, balance of payments and land use at a time of growing concern over the world's ability to meet future food demands.

The United States with its vastness and varied climate zones has a unique global position. For this country is, as one expert put it, the Saudi Arabia of the timber world.

With 100 marketable tree species the United States has enough forest land to cover every inch of Belgium, Great Britain, Denmark, Portugal, the Netherlands, Italy, France, Spain, Japan, Jordan and both Germanys with enough trees left over to blanket all of Algeria, Austria, Israel and an extra Netherlands.

The Forest Service, which presides over about one-quarter of the country's forest land, estimates that when Columbus landed, there were about one billion total acres of forests here. After almost 500 years of building, paving, burning, exporting and wasting by the nation's approximately two million timberland owners, about

75 per cent of that land is still tree-covered and about one-half is still available for commercial use. The rest has been set aside or cleared for homes or crops.

Of course, there are those who believe too much has been cleared already or cleared and replanted improperly. And there are those who see technology as only a more efficient threat to the pristine wilderness of the forests.

Such concerns are part of a fundamental split over what forest use provides the most social value—as a living wilderness museum, as a playground for city folk, or as a natural wood-producing factory turning out trees that make homes, toys, paper, exports, jobs and profits.

"We have an emotional problem here," said Jere Melo, a forestry foreman. "People like trees. And we're cutting them down. But we're also planting them. We're not running a big park. But we are using—and replenishing—a natural resource. Which is more than the oil and coal people can say."

Renewal has not always been a major concern for the disparate timber interests whose 83,-000 companies are the descendants of businessmen and lumberjacks who gave the English language such expressions as "skidroad" and "cut and run."

But in recent years environmental threats and lawsuits have combined with rising lumber and land prices and improved long-range planning to focus greatly increased attention on renewal of the forests and the most efficient use of existing timber.

Until recent years this forest renewal was left largely to the trees themselves. "Nature," said W. D. Hagenstein of the Industrial Forestry Association,

"does a first class job of growing trees. But she's awfully wasteful and time consuming. And with an earth full of people we have to do better."

And so Mr. Hagenstein, a former lumberjack, and other pioneers began vast tree farms and, more recently, the movement for "genetically improved" trees.

'Test-Tube' Trees Studied

The most dramatic step in that direction is the current research into "test-tube trees." Several projects are under way. Recently, the Oregon Graduate Center, a small independent research institute in Beaverton, announced a $1.25-million grant from the Weyerhauser Company.

This research, well along already, will attempt to grow superior Douglas fir trees from single cells without the time-consuming and uncertain natural sequence involving seeds and pollination.

The procedure operates on the theory that every living cell has locked within itself the information to regenerate the larger organism of which it is part.

The research objective is to provide an environment—a combination of light, heat, nutrition, humidity and other factors—that will cause the cell's hormones and other messenger molecules to trigger regeneration not only of similar cells but of dissimilar cells to form wood, bark, leaves, roots and so forth.

"Each cell," said Dr. Doyle Daves, the center's chemistry department chairman, "has the potential to become whatever you want it to be by manipulating the environment. All the techniques we're using with conifers have been accomplished in other species, carrots, tobacco, soybeans, barley.

"In terms of domestication for timber," he continued, "trees are at the stage that corn, wheat or rice were 10,000 years ago. It doesn't take much imagination to picture the dramatic changes in production and physical appearance of trees in the years to come."

When a superior tree variety is found, scientists would normally have to wait years before the plant matured and produced seeds to get sufficient numbers of offspring for planting. The seeds, formed after pollination by another, possibly inferior, tree, would not all contain the same desirable traits.

By culturing individual cells, however, virtually any number of offspring genetically identical to the parent can be obtained from an immature plant, shortening a process of years to days.

The cone-bearing trees, primarily Douglas fir (named for David Douglas, a British botanist), were selected for research for their strength and workability as lumber.

"This single cell work is revolutionary research," said Ira Keller, the center's president, "they did it to develop the high yield strains of rice. They're doing it now with sugar cane cells."

Mass Tree Production

If successful, this technology will permit eventual mass production of strong, fast-growing trees highly resistent to certain diseases and insects. When grown under progressive forestry techniques including thinning and fertilizing, it is estimated that these new trees will produce more and better wood in perhaps 20 per cent less time. That means an extra tree harvest every five forest generations.

The same result is the goal of numerous new tree breeding

ANDREW MALCOLM

programs. At Mosby Creek, Ore., for example, Philip Hahn, a research forester for the Georgia-Pacific Corporation, grafts the cone-producing tops of 50-year-old, well-formed Douglas firs onto the vibrant bottoms of two-year-old trees. The history, characteristics and growth rate of each tree is recorded in a kind of computerized yearbook for each nursery's graduating class.

The cones, carefully pollinated from trees with other desirable qualities, hopefully carry in their fertile seeds the best genetic traits of its parents' good girth, strong height, fast growth and adaptability to various altitudes, weather conditions and soils.

These seeds are meticulously planted by machines in sterile granite chips (to prevent fungi and rot) in holes drilled in styrofoam blocks.

The blocks sit on tables in vast greenhouses where fans suck in fresh air.

Within days millions of tiny green shoots, most with only a dozen needles on them, spring from the holes. In 40 years each fir can be harvested with enough wood fibers to make half a house.

The trees spend one to three years in the greenhouse, gradually being exposed to the elements to toughen them for their lives in distant woods.

There, they are planted by a special gun that digs a hole, drops in the treelet and tamps down the dirt. Here at Fort Bragg in recent days workers planted a quarter million redwoods, which will make handsome picnic tables or panel some den around the year 2026.

Some of the more potent and prolific "super trees," such as No. 62, nicknamed "Super Stud," have produced offspring that can adapt up to 1,000 miles from their original home and grow to be 20 inches tall in one year. This compares to five inches in some two-year-old "natural trees."

One latent danger is that these new hybrid trees might contain some unknown form of natural timebomb, a genetic weakness that could in, say, 20 years see vast forests fall victim to diseases or insects yet unknown with serious economic repercussions nationwide.

A similar catastrophe struck certain strains of hybrid corns in 1971. The exotic fungus cut harvests so much the bushel price of corn shot from $1.05 to $1.40 in weeks. A blight-resistant strain of corn was developed within months, but such steps for trees would take years.

Attention is also being focused on maximizing use of existing trees. Research, for instance, is under way on biological controls, helpful insects or bacteria used to control damaging ones, which according to some estimates destroy many more trees than fire.

Sawmills, spurred by rising prices, can now turn out usable lumber from logs up to 80 per cent rotten.

For Discussion and Further Application

1. The author uses specifics to dramatize his points. Notice, for example, how he describes the extent of his country's tree-producing capacity. How much forest land does the United States have?
2. Lumberjacks, like other specialized groups, have also contributed slang to the mainstream dialects. What kind of an attitude toward natural resources does the author imply dominated lumberjacks' vocabulary?
3. Write a working outline of the entire article.
4. Edit the article into longer paragraphs that you might use if you were writing a paper on the timber revolution.
5. Discuss the implications of the author's statement, ". . . every living cell has locked within itself the information to regenerate the larger organism of which it is part." How could this be called a "principle of organization"?
6. Editing considerations often determine format and length of articles. A page editor, for example, might have to fit together up to nine or ten articles under deadline pressure. Ends sometimes get chopped instead of being more carefully rewritten. Malcolm's article ends rather abruptly, perhaps a victim of such limited space and time requirements when it went to print. Provide a conclusion.
7. Reduce the article to a paragraph no longer than 200 words. Be sure you include all the essential points of the article and enough specifics to be convincing.

CHEMISTS IN TIMBER REVOLUTION ON VERGE OF TEST-TUBE TREES

LEWIS THOMAS

on societies
as organisms

The following article is excerpted from the first chapter of
Lewis Thomas' unique collection of scientific essays,
The Lives of a Cell. By shifting our perspectives, Thomas is able to make some startling
observations about human as well as animal behavior. He uses some specialized
vocabulary, but with the help of a good dictionary and some reasoning in context and
patient analysis, you should be able to understand him clearly. As you are reading,
you might want to consider the implications of viewing society as an organism.

Viewed from a suitable height, the aggregating
clusters of medical scientists in the bright sun-
light of the boardwalk at Atlantic City, swarmed there from everywhere for
the annual meetings, have the look of assemblages of social insects. There
is the same vibrating, ionic movement, interrupted by the darting back and
forth of jerky individuals to touch antennae and exchange small bits of
information; periodically, the mass casts out, like a trout-line, a long single
file unerringly toward Childs's. If the boards were not fastened down, it
would not be a surprise to see them put together a nest of sorts.

It is permissible to say this sort of thing about humans. They do
resemble, in their most compulsively social behavior, ants at a distance. It
is, however, quite bad form in biological circles to put it the other way
round, to imply that the operation of insect societies has any relation at all
to human affairs. The writers of books on insect behavior generally take
pains, in their prefaces, to caution that insects are like creatures from
another planet, that their behavior is absolutely foreign, totally inhuman,
unearthly, almost unbiological. They are more like perfectly tooled but
crazy little machines, and we violate science when we try to read human
meanings in their arrangements.

It is hard for a bystander not to do so. Ants are so much like human
beings as to be an embarrassment. They farm fungi, raise aphids as livestock, launch armies into wars, use chemical sprays to alarm and confuse
enemies, capture slaves. The families of weaver ants engage in child labor,
holding their larvae like shuttles to spin out the thread that sews the leaves
together for their fungus gardens. They exchange information ceaselessly.
They do everything but watch television.

What makes us most uncomfortable is that they, and the bees and termites and social wasps, seem to live two kinds of lives: they are individuals, going about the day's business without much evidence of thought for tomorrow, and they are at the same time component parts, cellular elements, in the huge, writhing, ruminating organism of the Hill, the nest, the hive. It is because of this aspect, I think, that we most wish for them to be something foreign. We do not like the notion that there can be collective societies with the capacity to behave like organisms. If such things exist, they can have nothing to do with us.

Still, there it is. A solitary ant, afield, cannot be considered to have much of anything on his mind; indeed, with only a few neurons strung together by fibers, he can't be imagined to have a mind at all, much less a thought. He is more like a ganglion on legs. Four ants together, or ten, encircling a dead moth on a path, begin to look more like an idea. They fumble and shove, gradually moving the food toward the Hill, but as though by blind chance. It is only when you watch the dense mass of thousands of ants, crowded together around the Hill, blackening the ground, that you begin to see the whole beast, and now you observe it thinking, planning, calculating. It is an intelligence, a kind of live computer, with crawling bits for its wits.

At a stage in the construction, twigs of a certain size are needed, and all the members forage obsessively for twigs of just this size. Later, when outer walls are to be finished, thatched, the size must change, and as though given new orders by telephone, all the workers shift the search to the new twigs. If you disturb the arrangement of a part of the Hill, hundreds of ants will set it vibrating, shifting, until it is put right again. Distant sources of food are somehow sensed, and long lines, like tentacles, reach out over the ground, up over walls, behind boulders, to fetch it in.

Termites are even more extraordinary in the way they seem to accumulate intelligence as they gather together. Two or three termites in a chamber will begin to pick up pellets and move them from place to place, but nothing comes of it; nothing is built. As more join in, they seem to reach a critical mass, a quorum, and the thinking begins. They place pellets atop pellets, then throw up columns and beautiful, curving, symmetrical arches, and the crystalline architecture of vaulted chambers is created. It is not known how they communicate with each other, how the chains of termites building one column know when to turn toward the crew on the adjacent column, or how, when the time comes, they manage the flawless joining of the arches. The stimuli that set them off at the outset, building collectively instead of shifting things about, may be pheromones released when they reach committee size. They react as if alarmed. They become agitated, excited, and then they begin working, like artists.

Bees live lives of organisms, tissues, cells, organelles, all at the same time. The single bee, out of the hive retrieving sugar (instructed by the dancer: "south-southeast for seven hundred meters, clover—mind you make corrections for the sundrift") is still as much a part of the hive as if attached by a filament. Building the hive, the workers have the look of embryonic cells organizing a developing tissue; from a distance they are like the viruses inside a cell, running off row after row of symmetrical polygons as though laying down crystals. When the time for swarming comes, and the old queen prepares to leave with her part of the population, it is as though the hive were involved in mitosis. There is an agitated moving of bees back and forth, like granules in cell sap. They distribute themselves in almost precisely equal parts, half to the departing queen, half to the new one. Thus, like an egg, the great, hairy, black and golden creature splits in two, each with an equal share of the family genome.

The phenomenon of separate animals joining up to form an organism is not unique in insects. Slime-mold cells do it all the time, of course, in each life cycle. At first they are single amebocytes swimming around, eating bacteria, aloof from each other, untouching, voting straight Republican. Then, a bell sounds, and acrasin is released by special cells toward which the others converge in stellate ranks, touch, fuse together, and construct the slug, solid as a trout. A splendid stalk is raised, with a fruiting body on top, and out of this comes the next generation of amebocytes, ready to swim across the same moist ground, solitary and ambitious.

Herring and other fish in schools are at times so closely integrated, their actions so coordinated, that they seem to be functionally a great multi-fish organism. Flocking birds, especially the seabirds nesting on the slopes of offshore islands in Newfoundland, are similarly attached, connected, synchronized.

Although we are by all odds the most social of all social animals—more interdependent, more attached to each other, more inseparable in our behavior than bees—we do not often feel our conjoined intelligence. Perhaps, however, we are linked in circuits for the storage, processing, and retrieval of information, since this appears to be the most basic and universal of all human enterprises. It may be our biological function to build a certain kind of Hill. We have access to all the information of the biosphere, arriving as elementary units in the stream of solar photons. When we have learned how these are rearranged against randomness, to make, say, springtails, quantum mechanics, and the last quartets, we may have a clearer notion how to proceed. The circuitry seems to be there, even if the current is not always on.

LEWIS THOMAS

1. What are the defining characteristics of an "organism"?
2. What does Thomas suggest might be the major function of a human social organism?
3. What does Thomas mean by the last sentence of the article, "The circuitry seems to be there, even if the current is not always on"?
4. What elements of good writing do you find in this article?
5. Discuss the article's organization. How do all the parts fit together to form a whole "organism"?
6. Describe a scene you might have witnessed where, seen from a distance, individuals form part of a mass that seems to have its own direction and purpose.

JESSICA MITFORD

the story of service

"The Story of Service" is a chapter from *The American Way of Death,* Jessica Mitford's controversial study of the American funeral "industry," published in 1963. This is a classic example of expository writing at its best. As you read, notice how the author organizes her arguments and piles up facts to support her conclusions. Notice, too, how she makes her very serious points in a very humorous way.

There was a time when the undertaker's tasks were clearcut and rather obvious, and when he billed his patrons accordingly. Typical late-nineteenth-century charges, in addition to the price of merchandise, are shown on bills of the period as: "Services at the house (placing corpse in the coffin) $1.25," "Preserving remains on ice, $10," "Getting Permit, $1.50." It was customary for the undertaker to add a few dollars to his bill for being "in attendance," which seems only fair and right. The cost of embalming was around $10 in 1880. An undertaker, writing in 1900, recommends these minimums for service charges: Washing and dressing, $5; embalming, $10; hearse, $8 to $10. As Habenstein and Lamers, the historians of the trade, have pointed out, "The undertaker had yet to conceive of the value of personal services offered professionally for a fee, legitimately claimed." Well, he has now so conceived with a vengeance.

When weaving in the story of service as it is rendered today, spokesmen for the funeral industry tend to become so carried away by their own enthusiasm, so positively lyrical and copious in their declarations, that the outsider may have a little trouble understanding it all. There are indeed contradictions. Preferred Funeral Directors International has prepared a mimeographed talk designed to inform people about service: "The American public receive the services of employees and proprietor alike, nine and one half days of labor for every funeral handled, they receive the use of automobiles and hearses, a building including a chapel and other rooms which require building maintenance, insurance, taxes and licenses, and depreciation, as well as heat in the winter, cooling in the summer and light and water." The writer goes on to say that while the process of embalming takes only about three hours, yet, "it would be necessary for one man to work two forty-hour weeks to complete a funeral service. This is coupled with an additional forty hours service required by members of other local allied professions, including the work of the cemeteries, newspapers, and of course, the most important of all, the service of your clergyman. These some 120 hours of labor are the basic value on which the cost of funeral rests."

Our informant has lumped a lot of things together here. To start with "the most important of all, the service of your clergyman," the average religious funeral service lasts no more than 25 minutes. Furthermore, it is not, of course, paid for by the funeral director. The "work of the cemeteries" presumably means the opening and closing of a grave. This now mechanized operation, which takes 15 to 20 minutes, is likewise not billed as part of the funeral director's costs. The work of "newspapers"? This is a puzzler. Presumably reference is made here to the publication of an obituary notice on the vital statistics page. It is, incidentally, surprising to learn that newspaper work is considered an "allied profession."

Just how insurance, taxes, licenses and depreciation are figured in as part of the 120 man-hours of service is hard to tell. The writer does mention that his operation features "65 items of service." In general, the funeral salesman is inclined to chuck in everything he does under the heading of "service." For example, in a typical list of "services" he will include items like "securing statistical data" (in other words, completing the death certificate and finding out how much insurance was left by the deceased), "the arrangements conference" (in which the sale of the funeral to the survivors is made), and the "keeping of records," by which he means his own bookkeeping work. Evidently there is some confusion here between items that properly belong in a cost-accounting system and items of *actual* service rendered in any given funeral. In all likelihood, idle time of employees is figured in and prorated as part of the "man-hours." The up-to-date funeral home operates on a 24-hour basis, and the mimeographed speech contains this heartening news:

The funeral service profession of the United States is proud of the fact that there is not a person within the continental limits of the United States who is more than two hours away from a licensed funeral director and embalmer in case of need. That's one that even the fire fighting apparatus of our country cannot match.

While the hit-or-miss rhetoric of the foregoing is fairly typical of the prose style of the funeral as a whole, and while the statement that 120 man-hours are devoted to a single man- (or woman-) funeral may be open to question, there really is a fantastic amount of service accorded the dead body and its survivors.

Having decreed what sort of funeral is right, proper and nice, and having gradually appropriated to himself all the functions connected with it, the funeral director has become responsible for a multitude of tasks beyond the obvious one of "placing corpse in the coffin" recorded in our nineteenth-century funeral bill. His self-imposed duties fall into two main categories: attention to the corpse itself, and the stage-managing of the funeral.

249

The drama begins to unfold with the arrival of the corpse at the mortuary.

Alas, poor Yorick! How surprised he would be to see how his counterpart of today is whisked off to a funeral parlor and is in short order sprayed, sliced, pierced, pickled, trussed, trimmed, creamed, waxed, painted, rouged and neatly dressed—transformed from a common corpse into a Beautiful Memory Picture. This process is known in the trade as embalming and restorative art, and is so universally employed in the United States and Canada that the funeral director does it routinely, without consulting corpse or kin. He regards as eccentric those few who are hardy enough to suggest that it might be dispensed with. Yet no law requires embalming, no religious doctrine commends it, nor is it dictated by considerations of health, sanitation, or even of personal daintiness. In no part of the world but in Northern America is it widely used. The purpose of embalming is to make the corpse presentable for viewing in a suitably costly container; and here too the funeral director routinely, without first consulting the family, prepares the body for public display.

Is all this legal? The processes to which a dead body may be subjected are after all to some extent circumscribed by law. In most states, for instance, the signature of next of kin must be obtained before an autopsy may be performed, before the deceased may be cremated, before the body may be turned over to a medical school for research purposes; or such provision must be made in the decedent's will. In the case of embalming, no such permission is required nor is it ever sought. A textbook, *The Principles and Practices of Embalming,* comments on this: "There is some question regarding the legality of much that is done within the preparation room." The author points out that it would be most unusual for a responsible member of a bereaved family to instruct the mortician, in so many words, to "embalm" the body of a deceased relative. The very term "embalming" is so seldom used that the mortician must rely upon custom in the matter. The author concludes that unless the family specifies otherwise, the act of entrusting the body to the care of a funeral establishment carries with it an implied permission to go ahead and embalm.

Embalming is indeed a most extraordinary procedure, and one must wonder at the docility of Americans who each year pay hundreds of millions of dollars for its perpetuation, blissfully ignorant of what it is all about, what is done, how it is done. Not one in ten thousand has any idea of what actually takes place. Books on the subject are extremely hard to come by. They are not to be found in most libraries or bookshops.

In an era when huge television audiences watch surgical operations in the comfort of their living rooms, when, thanks to the animated cartoon, the geography of the digestive system has become familiar territory even to the nursery school set, in a land where the satisfaction of curiosity about almost all matters is a national pastime, the secrecy surrounding embalming can, surely, hardly be attributed to the inherent gruesomeness of the subject.

JESSICA MITFORD

Custom in this regard has within this century suffered a complete reversal. In the early days of American embalming, when it was performed in the home of the deceased, it was almost mandatory for some relative to stay by the embalmer's side and witness the procedure. Today, family members who might wish to be in attendance would certainly be dissuaded by the funeral director. All others, except apprentices, are excluded by law from the preparation room.

A close look at what does actually take place may explain in large measure the undertaker's intractable reticence concerning a procedure that has become his major *raison d'être*. Is it possible he fears that public information about embalming might lead patrons to wonder if they really want this service? If the funeral men are loath to discuss the subject outside the trade, the reader may, understandably, be equally loath to go on reading at this point. For those who have the stomach for it, let us part the formaldehyde curtain. . . .

The body is first laid out in the undertaker's morgue—or rather, Mr. Jones is reposing in the preparation room—to be readied to bid the world farewell.

The preparation room in any of the better funeral establishments has the tiled and sterile look of a surgery, and indeed the embalmer-restorative artist who does his chores there is beginning to adopt the term "dermasurgeon" (appropriately corrupted by some mortician-writers as "demisurgeon") to describe his calling. His equipment, consisting of scalpels, scissors, augers, forceps, clamps, needles, pumps, tubes, bowls and basins, is crudely imitative of the surgeon's, as is the technique, acquired in a nine- or twelve-month post-high-school course in an embalming school. He is supplied by an advanced chemical industry with a bewildering array of fluids, sprays, pastes, oils, powders, creams, to fix or soften tissue, shrink or distend it as needed, dry it here, restore the moisture there. There are cosmetics, waxes and paints to fill and cover features, even plaster of Paris to replace entire limbs. There are ingenious aids to prop and stabilize the cadaver: a Vari-Pose Head Rest, the Edwards Arm and Hand Positioner, the Repose Block (to support the shoulders during the embalming), and the Throop Foot Positioner, which resembles an old-fashioned stocks.

Mr. John H. Eckels, president of the Eckels College of Mortuary Science, thus describes the first part of the embalming procedure: "In the hands of a skilled practitioner, this work may be done in a comparatively short time and without mutilating the body other than by slight incision— so slight that it scarcely would cause serious inconvenience if made upon a living person. It is necessary to remove the blood, and doing this not only helps in the disinfecting, but removes the principal cause of disfigurements due to discoloration."

Another textbook discusses the all-important time element: "The earlier this is done, the better, for every hour that elapses between death and embalming will add to the problems and complications encountered. . . ."

Just how soon should one get going on the embalming? The author tells us, "On the basis of such scanty information made available to this profession through its rudimentary and haphazard system of technical research, we must conclude that the best results are to be obtained if the subject is embalmed before life is completely extinct—that is, before cellular death has occurred. In the average case, this would mean within an hour after somatic death." For those who feel that there is something a little rudimentary, not to say haphazard, about this advice, a comforting thought is offered by another writer. Speaking of fears entertained in early days of premature burial, he points out, "One of the effects of embalming by chemical injection, however, has been to dispel fears of live burial." How true; once the blood is removed, chances of live burial are indeed remote.

To return to Mr. Jones, the blood is drained out through the veins and replaced by embalming fluid pumped in through the arteries. As noted in *The Principles and Practices of Embalming*, "every operator has a favorite injection and drainage point—a fact which becomes a handicap only if he fails or refuses to forsake his favorites when conditions demand it." Typical favorites are the carotid artery, femoral artery, jugular vein, subclavian vein. There are various choices of embalming fluid. If Flextone is used, it will produce a "mild, flexible rigidity. The skin retains a velvety softness, the tissues are rubbery and pliable. Ideal for women and children." It may be blended with B. and G. Products Company's Lyf-Lyk tint, which is guaranteed to reproduce "nature's own skin texture . . . the velvety appearance of living tissue." Suntone comes in three separate tints: Suntan; Special Cosmetic Tint, a pink shade "especially indicated for young female subjects"; and Regular Cosmetic Tint, moderately pink.

About three to six gallons of a dyed and perfumed solution of formaldehyde, glycerin, borax, phenol, alcohol and water is soon circulating through Mr. Jones, whose mouth has been sewn together with a "needle directed upward between the upper lip and gum and brought out through the left nostril," with the corners raised slightly "for a more pleasant expression." If he should be bucktoothed, his teeth are cleaned with Bon Ami and coated with colorless nail polish. His eyes, meanwhile, are closed with flesh-tinted eye caps and eye cement.

The next step is to have at Mr. Jones with a thing called a trocar. This is a long, hollow needle attached to a tube. It is jabbed into the abdomen, poked around the entrails and chest cavity, the contents of which are pumped out and replaced with "cavity fluid." This done, and the hole in the abdomen sewn up, Mr. Jones's face is heavily creamed (to protect the skin from burns which may be caused by leakage of chemicals), and he is covered with a sheet and left unmolested for a while. But not for long—there is more, much more, in store for him. He has been embalmed, but not yet restored, and the best time to start the restorative work is eight to ten hours after embalming, when the tissues have become firm and dry.

The object of all this attention to the corpse, it must be remembered, is to make it presentable for viewing in an attitude of healthy repose. "Our customs require the presentation of our dead in the semblance of normality . . . unmarred by the ravages of illness, disease or mutilation," says Mr. J. Sheridan Mayer in his *Restorative Art*. This is rather a large order since few people die in the full bloom of health, unravaged by illness and unmarked by some disfigurement. The funeral industry is equal to the challenge: "In some cases the gruesome appearance of a mutilated or disease-ridden subject may be quite discouraging. The task of restoration may seem impossible and shake the confidence of the embalmer. This is the time for intestinal fortitude and determination. Once the formative work is begun and affected tissues are cleaned or removed, all doubts of success vanish. It is surprising and gratifying to discover the results which may be obtained."

The embalmer, having allowed an appropriate interval to elapse, returns to the attack, but now he brings into play the skill and equipment of sculptor and cosmetician. Is a hand missing? Casting one in plaster of Paris is a simple matter. "For replacement purposes, only a cast of the back of the hand is necessary; this is within the ability of the average operator and is quite adequate." If a lip or two, a nose or an ear should be missing, the embalmer has at hand a variety of restorative waxes with which to model replacements. Pores and skin texture are simulated by stippling with a little brush, and over this cosmetics are laid on. Head off? Decapitation cases are rather routinely handled. Ragged edges are trimmed, and head joined to torso with a series of splints, wires and sutures. It is a good idea to have a little something at the neck—a scarf or high collar—when time for viewing comes. Swollen mouth? Cut out tissue as needed from inside the lips. If too much is removed, the surface contour can easily be restored by padding with cotton. Swollen necks and checks are reduced by removing tissue through vertical incisions made down each side of the neck. "When the deceased is casketed, the pillow will hide the suture incisions . . . as an extra precaution against leakage, the suture may be painted with liquid sealer."

The opposite condition is more likely to present itself—that of emaciation. His hypodermic syringe now loaded with massage cream, the embalmer seeks out and fills the hollowed and sunken areas by injection. In this procedure the backs of the hands and fingers and the under-chin area should not be neglected.

Positioning the lips is a problem that recurrently challenges the ingenuity of the embalmer. Closed too tightly, they tend to give a stern, even disapproving expression. Ideally, embalmers feel, the lips should give the impression of being ever so slightly parted, the upper lip protruding slightly for a more youthful appearance. This takes some engineering, however, as the lips tend to drift apart. Lip drift can sometimes be remedied by pushing one or two straight pins through the inner margin of the lower lip and then inserting them between the two front upper teeth. If Mr. Jones happens to have no teeth, the pins can just as easily be anchored in his

253

Armstrong Face Former and Denture Replacer. Another method to maintain lip closure is to dislocate the lower jaw, which is then held in its new position by a wire run through holes which have been drilled through the upper and lower jaws at the midline. As the French are fond of saying, *il faut souffrir pour être belle.*

If Mr. Jones has died of jaundice, the embalming fluid will very likely turn him green. Does this deter the embalmer? Not if he has intestinal fortitude. Masking pastes and cosmetics are heavily laid on, burial garments and casket interiors are color-correlated with particular care, and Jones is displayed beneath rose-colored lights. Friends will say, "How *well* he looks." Death by carbon monoxide, on the other hand, can be rather a good thing from the embalmer's viewpoint: "One advantage is the fact that this type of discoloration is an exaggerated form of a natural pink coloration." This is nice because the healthy glow is already present and needs but little attention.

The patching and filling completed, Mr. Jones is now shaved, washed and dressed. Cream-based cosmetic, available in pink, flesh, suntan, brunette and blond, is applied to his hands and face, his hair is shampooed and combed (and, in the case of Mrs. Jones, set), his hands manicured. For the horny-handed son of toil special care must be taken; cream should be applied to remove ingrained grime, and the nails cleaned. "If he were not in the habit of having them manicured in life, trimming and shaping is advised for better appearance—never questioned by kin."

Jones is now ready for casketing (this is the present participle of the verb "to casket"). In this operation his right shoulder should be depressed slightly "to turn the body a bit to the right and soften the appearance of lying flat on the back." Positioning the hands is a matter of importance, and special rubber positioning blocks may be used. The hands should be cupped slightly for a more lifelike, relaxed appearance. Proper placement of the body requires a delicate sense of balance. It should lie as high as possible in the casket, yet not so high that the lid, when lowered, will hit the nose. On the other hand, we are cautioned, placing the body too low "creates the impression that the body is in a box."

Jones is next wheeled into the appointed slumber room where a few last touches may be added—his favorite pipe placed in his hand or, if he was a great reader, a book propped into position. (In the case of little Master Jones a Teddy bear may be clutched.) Here he will hold open house for a few days, visiting hours 10 A.M. to 9 P.M.

All now being in readiness, the funeral director calls a staff conference to make sure that each assistant knows his precise duties. Mr. Wilber Krieger writes: "This makes your staff feel that they are a part of the team, with a definite assignment that must be properly carried out if the whole plan is to succeed. You never heard of a football coach who failed to talk to his entire team before they go on the field. They have drilled on the plays they are to execute for hours and days, and yet the successful coach knows the importance of making even the bench-warming third-string substitute feel that he is important if the game is to be won." The winning of this game is predicated upon glass-smooth handling of the logistics. The funeral director has notified the pallbearers whose names were furnished by the family, has arranged for the presence of clergyman, organist, and soloist, has provided transportation for everybody, has organized and listed the flowers sent by friends. In *Psychology of Funeral Service* Mr. Edward A. Martin points out: "He may not always do as much as the family thinks he is doing, but it is his helpful guidance that they appreciate in knowing they are proceeding as they should. . . . The important thing is how well his services can be used to make the family believe they are giving unlimited expression to their own sentiment."

The religious service may be held in a church or in the chapel of the funeral home; the funeral director vastly prefers the latter arrangement, for not only is it more convenient for him but it affords him the opportunity to show off his beautiful facilities to the gathered mourners. After the clergyman has had his say, the mourners queue up to file past the casket for a last look at the deceased. The family is never asked whether they want an open-casket ceremony; in the absence of their instruction to the contrary, this is taken for granted. Consequently well over 90 per cent of all American funerals feature the open casket—a custom unknown in other parts of the world. Foreigners are astonished by it. An English woman living in San Francisco described her reaction in a letter to the writer:

I myself have attended only one funeral here—that of an elderly fellow worker of mine. After the service I could not understand why everyone was walking towards the coffin (sorry, I mean casket), but thought I had better follow the crowd. It shook me rigid to get there and find the casket open and poor old Oscar lying there in his brown tweed suit, wearing a suntan makeup and just the wrong shade of lipstick. If I had not been extremely fond of the old boy, I have a horrible feeling that I might have giggled. Then and there I decided that I could never face another American funeral—even dead.

The casket (which has been resting throughout the service on a Classic Beauty Ultra Metal Casket Bier) is now transferred by a hydraulically operated device called Porto-Lift to a balloon-tired, Glide Easy casket carriage which will wheel it to yet another conveyance, the Cadillac Funeral Coach. This may be lavender, cream, light green—anything but black. Interiors, of course, are color-correlated, "for the man who cannot stop short of perfection."

At graveside, the casket is lowered into the earth. This office, once the prerogative of friends of the deceased, is now performed by a patented mechanical lowering device. A "Lifetime Green" artificial grass mat is at the ready to conceal the sere earth, and overhead, to conceal the sky, is a portable Steril Chapel Tent ("resists the intense heat and humidity of

THE STORY OF SERVICE

summer and the terrific storms of winter . . . available in Silver Grey, Rose or Evergreen"). Now is the time for the ritual scattering of earth over the coffin, as the solemn words "earth to earth, ashes to ashes, dust to dust" are pronounced by the officiating cleric. This can today be accomplished "with a mere flick of the wrist with the Gordon Leak-Proof Earth Dispenser. No grasping of a handful of dirt, no soiled fingers. Simple, dignified, beautiful, reverent! The modern way!" The Gordon Earth Dispenser (at $5) is of nickel-plated brass construction. It is not only "attractive to the eye and long wearing"; it is also "one of the 'tools' for building better public relations" if presented as "an appropriate non-commercial gift" to the clergyman. It is shaped something like a saltshaker.

Untouched by human hand, the coffin and the earth are now united.

It is in the function of directing the participants through this maze of gadgetry that the funeral director has assigned to himself his relatively new role of "grief therapist." He has relieved the family of every detail, he has revamped the corpse to look like a living doll, he has arranged for it to nap for a few days in a slumber room, he has put on a well-oiled performance in which the concept of *death* has played no part whatsoever—unless it was inconsiderately mentioned by the clergyman who conducted the religious service. He has done everything in his power to make the funeral a real pleasure for everybody concerned. He and his team have given their all to score an upset victory over death.

Dale Carnegie has written that in the lexicon of the successful man there is no such word as "failure." So have the funeral men managed to delete the word death and all its associations from their vocabulary. They have from time to time published lists of In and Out words and phrases to be memorized and used in connection with the final return of dust to dust; then, still dissatisfied with the result, have elaborated and revised the lists. Thus a 1916 glossary substitutes "prepare body" for "handle corpse." Today, though, "body" is Out and "remains" or "Mr. Jones" is In.

"The use of improper terminology by anyone affiliated with a mortuary should be strictly forbidden," declares Edward A. Martin. He suggests a rather thorough overhauling of the language; his deathless words include: "service, not funeral; Mr., Mrs., Miss Blank, not corpse or body; preparation room, not morgue; casket, not coffin; funeral director or mortician, not undertaker; reposing room or slumber room, not laying-out room; display room, not showroom; baby or infant, not stillborn; deceased, not dead; autopsy or post-mortem, not post; casket coach, not hearse; shipping case, not shipping box; flower car, not flower truck; cremains or cremated remains, not ashes; clothing, dress, suit, etc., not shroud; drawing room, not parlor."

This rather basic list was refined in 1956 by Victor Landig in his *Basic Principles of Funeral Service*. He enjoins the reader to avoid using the word "death" as much as possible, even sometimes when such avoidance may seem impossible; for example, a death certificate should be referred to as a

JESSICA MITFORD

"vital statistics form." One should speak not of the "job" but rather of the "call." We do not "haul" a dead person, we "transfer" or "remove" him— and we do this in a "service car," not a "body car." We "open and close" his grave rather than dig and fill it, and in it we "inter" rather than bury him. This is done, not in a graveyard or cemetery but rather in a "memorial park." The deceased is beautified, not with makeup, but with "cosmetics." Anyway, he didn't die, he "expired." An important error to guard against, cautions Mr. Landig, is referring to "cost of the casket." The phrase, "amount of investment in the service" is a wiser usage here.

Miss Anne Hamilton Franz, writing in *Funeral Direction and Management,* adds an interesting footnote on the use of the word "ashes" to describe (in a word) ashes. She fears this usage will encourage scattering (for what is more natural than to scatter ashes?) and prefers to speak of "cremated remains" or "human remains." She does not like the word "retort" to describe the container in which cremation takes place, but prefers "cremation chamber" or "cremation vault," because this "sounds better and softens any harshness to sensitive feelings."

As for the Loved One, poor fellow, he wanders like a sad ghost through the funeral men's pronouncements. No provision seems to have been made for the burial of a Heartily Disliked One, although the necessity for such must arise in the course of human events.

For Discussion and Further Application

1. Are you able to separate the author's opinions from her facts? Analyze some examples to prove your point.
2. The author sometimes uses sarcasm to punctuate an argument. Can you find the examples? Is it effective or should she have maintained a more direct and objective manner?
3. Like many other authors included in this reader, Mitford uses numerous details to build up her writing. Analyze what kinds of details she selects and how she uses them.
4. Go through the article and analyze how Mitford uses transitions to help develop her reading.
5. What are the implications of the morticians' vocabulary and use of language as it is described in the article?

B 6
C 7
D 8
E 9
F 0
G 1
H 2
I 3
J 4
5